£2·00

West Midland Gardens

West Midland Gardens

The Gardens of
Hereford & Worcester,
Shropshire, Staffordshire,
Warwickshire & West Midlands

Ron Sidwell

**Alan
Sutton**

Alan Sutton Publishing Limited
17a Brunswick Road
Gloucester GL1 1HG

First Published 1981
Copyright © Ron Sidwell 1981

ISBN 0-904387-71-2 (case edition)
ISBN 0-86299-001-7 (paper edition)

Cover Photographs
Front: Bredon Springs
Back: Spetchley Park

Typesetting and origination by
Alan Sutton Publishing Limited.
Photoset Bembo 10/11
Printed in Great Britain
by Redwood Burn Limited
Trowbridge

Contents

List of Black and White Photographs

List of Colour Photographs

County Maps

List of Garden Plans

Acknowledgements

I would like to thank the garden owners who have given their time to provide the backgrounds to the garden descriptions. One great bonus in writing a book of this kind is the large number of nice people one meets.

My thanks must also go to Margaret Satchell for typing the whole book, correcting my spelling and taking some of the photographs; to Jacquie Terry for producing the garden plants and to James Usher for helping with plans in the early stages.

To my College colleagues who have contributed little pearls of wisdom, perhaps unwittingly, I am grateful but especially to Pat Blockley whose gems on Garden History and Design give much inspiration and to Pam Lewis whose help with Library facilities far exceeded what one has a right to expect. To Stuart Whittall for his help and professional advice on the photography I am also indebted.

Ron Sidwell

Introduction

Starting in the north east corner much of the boundary with Derbyshire is formed by the River Dove. The land west of the river rises to over 1,000 feet. South west of this area lies the river Trent which flows more or less south eastwards and leaves Staffordshire at Burton-upon-Trent, on its way to the river Humber. Before reaching this point it is joined by the Thame which with its tributaries drains the Birmingham and South Staffordshire Plateau.

To the south east of this area is the main body of Warwickshire through which the Avon flows southwesterly from the Northamptonshire border down to the Severn at Tewkesbury. The south east border of Warwickshire runs along the fringe of the Northamptonshire uplands and includes the interesting area of Edge Hill. A little further to the south are the Cotswolds, mostly in neighbouring Gloucestershire, but Worcestershire does claim Broadway Hill, just over 1,000 feet. Bredon Hill (960 feet), a Cotswold outlier on our southern boundary, has many attractive villages around its lower slopes.

West of Bredon Hill, and running north and south is the steep ridge of the Malvern Hills where the highest point, the Worcester Beacon is a little more than 1,400 feet.

The western boundary of Hereford and Shropshire is formed by the Welsh hills. The Long Mynd, just west of Church Stretton in Shropshire, reaches a height of 1,696 feet and a little to the south east of this is Wenlock Edge rising steeply from relatively low land to just short of 1,000 feet. Still further to the south east between the valleys of the Corfe and the Severn are the twin hills of Clee and Brown Clee, the latter with a height of 1,790 feet is the highest ground in our area. Local people like to remind one that travelling eastwards there is nothing as high until one reaches the Urals.

The rivers Severn, Wye, Lugg and Teme all rise in Wales and their waters together with that of the Avon ultimately reach the Bristol Channel.

There is one further catchment area. A small part of north Shropshire drains into the river Weaver which flows northwards into the Mersey.

GEOLOGY AND SOILS

The solid geology of Staffordshire and North Shropshire is mostly Triassic, consisting of sandstones and marls but the solid formations are largely overlaid by glacial drifts of sands and gravels. Soils derived from these drifts are usually base depleted and are well suited to the growing of calcifuge plants such as rhododendrons.

Old Red Sandstone covers an area of south Shropshire, much of Hereford and the west side of the old county of Worcester. Here again there is some surface drift but many of the soils are derived from the solid formation itself. These soils are often around neutral but are frequently sufficiently acid to grow calcifuge plants. Hops and fruit are important commercial crops on these soils.

The upland country along the Welsh border includes much older geological formations and the soils derived from these are usually acid in reaction. Over east Worcestershire and south of Birmingham is a substantial belt of Keuper Marl which usually produces soils neutral to slightly acid.

The only strongly calcareous soils lie along the south east border where a belt of lower lias clay gives rise to very heavy soils with remarkable powers of flocculation when properly managed. These are the soils on which Evesham asparagus has been grown for the last century and a half, a crop which, alas, has now shrunk to insignificance. The clay is in places overlaid by drifts of Jurassic gravels, also strongly calcareous.

Further to the south east, along the Warwickshire fringe, are some outcrops of Middle Lias, notably at Edge Hill. This formation gives rise to a remarkably free working loam which is sometimes base depleted but is usually near neutral in reaction.

A notable feature of the Avon valley and the lower part of the Severn within our area is the presence of river terraces consisting of sandy loams with varying quantities of Bunter pebble. These are sometimes of considerable depth and form the early market garden soils of the Vale of Evesham, but, partly because of their value for commercial production they contain few private gardens of note.

THE RANGE OF GARDENS

In an area with such diversity of conditions, natural and man made, one must expect a great diversity of gardens. Country gardens may be quite different from town gardens. But even in areas of high population density it is surprising how remote from the scurry and bustle of modern town life some of these gardens are. This applies particularly to Edgbaston where, owing to the altruistic policy of the Calthorpe Estate some 500 acres of open space, including two nature reserves, have been preserved within about one to two miles of Birmingham city centre. One shudders to think what might have happened if the estate had got into the hands of modern property speculators.

Whilst many of the gardens included are quite ordinary and contain little that could not be imitated by the average visitor there are others with very special features.

Great gardens of the past are preserved by commercial enterprise at Alton Towers and, perhaps less successfully at Trentham, both in Staffordshire.

The National Trust has in its care many fine gardens. Whilst the West Midlands cannot claim any of the calibre of Bodnant, Hidcote or Sissinghurst, there are many of interest. Upton House is among the finest of gardens, with its deep coombs.

The Yew Garden at Packwood House and the Long Terrace at Farnborough are features of special interest.

Associations with historic personages are often worth noting. Charles II was at Madresfield Court before the Battle of Worcester and at Moseley Old Hall shortly after. The garden at the latter has been designed in mid-seventeenth century style to commemorate the fact.

Congreve once lived at Stretton Hall, Jenny Lind at Wind's Point, Malvern and Mary Anderson at Court Farm, Broadway, where she created the garden much as it is today.

George Eliot was born at Arbury and apart from changes in farming methods one feels that this estate is much as it was in her time when her father was agent for the estate.

Izaak Walton's cottage near Stafford has been restored and the garden stocked with plants that were in Britain at the time of his death.

But most important of the historic personages, of course, is Shakespeare himself. He was born and he died at Stratford-upon-Avon. Five properties are owned by the Shakespeare Birthplace Trust. The recreated knot garden at New Place, where Shakespeare died is perhaps the most important of the gardens and attracts a lot of attention from visitors.

Abbreviations

The following abbreviations are used

NT   National Trust
NGS   National Gardens Scheme
GS   Gardeners' Sunday

The Gardens of
Hereford and Worcester

Shropshire

B

Powys

Gatley Park •

• **Croft Castle**

• **Berrington**

■ LEOMINSTER

• Hergest Croft

Broadfield Court •

■ BROM

• **Dinmore Manor**

W
Broc

Garnons
•
• **Monnington Court**

HAY ON WYE

Moccas Court

• **The Weir**

■ HEREFORD

LEDBUR

Haf

• **Whitfield**

• **Old Post Office**
Abbey Dore Court •

Fawley Court •

Pontrilas Court •

ROSS ON WYE ■

Gwent

The Gardens of
Hereford and Worcester

Abbey Dore Court
Mrs C.L. Ward

17.5 km (11 miles) SW of Hereford. 4km (2½ miles) NW of A465 Hereford — Abergavenny at point about midway between the two towns. Area: 1.25 ha (3 acres). Altitude: 75 m (250 ft). Soil: loam to clay loam slightly acid. Rainfall: 750 mm (29.5 m). Open daily 1 March to 31 October for NGS and GS.

The garden has been developed by the present owner since 1968 on the site of a one time fine garden which had fallen into complete neglect.

On the lower side the River Dore forms the boundary for the full length of the garden. As with all rivers supplied with surface water from hill country the flow fluctuates greatly. Flooding follows quickly after heavy rains and the flow is soon reduced to a trickle in dry weather.

Nevertheless the river is the main feature of the garden. A substantial number of alders were cleared from the riverside to create an open woodland effect. A riverside walk has been created with many low growing plants, especially ferns, of which there is large collection.

There is one acre of walled garden half of which has been planted with dessert applies on dwarfing rootsticks. The management of these is excellent and they are an interesting feature to those visitors who have utilitarian leanings. The remainder of the walled garden is mainly devoted to kitchen garden.

A large herb collection, together with shrubs and herbaceous plants make this a garden of great interest.

Two fine though rather stumpy looking Wellingtonias, *Sequoiadendron giganteum*, stand on the lawn, links with the garden of the past.

Arley House
R.D. Turner Esq.

Upper Arley, Kidderminster, 8km (5 miles) NW Kidderminster on A442 turn left for Arley. Area: 7.6ha (19 acres). Altitude: 39m (130ft). Soil: sandy, lime free. Rainfall: 700mm(27.5m). Labour employed: three full time plus casual. Open for NGS.

The gardens at Arley House have a distinguished history. The present house — a modern one — is built on the site of Arley Castle, now demolished. There are some ancient oaks and beeches in the parkland but the main early plantings started in 1800 and reached their peak around 1820. This was the work of the second and last Earl of Mountnorris who succeeded to the title in 1816 and died in 1844.

Trees planted during this period included many American oaks, caryas, thujas, junipers, pines, maples, taxodiums, Eastern Hemlock, and others including many rare and newly introduced species. Pride of place among the rarieties must go to the fine specimen *Sorbus domestica* which we will deal with more fully in due course.

After the death of Lord Mountnorris, Arley passed into the possession of his nephew Arthur Lyttelton Macleod who a few years later, in 1852, sold the estate to Robert Woodward. Woodward's son, another Robert, succeeded his father in 1882 and the estate remained in the Woodward family until 1956 when the present owner purchased it from Lady Woodward, widow of Sir Chad Woodward.

The Woodwards added substantially to the tree and plant collection and took great care of the estate. An indication of this care is recorded by Robert Woodward II. A *Juniperus virginiana* planted in 1820 and 70 ft high in 1903 blew down in the gale of Sunday 24 March 1895 at 1.30 pm. How good to have such precise records! The tree was pulled back by wires which broke in the high winds of 1902. The wires were again affixed. The tree does not appear to be standing today.

The above note is contained in 'Hortus Arleyensis' published in 1907. This work lists 424 specimens, mostly trees covering over 300 species planted over the previous century.

As for *Sorbus domestica* this tree is surrounded by legend, and no little romance. It has appeared in lists of the British Flora on the strength of a solitary specimen in the Wye Forest, just across the river from Arley. Edmund Pitt, a distinguished citizen of Worcester, discovered it in 1677 and in a letter to the Royal Society, published in their 'Philosophical

Transactions' of 1678 calls attention to the fact that no other botanist has recorded the tree as growing wild in England. Indeed no other record has appeared to this day. The true wildness of this solitary tree has been disputed. It was an old specimen when discovered by Pitt. Lees in his 'Botany of Worcestershire' (1867) suggests that it may have been planted by a hermit who lived in the forest.

Whatever its origin it attracted more than a little interest locally where it was known as the Quicken Pear, quicken being an old name for Mountain Ash, *Sorbus aucuparia*. More recently it seems to have been known as the witty pear. The old tree was burnt down by a vagrant in 1862.

Various unsuccessful attempts at vegetative propagation were made by skilled local gardeners but Lord Mountnorris succeeded in raising two seedlings which were planted at Arley between 1800 and 1820. The best of these measured 55ft in height and 7ft 4ins in girth in 1907. In 1975 it measured 65ft and 11ft. Today it looks very well and is good for another century or two.

By the end of the second world war the maintenance problems at Arley Castle were increasing and when the present owner purchased the property in 1956 much of the garden area was derelict. This allowed considerable replanning.

Fortunately the ten acre arboretum is in its original state with a superb *Liriodendron tulipifera* and an immense Corsican pine together with cedars, redwoods, wellingtonia, beeches and oaks. There is a fine trunkless beech, its multi-multi-stemmed crown starting at ground level. Not exactly a forester's tree but pleasing nevertheless. These and many other good specimens keep the witty pear company.

The remainder of the garden has been completely remodelled during the last 16 years (the period served by Mr David Lee, the present head gardener). The old glasshouses have gone and have been replaced by modern aluminium houses of the best design. One of these is used for orchids and one for pot plants. Others are tomato and general plant houses. The paving between and around the houses makes possible a neat and tidy finish which is well maintained. Within this same walled area is a block of apples on dwarfing rootstock partly surrounded by a hedge of *Chamaecyparis lawsoniana* 'Pottenii'. Peaches and morello cherries are on the walls.

South of this is the so called Italian Garden. This is walled all round. The walls are planted with camellias with heather in front. In a wide gravel path two yards or so from the wall is a row of pleached limes, *Tilia tomentosa*.

The central area of the Italian garden is mostly taken up with water. At the west end is an octagonal pool. In the centre is a square pool with an elaborate fountain. Two rectangular pools abut this and a further

Above: Arley House. The range of modern glass is maintained at a level of cultivation and tidiness rarely found in private gardens.

Left: Arley House. *Sorbus domestica.* This tree is the only surviving seedling from the only specimen recorded wild in Britain. It is about 160 years old and still in fine trim.

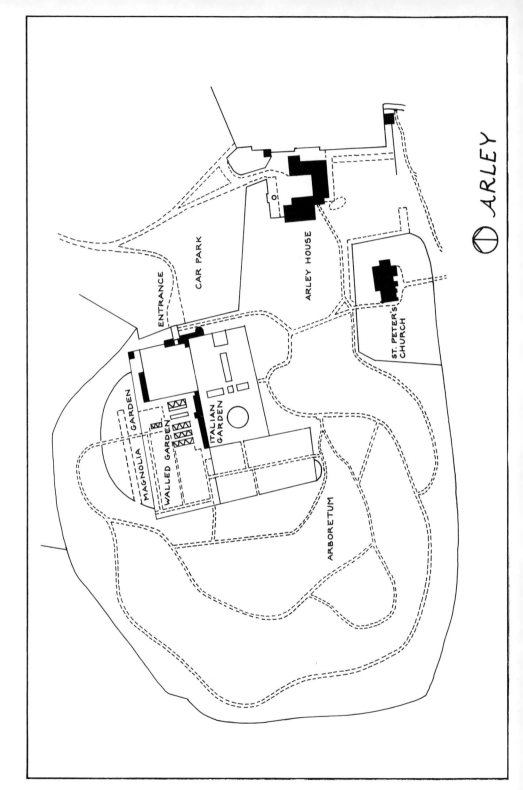

ARLEY

ENTRANCE

CAR PARK

ARLEY HOUSE

ST. PETER'S CHURCH

MAGNOLIA GARDEN

WALLED GARDEN

ITALIAN GARDEN

ARBORETUM

rectangular pool runs up to the east end with heather beds set back behind wide gravel paths. Jets of water play from the pool margins. A few vases on pedestals complete the scene.

The effect is one of impressive, if somewhat contrived elaboration. It is in complete contrast to the quiet naturalness of the nearby arboretum. However, since it is completely enclosed and one cannot get partial glimpses of it as one walks about it must be counted a great success. The impact on entering is considerable.

There are about five acres of modern garden around the modern house. This consists of terraced lawns with beds of roses and bedding plants. Smallish conifers such as junipers and *Chamaecyparis lawsoniana* 'Ellwoodii'. Conventional but well done. At this point the ground falls away steeply to the River Severn which lies below the south west boundary of the garden and arboretum.

North of the walled garden is the magnolia garden. This consists of a large rectangular block with a broad central grass path and wide borders of magnolias on each side. On the south side is the wall; on the north a yew hedge. The central grass path is edged with box. How rarely one sees dwarf edging box planted nowadays.

For those with wider interests there is a large collection of ornamental pheasants.

Ballards Farm
Mrs M.J. Eaton

Hinton on the Green, Evesham, 3.2km (2 miles S of Evesham, turn R at Hinton Cross through Hinton village. Area: 0.4ha (1 acre). Altitude: 33m (110ft). Soil: heavy calcareous clay. Rainfall: 660mm (26in). Labour employed: casual. Open occasionally for NGS and Red Cross.

The outstanding feature of this garden is the high standard of cultivation which has been attained on the most intractible of Lower Lias clays. Those who do not understand this type of clay might well despair of ever growing anything on it. Experienced cultivators who know when to work it and when to keep off, and how to take advantage of the remarkable powers of flocculation which this calcareous clay possesses can achieve remarkable results.

For centuries these clays have been among the heaviest yielding wheat soils in Britain. They have borne most of the Evesham plums and, oddly enough, most of the Evesham asparagus when this was an important crop.

Ten years ago this garden was a typical farm garden, a small lawn, a few roses, some rather neglected soft fruit and a small area of rough grass and fruit trees where the odd cade lamb was reared.

If asked what use this soil was least suited to it would probably be lawn. Yet here is to be found a lawn so near perfection that even the present writer who has lived with these soils for 40 years cannot quite understand how it has been done.

In addition to lawn there is a good collection of shrub roses, many choice and interesting shrubs and herbaceous plants. Three *Calocedrus decurrens* form a well sited group and in years to come will be a noteworthy feature. *Metasequoia glyptostroboides* is establishing well as is *Picea pungens glauca* after a shaky start. *Parottia persica* is also at home on this heavy soil.

There is a small garden pool and two greenhouses. Management is of the highest order and weeds are almost non-existent.

Beaucastle

G. Clancey Esq.

Bewdley, about three miles from Bewdley on the A456 Bewdley to Cleobury Mortimer Road. Area: 4ha (10 acres). Altitude: 135m (450ft). Soil: sandy loam, lime free. Rainfall: 700mm (27.5in). Labour employed: one full-time, one part-time.

Beaucastle lies on the southern edge of the Wyre Forest. The house, which is rather an architectural oddity was built in 1877 by George Baker following his retirement as Lord Mayor of Birmingham. John Ruskin is said to have been involved with the design and the architect was William Doubleday.

With its steep gables, wooden balcony and central tower it shows continental influence.

The present owner acquired the property in 1950. The garden at that time was quite small and mostly on the south east side. Most of the present ten acre garden was then part of the Wyre Forest itself.

Development since 1950 has been done in stages with local casual labour and general contractors. Mr. Clancey has one full-time gardener, Mr. K. Williams, with extra casual help when needed. Mrs. Williams looks after the greenhouse.

The soil is mainly a hungry sandy loam but clay occurs in places, notably on the site of the pools. The soil reaction is acid throughout.

Apart from an avenue of oaks, with a few beech and limes along the main drive few mature trees remain. There is thus a newness about the planting and no outstanding specimen trees.

The central features on the left, north west, side of the approach drive is a chain of pools supplied by pumping the water from a pool in the Forest. These pools are on the site of a former clay pit and were commenced in 1960. Westmorland limestone has been used throughout for waterfalls, stepping stones · and marginal support. With lavish planting of rhododendrons and other shrubs the contrast with the oak birch and bracken of the nearby woodland is extreme. A solitary flamingo now survives of the three or four originally introduced. There are numerous resident ducks as well as large numbers of visiting mallards. At the north east end of the pools is a large collection of dwarf and not so dwarf conifers.

The main part of the garden consists of a large expanse of grass with numerous solitary trees such as prunus etc. Sweeping informal borders and beds are planted with a wide range of shrubs. As one would expect on such a soil rhododendrons figure prominently and pernettyas and pieris are also to be found. The shrubs, in the main, are noteworthy for their variety rather than their rarity. Many cotoneasters, berberis, hebes and such like are used. On one of my visits *Decaisnea fargesi* and *Hippophae rhamnoides* were fruiting particularly well. The planting of this area is wholly informal and there are few hard surfaces.

The older plantings are tending to get overcrowded. Thinning out and transplanting now takes place annually. Even large shrubs transplant quite well on this soil provided water is given when needed and provided adequate equipment and labour are available.

On the subject of equipment it should be noted that Mr Clancey is an engineer by profession and as he does a lot of the work himself, he is able to assess the merits and shortcomings of existing machinery at first hand and to design and build improved items if necessary.

In front of the house is the original garden. This now consists of a formal terrace with lawns and rose beds. Below this is a rock garden of Westmorland limestone mainly planted with prostrate conifers, cotoneasters and similar low shrubs. There is a noteworthy large patch of *Hebe pagei* which is quite effective. The upright conifers are getting rather large for their sites and some removals are planned for the near future. There are a few conventional 'rock plants' and the gaps are often filled with annuals.

The greenhouse is well stocked and well managed. Its contents include cymbidiums, begonias in variety, *Dipladenia, Hoya, Monstera, Ficus, Columnea* etc.

Beaucastle. The late nineteenth century house looks down over the main pool, the central feature of this attractive garden.

Development is continuing especially at the north end of the garden and as trees mature a change in character can be anticipated.

Although there are as yet no outstanding specimens one has hopes of *Liquidambar styraciflua* and *Liriodendron tulipifera* making it one day. There is an attractive small specimen of *Sophora japonica* 'Pendula'.

Bell's Castle

Lady Holland-Martin

Kemerton, about 10km (6 miles) NE of Tewkesbury on SW side of Bredon Hill. Area: 0.4ha (1 acre). Altitude: 150m (500ft). Soil: brashy loam over rock. Calcareous. Rainfall: 660mm (26in). Labour employed: one part-time. Open for NGS.

A certain Captain Bell, who is said to have acquired his wealth through smuggling built his castle in 1820. His enjoyment of it was comparatively short lived for he is reputed to have been hanged in 1841. Raymond Bush, once a well known writer on fruit growing, lived here between the wars when he was fruit farm manager of Overbury Orchards.

The house is perched on a steep part of Bredon Hill looking down to the lower Avon valley some four hundred and fifty feet below. The superb view is one of the garden's attractions.

The present owner came here in 1964 with her late husband Admiral Sir Derek Holland-Martin and the present garden is largely her creation. A Yellow Banksian rose covers a large part of the south west front of the house. A north west facing wall at the end of the terrace has a vigorous rose 'Albertine', beautiful while it lasts but too short a flowering season, Lady Holland-Martin thinks.

The terrace below has a swimming pool that is more like an ornamental pool. No blue tiles or chromium plate and therefore no need to hide it behind hedges as is usually necessary. A large rectangular level lawn extends beyond and calls for a high retaining wall on the ramparts of which are statues brought from Venice.

Further below a final high retaining wall with castellated ramparts provides a fine point for viewing the country below. There is an even better look-out point at the west corner. A little summer house is tucked under the wall of the terrace behind.

The main interest in this garden apart from the simple and effective layout and the view is a considerable collection of shrub roses. Other

plants include mostly soft greys and pinks toning with the grey stone
which in the form of buildings, walls and ramparts is never out of sight.
Cyclamen repandum was flowering profusely at the time of my visit.

On the other, north east, side of the house is the kitchen garden
containing many roses grown for cutting, hedges of sweet briar, *Rosa
rubiginosa* and a forgotten old variety Duc de Fitzjames. There are
substantial herbaceous borders in this area.

Berrington Hall
The National Trust

---

*Leominster, 5.6km (3½ miles) N of Leominster on W side of A49. Area: 4ha (10 acres).
Altitude: 106m (350ft). Soil: medium loam, lime free. Rainfall: 750mm (29.5in). Open for NT
and NGS.*

The Berrington estate was, until about 1775-6, in the possession of the
Cornewall family who also owned Moccas. In that year the Hon. Thomas
Harley purchased the estate and 'Capability' Brown was consulted about
siting the house and developing the park. At that time there was no house
of consequence on the estate.

Harley had been Lord Mayor of London in 1767 and was elected
Member of Parliament for Herefordshire in 1776. He engaged Brown and
his architect son-in-law, Henry Holland, to design house and park.
Brown's love for damming small streams to create lakes was demonstrated
here as elsewhere and the result was a 14 acre lake with a four acre island
in the south east corner of the park.

Work on the house covered the period 1778-81. The house is faced with
an attractive red sandstone quarried locally.

In 1900 the estate was purchased by Mr Frederick Cawley (later the first
Lord Cawley). The estate was given to the National Trust in 1957 but the
present Lord Cawley has remained interested, especially in the garden.

Brown's original landscape would have left little room for flower
gardens but doubtless over the next century or so beds and borders would
have appeared. There does not appear, however, to have been any large
formal gardens such as are often associated with such houses.

Today the garden is chiefly of note for its interesting collection of choice
and often rare shrubs and other plants, the planting of which has been the
responsibility of Lord Cawley.

The entrance drive passes under an impressive gatehouse arch north of the house and follows a curved line to the south front. Lawns cover much of the garden south and east of the house. Shrub borders flank the drive until the lawns are reached. Here one finds *Ginkgo biloba*, *Hibiscus syriacus*, *Chimonanthus fragrans* and *Magnolia* and *Sorbus* species among other things.

On the right (west) of the entrance drive is a large lawn of four shallow terraces and crossing it is a gravel path flanked by a series of small dome-clipped golden yews. This is one of the few formal features of the present garden.

At one time substantial herbaceous beds and borders were to be found but some of these have now gone. The west side of the north garden is bounded by the east wall of the walled garden. This contains several plants and climbers of interest. *Garrya elliptica*, *Solanum crispum*, *Buddleia colvilei*, *Clematis orientalis*, *Campsis tagliabuana*, *Carpenteria californica* and four ancient wistarias were noted but most exciting of all that rare perennial cucurbit *Thladiantha oliveri* with yellow flowers and cucumber foliage.

Outside the west wall of the walled garden is a second wall creating a small enclosure. The walls here are mostly planted with camellias but there is also a smallish specimen of *Eriobotryta japonica* its foliage bedraggled as usual and one of the rarest items, *Crinodendron patagua*. Near the gate on the inside is *Celastrus scandens* and outside *Actinidia kolomikta*.

A woodland garden runs along most of the west boundary. This is planted with a wide range of shrubs including dwarf rhododendrons, kolkwitzia, deutzia, philadelphus, escallonia and many herbaceous plants.

Cyclamen neapolitanum covers considerable areas along the lawn/woodland margin and bulbs are abundant in the spring.

This is a garden for those who like plants rather than those who look for overall design. But whatever one's interests it is a pleasant place to visit.

Bickmarsh Hall

Mr and Mrs Jeremy Green

Bidford-on-Avon, 2.5km (1½ miles) S of Bidford, midway between Stratford and Evesham on A439, on Buckle Street (old Roman road). Area: 0.3ha (¾ acre). Altitude: 48m (160ft). Soil: calcareous clay. Rainfall: 660mm (26in). Open from time to time for NGS.

Bickmarsh Hall is built in the cold grey limestone of the Lower Lias as are so many of the older houses in this Warwickshire/Worcestershire border country. A chapel existed here in the twelfth century and the present house has traces of buildings of several periods. It was in the hands of the Griffin family for many centuries and it is recorded that one of the Griffin women married Richard Shakespeare, grandfather to the illustrious William, for this is in the heart of Shakespeare country.

The garden is of fairly conventional form for an old farmhouse and much of the planting has been done by the present owners since 1947. On the west side is the main garden enclosed in a stone wall. A broad paved terrace with mixed shrub and herbaceous beds runs along the house front. A healthy Double Banksian rose was noted on the house wall. West of the terrace is a large lawn with border plantings. A weeping ash is a prominent feature on a raised paved area in the south west corner. Under it are naturalised *Cyclamen neapolitanum*, *Helleborus argutifolius*, and the native Tutsan.

Cercis siliquastrum, the Judas Tree bears its pink flowers freely in early summer and there is a good sized specimen of *Cornus mas*, bright with yellow flowers in winter. Roses include 'Canary bird' and the tiny pink 'Farrar's Threepennybit rose'. The threepennybit in question was, of course, the old silver coin. Sprawling over a tree is *Clematis* 'Mrs Spencer Castle' with mauvy pink flowers, double on its first flush of bloom. A swimming pool fits neatly into the north east corner.

North of this garden is a wild woodland garden with recent plantings of birch, larch etc. and various shrubs. A large walnut is just over the boundary in the field.

Birtsmorton Court
N.G.K. Dawes Esq.

Just N of A438 Tewkesbury — Ledbury road at midway point. 11km (7 miles). Altitude 18m (60ft). Rainfall 750mm (29.5in). One full-time gardener. Open under NGS.

The house is completely surrounded by a large moat which sets the tone for the whole place. On the west side, separated by an area of mown grass is the large rectangular Westminster Pool, said to derive its name from the fact that it was constructed in the year of the consecration of the nave of Westminster Abbey.

The garden consists largely of mown grass with numerous native deciduous trees. There are some good specimens of Lawson's Cypress and *Thuja plicata* dating from the earlier part of this century and I noted *Chamaecyparis nootkatensis* also. There are some fine *C. lawsoniana erecta* which, with the help of a little corsetting have kept their shape remarkably well.

But the prize of the garden is a magnificent yew of great age; its low, wide spreading branches reaching the ground on all sides. Tradition has it that Cardinal Wolsey sat under this tree. Since there is abundant evidence that Wolsey stayed at Birtsmorton as a young man and as the tree is probably old enough there is no reason to dispute the legend. After all, he must have sat down somewhere.

A topiary garden, consisting of a double row of clipped yews forms the boundary of a large square with a mown grass centre. The yews are partly clipped to form a continuous square hedge topped with domes and partly separate rectangular blocks, also surmounted by domes. The topiary garden is surrounded on a little more than two sides by an old wall. One cannot help thinking that this was originally a traditional type walled kitchen garden. Today herbaceous borders have been planted between the wall and the topiary.

The age of the topiary is a little puzzling. It has the ring of 19th century and is almost certainly of that date. What is surprising is that a walled kitchen garden of that date should have been converted to topiary. Most of these gardens were maintained well into the 20th century, and then not converted into another high labour feature.

The greenhouses were demolished some years ago but Mrs Dawes treasures a good collection of orchids which she cares for herself in two small greenhouses.

This garden is now being cared for very well after a long period of neglect and new plantings of trees are continuing but the character is being retained. There are no shrub roses, no flowering cherries. It belongs to some ill defined period of the past and I hope it will remain that way.

Bredon Springs, Paris

Ronald Sidwell Esq

Ashton-under-Hill, 10km (6 miles) SW of Evesham. N of A435 Evesham — Cheltenham road. Area: 0.6ha (1½ acres). Altitude: 75m (250ft). Soil: Light to heavy loam, highly calcareous. Rainfall: 660mm (26in). Labour employed: Occasional casual. Open weekends and Wednesdays April — October for NGS.

This is the writer's own garden. Compared with many in this book it is untidy but, it is hoped, not uninteresting.

The original purchase in 1948 was a 1781 Cotswold stone cottage with about ¾ acre of 'garden'. In 1953 the adjoining 1735 cottage and small garden were added and also the front bank which until then had been part of the field. Finally in 1974 a realignment of the south west boundary took place, involving an exchange of land with the adjoining cottage.

Owing to the unlimited supply of excellent water and rich deep soil the site has been a settlement for many centuries. At the time of our purchase it consisted of many dead fruit trees in a waterlogged part and a general impenetrable jungle elsewhere. There seemed to be many hundreds of yards of buried wire netting of various vintages from the days when fruit and poultry were the crops produced.

Today the jungle has, to some extent, persisted but the rich moist soil has allowed *Gunnera manicata, Ligularia spp, Iris kaempferi, I. siberica,* moisture loving primulas, astilbes etc to be grown successfully.

The old fruit trees have been preserved where possible and a fine Pitmaston Duchess pear is the tallest tree in the garden at the moment but a *Thuja plicata* planted in 1958 will soon overtake it. A beautifully gnarled old Blenheim Orange apple leans over the steps as one enters, its principal crop is now mistletoe. It sets the pattern for the whole garden, that of slightly controlled wildness where most things, birds, mammals and insects included are allowed to live their own lives unmolested. Safe herbicides are used on paths but all noxious chemicals are avoided. Sparrows and tits keep the few roses free of aphids and moles enjoy their worm hunting on the moist green 'lawn' when most lawns are parched dry in a summer drought.

Broadfield Court

Mr and Mrs Keith James

Bodenham, Leominster, one mile N of A417 at point two miles W of Junction with A49 Hereford — Leominster at Hope under Dinmore. Garden (1.67ha) 4 acres. Vineyard (2.5ha) 6 acres. Soil: clay loam derived from Old Red Sandstone. Open for NGS and local functions.

Broadfield is mentioned in Domesday Book and parts of the present house date from the fourteenth century. Otherwise the house is part Tudor and part Regency. Edwardian additions have been demolished. Today it is essentially a farmhouse from which four farms totalling over 1,000 acres are run.

The present owner came here in 1968. Prior to that it was in the Romilly family for about forty years.

The quarter mile entrance drive has horse chestnuts on one side and is heavily planted with daffodils. A fine copper beech stands near the courtyard entrance. Pleached beeches surround the courtyard and one is immediately aware of the high standards of care and management which characterise the whole estate. The garden is mainly a nineteenth century creation with twentieth century additions and alterations.

The south front of the house looks over a formal paved terrace of random rectangular stone. Below this is an area of crazy paving in the centre of which is a well with an imposing well-head of wrought iron. Still further south is a paved rose garden with central fountain and lawn surround. The whole area is enclosed in neatly clipped yew hedges six to seven feet high.

A woodland walk links the entrance drive with the yew enclosed rose garden. Trees in this woodland area include Blue Cedar, beech, Scots Pine, hornbeam and *Calocedrus decurrens*. Spring bulbs are freely naturalised.

East of the rose garden is a large lawn area with an old mulberry and a cherry. Running east to west below this and the rose garden is a gravel path flanked by pear trees. This typifies gardens of this kind that have evolved through a series of stages. One cannot conceive a garden designer creating such a feature if he were designing the garden as a whole but it is to features of this kind that Broadfield Court owes so much of its old world charm.

A Ha-Ha constructed by the Romillies in the 1960s forms the south boundary of this part of the garden.

Moving further to the east we find a shrub border under a west facing wall. Beyond the wall is the kitchen garden. Walled gardens of old houses are so often abandoned nowadays. Here we find traditional standards maintained. A greenhouse provides tomatoes and house plants. The south boundary of the walled garden is actually a clipped yew hedge, south of which is a large herbaceous border. Below this in turn is an area of young fruit trees. Hornbeam hedges enclose this part of the garden.

The six acre vineyard lies to the east. This interesting commercial venture is, like everything else here, very well run. The varieties grown are the traditional Müller Thurgau, the newer Reichensteiner, the Seyve — Villard hybrid now renamed Seyval blanc and another new grape Huxelrebe. The double Guyot system of pruning is adopted throughout. About two and a half acres were fruiting in 1979. Within two years full production should be reached.

The garden is managed by the head gardener Mr Leon Cook with one full time assistant and a part-time helper for lawn mowing.

The Brook House
J.D. Milne Esq

Colwall, on B4218 mid-way between Malvern and Ledbury opp. Horse and Jockey Hotel. Area: 1.6ha (4 acres). Altitude: 120m (400ft). Soil: medium loam. Neutral to slightly acid. Rainfall: 750mm (29.5in). Labour employed: one full-time. Open for NGS and GS.

This is one of the most complete gardens in the West Midlands and certainly one of the most beautiful. The house is partly 1630 and it seems to have been a farmhouse with millstream for almost three centuries. In 1912 Sir Guy Dawber was engaged to enlarge and extend the house to create the 'gentleman's residence' we have today.

The garden at that time was close around the house and east of the stream which flows along the west front of the house.

In 1936 the present owner came here and the garden has developed from that time but especially since 1968. The old part of the garden has not been greatly altered, except in detail. Expansion west of the stream has created a new modern garden with shrubs and trees in rough mown grass.

The garden is divided by a wide gravel path running more or less north and south. This is continuous with a paved terrace on the west side of the house.

Above: The Brook House. The old cider mill at the garden entrance. A link with one of Herefordshire's oldest industries.

Below: The Brook House. The streamside garden in early spring. Hellebores and ericas are a feature of the bank on the right.

The garden is entered by a door in a wall at the north east corner over which a good specimen of *Cotoneaster henryanus* hangs. Before going through the door an old stone cider mill is worth a little study. The woodwork is beginning to crumble and the pony shafts hve become vestigial but it is an interesting museum piece and a reminder of the old cider making industry of this area.

On passing into the garden one finds a narrow strip garden on the left some four metres wide with the west facing wall on its left and a clipped yew hedge on the right. There are two grass strips with a middle strip of small plants and a narrow border under the wall. Under the wall are many somewhat tender shrubs including *Buddleia colvilei*, the Kew red form, *Vestia foetida, Solanum jasminioides, Ceanothus papillosus, Cytisus battandieri, Abutilon vitifolium* among others.

Continuing up this enclosed strip we open out on to a large lawn. The wall continues and joins a north facing wall at right angles. This wall, it seems, was built by German prisoners during the 1914–18 war. A neat little gazebo occupies a middle position on the north wall. On the west side of this lawn is the main gravel path mentioned above.

North of the lawn and south of the house is a formal rose garden with six rectangular beds divided by grass strips with a central paved path.

Narrow grass strips and paths are a feature of this garden. This makes for much work in mowing and edging but it is all done with impeccable tidiness. It is noticeable also that hard surface materials are always used where wear and tear is heavy.

The main entrance to the house is on the north side and this opens on to a small formal garden with rose beds and a large *Magnolia soulangeana* some 50 years old.

The mill stream is the central feature of this garden. It gives it a character that cannot be obtained by any artificial water schemes and full use has been made of it. At the highest point at the southern end of its course the stream garden is at its wildest. Here are found *Ligularia* species, *Peltiphyllum peltatum*, and other plants capable of holding their own with native vegetation. This area is small — north of a bridge which crosses at this point a much more managed garden is found. Here one can find almost all of the moisture loving primulas, meconopsis, hostas, lysichitums, astilbes, and others of their kind. A bank between the stream and the main lawn has had large additions of peat and the smaller rhododendrons and other peat lovers are planted here. The plant collection here is very great and includes many choice items. I noted a particularly good clump of *Adiantum pedatum* among other things.

A little downstream is a bridge of railway sleepers under a massive yew tree and further still we reach the house with the paved terrace alongside. This is approached down steps with pewter urns on pillars on each side.

An attractive wooden bridge crosses the stream from the terrace. It has *Clematis montana* and *Vitis coignetae* on its side rails. Westwards is a vista of herbaceous borders with a central grass path culminating in a clipped yew alcove and a liquidamber as an end stop beyond. Looking back from this point the house is seen in a perfect setting.

A little to the south of the herbaceous borders is a massive cherry tree of great age. Some of the branches are braced but the tree still has most of its branch system intact and may remain so for quite a time yet. Nearby is a fine hornbeam in very sound condition and a large spread. It has obviously had plenty of room over the years and has been able to develop to its full potential.

In this south western part of the garden we find the most recent development. Trees and shrubs of great variety and interest are planted in rough mown grass. Autumn colour is one of the features. *Acer nikoense* and other maples, *Parotia persica, Euonymus* all contribute. A ten year old *Davidia* is growing well and an *Ailanthus* will have to be moved to make way for it. Mr Milne hopes to see flowers on it soon. New plantings are being made of many rare and interesting subjects.

A surprising feature of this area is a small water garden — static not running — and carrying a full range of appropriate plants.

A walled kitchen garden lies south of the main lawn and greenhouses and frames provide plants for the garden as well as the usual fruit and vegetables.

Clent Hall
C. Parkes Esq.

Stourbridge, three miles S of Stourbridge, just off A491 Stourbridge to Bromsgrove road. Area: 2.5ha (6 acres). Altitude: 210m (700ft). Soil: light loam over sandy gravel. Acid. Open frequently under NGS and at other times by appointment and for GS.

This is an ancient site with records going back to 760 A.D. The first Clent Hall is mentioned in Domesday Book. The present house dates from about 1685 but thirteenth century foundations exist.

No evidence of great antiquity is to be found in the garden which is essentially late Victorian. Trees, shrubs and especially rhododendrons form a roadside boundary to the garden. It is said that the then owner was a friend of Joseph Dalton Hooker and that Hooker may have influenced the planting.

The garden consists substantially of lawns of differing levels with rose beds, conifers and other trees. A fine young Western Hemlock, Tsuga heterophylla, is on the lawn in front of the house.

There is a small semi-formal water garden with stream and waterfalls and a small rock garden of local stone. A pet's cemetery dating from 1903–1925 period sets the tone of the whole garden.

The garden is kept colourful by seasonal bedding and the standard of management is high, entirely with family labour.

Included in the area to which the public has access is the field above, from which magnificent views may be obtained. Above that lies the National Trust area of the Clent Hills rising to over 1,000 ft.

This is a deservedly popular spot for the town dweller seeking an afternoon out near at hand. It is not a plantsman's garden, nor will the designer find much inspiration.

Conderton Manor
Mr and Mrs Wm. Carr

(5½ miles) NE of Tewkesbury, between A435 and B4079. Area: 2.2ha (7 acres). Altitude: 69m (230ft). Soil: clay loam calcareous. Rainfall: 660mm (26in). Labour employed: one full-time. Open for NGS.

Apart from a few fine old trees, notably a couple of Lebanon Cedars and a walnut, there is little in this garden, apart from some yew hedges, that can claim origins before the second world war. Around 1950 the late Thurstan Holland-Martin came to live in this late seventeenth century house and started a programme of enlarging the garden and planting a very large collection of trees, many quite rare. Since 1970 the present owners have continued to add to the collection, especially by creating new areas for shrubs. It must now be reckoned as one of the most important collections of woody plants in our area.

On approaching the entrance gate the first thing to catch our eye is a row of pleached limes along the roadside boundary and just behind a retaining wall. Behind this is a yew hedge. The drive will take us round to the west front into a courtyard, part gravel, part lawn on the other side of the hedge. Viewed from this side the upper half of the limes seems to sit on top of the hedge. The contrast in foliage is most effective.

The general character of this garden is best described as that of informally grouped trees and shrubs in mown grass. There are plenty of open stretches of lawn to create vistas and some denser planted areas with that feeling of intimacy which one associates with the 'secret garden'. There are some formal features but the wide open space effect predominates.

A lawn terrace is on the south and east fronts of the house. Along the middle of the east terrace is a wide paved path co-axial with an even wider grass path to the south. This is bordered with the Hybrid Musk Rose 'Felicia'. Still on the same axis but much more widely spaced are two rows of cider apples in the field below. The effect is striking. We often see rows of trees converging to give the effect of distance through exaggerated perspective. Here we have the opposite. But there is no need to create the illusion of distance. We have distance — several hundred yards of it. One has a feeling of reaching out into wide open spaces.

On the terrace are several features of note. Rose beds have been removed and two simple rectangles have been planted with a medley of dwarf spreading plants such as *Helianthemum* cvs, *Santolina* spp. and *Senecio laxifolius*. The dainty little rose 'The Fairy' fills a border under the south wall of the house and nearby an espalier trained Fuchsia Flowered Gooseberry *Ribes speciosus* always attracts attention. The training seems to accentuate the fuchsia — like character of the flowers. Just around the corner to the west is a flourishing *Itea ilicifolia* with evergreen holly-like leaves and pendant spikes of scented greenish flowers in late summer.

Below the wall of the south terrace a border of *Paeonia moutan* cvs are a notable feature. A south facing border backed by conifers supporting a 'Kiftsgate' rose has an assortment of shrubs and ground cover that is effective, *Choisya ternata, Tiarella cordifolia,* that most admirable of ground coverers, the variegated *Kerria japonica* and, unexpectedly gold laced polyanthus.

A rare small tree that I first took to be *Acer nikoense* is, in fact *A. triflorum*, brilliant in autumn colour. It has peculiarly furrowed bark. A fastigiate Tulip Tree is making good progress. Near the middle of the garden is a group of low topped spreading white flowered cherries of uncertain identity. They are quite spectacular when in bloom.

The previous owner extended the garden considerably on the east side and built a high retaining wall level with the garden so that one may now look out over open fields on that side. This does mean that the garden is exposed to cold winds from that quarter but as the trees grow up they will be, to some extent, self protecting.

A long narrow tongue of the garden runs eastwards from the north east corner. A sloping bank is densely planted with beech, larch and other things originally to provide a game covert. Below it on more level ground is a wide mown ride with many choice trees, including *Sorbus* in variety and the little known *Aesculus x mutabilis induta* with golden pink young leaves and a rate of growth of an inch or two a year. Among the many sorbus 'Wilfred Fox' may be mentioned as making a bold, upright — almost fastigiate — tree and *S. sargentiana* with its heavy twigs and big red buds, reminding one of horsechestnut.

A bog garden with double *Caltha palustris, Iris siberica*, hostas, trollius, primulas and astilbes and such items extends the plant range and substantial herbaceous borders extend it further.

Formality reaches its peak in an enclosed area near the middle of the garden. A swimming pool in a sunken garden with neat box hedges above the boundary walls adjoins another garden enclosed with hedges of *Cotoneaster lacteus*. This has a central round pool with fountain and lawn surround.

Court Farm

Mrs de Navarro

Broadway, on A44 in Broadway on S side of road at foot of Broadway Hill. Area: 2.8ha (7 acres) plus 3 acres orchard. Altitude: 114m (380ft). Soil: clay. Rainfall: 660mm (26in). Labour employed: one full-time plus one if obtainable. Open from time to time for NGS.

When the greatest American actress of her day and one of the greatest of all Shakespearean actresses decided to retire at the age of thirty, marry and create a garden in the heart of England there must have been many who mourned the loss to the stage. Yet this is just what happened. For Mary Anderson married Antonio de Navarro in 1890 and apart from a possible charity performance never appeared on the stage again.

Alfred Parsons, who is well known to horticulturists as the illustrator of Ellen Willmott's 'The Genus Rosa', also lived at Broadway, as indeed did several other noted artists, and it was Parsons in conjunction with Mary de Navarro who made the garden at Court Farm. The work was completed by the end of last century and in over eighty years it has not been changed. New trees have been planted and doubtless some old ones have gone but the basic design is unaltered and in spite of difficulties an impeccable standard of maintenance has been consistently kept up. It is therefore perhaps the least altered of nineteenth century gardens in the area covered by this book.

The house is close to the main street in Broadway so that the garden lies wholly behind on the south side, apart from a little semi-formal roadside garden to the east of the house. The ground rises slightly to the south-east giving lawns of varying levels maintained with low retaining walls. The drive entrance is on the west side of the house and is separated from the north end of the garden by a high yew hedge. More yew hedges are used as internal divisions.

Near the house are topiary peacocks and patterns of formal beds edged with dwarf box. A row of golden Irish yews runs east to west across one section, dividing the lawn near the house from the one above. Narrow borders on the tops of the retaining walls are planted with numerous small plants and many fine daffodils.

The mention of daffodils prompts the writer to digress. The late Mr de Navarro son of Mary Anderson was a noted amateur daffodil breeder and a winner of the Engleheart Cup. Many cultivars of his raising are still valued as parents by breeders.

Moving east but still at the north of the garden we find a rectangular pool with clipped yew corner pieces and *Cotoneaster horizontalis* breaking the hard edge. West of the pool is a design of elaborate beds separated by very narrow grass paths. The beds are now filled with roses. One suspects they once contained bedding plants. In most gardens they would have been scrapped long ago to reduce labour but here they are faithfully maintained. One can almost hear the actress saying 'Whatever happens the show goes on'.

East of the pool is a series of north to south running features. On the bank of the pool itself are shrubs, then a row of climbing roses up pillars with a connecting top-rail, a mown grass strip, a wide gravel path with a curved iron seat as an end stop at the south end, — another grass strip, a wide border of shrubs and shrub roses, more grass with a row of stepping stones down the middle, a row of lopped limes, not pleached but cut back hard each year, *Lilium monadelphum* in beds under the limes, roses up pillars in narrow border, more shrub roses with spring bulbs underneath, more grass and finally the east boundary hedge.

Here one can detect the influence of Wm Robinson for this is in many ways a garden of transition. There are links with Victorian formality and yet the freer use of plants which came with the twentieth century is anticipated.

South of all this we pass into mown grass with trees, some old, some young. A row of lombardy poplars is at the southern end of the east boundary. Along the south boundary itself is a stream, crossed by a little stone bridge leading to a wild woodland area filled with *Anemone appenina, A. blanda, A. nemorosa* and later in the year masses of *Lilium martagon,* later still *Colchicum spp.*

A nut walk is near the west boundary and links with the entrance drive. Among the older trees may be mentioned a large *Robinia pseudoacacia* and two limes near the house, a walnut and the rather uncommon *Malus trilobata*, narrow, upright with pointed top, a most pleasing and attractive tree well suited to the small garden.

Although this is an old garden preserved it is no mere museum piece. New plantings of trees and shrubs have gone on continuously, ensuring a fine garden for years to come given good maintenance.

For some twenty three years the head gardener, Mr J.E. Hood, trained at Barnwell Manor and Luton Hoo, has tended this garden with love and care with such help as has been available. One hopes that it will long continue.

The Courthouse
Mr & Mrs Ian Macpherson

Birlingham, two miles south of Pershore on A4104, Pershore to Upton-on-Severn. First turning left to Birlingham village. Area: 1.6ha (4 acres). Altitude 33m (110ft). Soil: loam to clay loam, slightly alkaline. Rainfall: 660mm (26in). Labour employed: one full-time gardener.

The garden is pleasantly situated with a view of Bredon Hill three miles to the south east and a steep drop of about 60 feet to the River Avon on the north side, giving views over the river meadows.

The house dates from early 19th century with substantial additions a century later. The present owners purchased the house in 1970 when the garden was in a state of some neglect although it did contain a number of mature trees.

Tree and shrub planting, some isolated specimens and some in beds, has been carried out by the present owners and is still continuing so that we now have an eight year old garden superimposed on the framework of an earlier one.

Mown grass covers most of the area and this is bisected by the entrance drive leaving most of the garden on the east or right hand side of the drive as one enters. The smaller area of lawn in front of the house contains a number of mature trees, most prominent of which is a good specimen of Corsican pine with an abnormally large witches broom in it. There is a weeping ash, a small cedar, robinias, and three mulberry trees. The latter are small by 'stately homes' standards and probably date from the earlier part of this century.

Care has been taken to maintain large areas of unplanted lawn near to the house so that there is a feeling of space and the effect of the planting is enhanced.

It is very much the modern labour saving garden with small cultivated areas and well handled ground cover. An unexpected item hidden behind a shrub border is a small swimming pool.

A prominent feature is a very fine specimen holly, *Ilex aquifolium* with a dense mass of foliage down to ground level. There is also a good specimen of the hybrid holly *I. x altaclarensis*. A group of silver birch near the east boundary is a focal point and a break of Norway spruce form a screen near the roadside.

An old cider mill has been planted with rock plants and provides one of the few hard surface items in the garden.

A grass walk along the top of the bank is partially screened by shrubs from the rest of the garden and forms an attractive feature. Bulbs are a prominent feature in the Spring.

The walled kitchen garden is very well maintained and although mainly cropped with vegetables the only herbaceous plants in the garden are to be found here.

Croft Castle
The National Trust

Leominster, take B4361 N of Leominster 5 miles and turn left on B4362 2½ miles. Croft Castle is on right. Area: 2ha (5 acres). Altitude: 167m (550ft). Soil: lime free. Rainfall: 750mm (29.5in). Labour employed: two. Open for NT and NGS.

Croft Castle dates from about the fourteenth or fifteenth century but it is probable that the site accommodated an earlier building as the Croft family was here at the time of the Domesday Book.

Trees are the main attraction at Croft. The Sweet Chestnut avenue is famous. The older row is thought to be 350 years old and its companions perhaps about 100. This runs westward from the castle along the line of a former approach drive. The present drive passes through avenues of oak and beech. Fortunately the mid eighteenth century landscape movement passed Croft by and the avenues remain. New avenues of lime and beech have recently been planted.

Approaching the gateway entrance through the beech avenue one finds a vigorous specimen of the Kiftsgate rose covering the wall. Beyond the gateway the east lawn lies to the left of the drive and at this point is a large layered lime, a survivor of an earlier avenue. Nearby is a group of young *Parotia persica* which will be a feature in the next century.

The lawn on east, south and west of the castle is divided from the parkland by a Ha-Ha. There are three large limes on the south lawn and others have been planted to complete a row. Near the small church is a good specimen of the Monterey Pine *Pinus radiata*.

All these trees are sufficiently far from the castle for the building to stand clear and isolated behind the lawns. Shrubs, including some climbers break the hard lines at ground level but do not cover great areas of the walls. A climbing Lady Hillingdon rose was tall and looking particularly happy.

Near the north west corner of the castle is a tiny secret garden divided into four sectors by gravel cross paths.

The old walled garden, north of the castle, is being organised, planned and planted, largely through the energies of Mrs Uhlman, Lord Croft's sister. Many differing treatments are meted out to the walled gardens of stately homes. Here a creditable attempt has been made to create a garden of interest but above all do something with the site and not abandon it.

The garden has been partly grassed down and two rows of *Juniperus communis hibernica* border a wide path running east to west. Near the centre a formal rose garden has been made with a retaining wall on the lower (south) side so creating a level garden on a sloping site. There is another small rectangular garden with bamboos, semi-formal walling and odd shrubs. The borders under the east and north facing walls have been planted with shrubs and some herbaceous plants. Apples and other trees have been planted. Much of this work has been done with unskilled labour and some features lack professional finish but how good it is to see something being done.

North of the entrance drive at the bottom of a steep woodland bank lies Fishpool Valley, a chain of connected pools created in the eighteenth century.

But above all Croft Castle is a place of parkland trees. Oaks, wellingtonias, pines and others all contribute to the general atmosphere of peace and serenity.

Dinmore Manor

J.S. Murray Esq

Herefordshire, on W side of A49 Hereford — Leominster road. Six miles N of Hereford. Area: .4ha (1 acre). Altitude: 120m (400ft). Soil: lime free. Rainfall: 750mm (29.5in). Open daily.

The Manor of Dinmore has ancient connections with the Order of St John of Jerusalem. The Chapel dates from about 1370 but much of the present Manor House including the Cloisters was built by Richard Hollins Murray who purchased the estate in 1927. Building was completed in 1936.

The garden is not large. It consists substantially of a rock garden typical of the period between the wars when interest in this type of garden was at its height. The cloisters form the boundary on two sides.

A stream flows through and there are small pools. A stone bridge crosses the stream.

Planting consists of numerous *Acer palmatum*, smallish conifers and other dwarf shrubs, in addition to the commoner rock plants such as aubrieta, alyssum and the like. Whilst it is not a plantsman's garden there is plenty of variety and it is colourful and attractive.

An ancient yew stands close to the chapel. The ground falls away steeply to the south giving magnificent views.

Duckswich House

Mr and Mrs E.C.S. Howard

Upton-on-Severn, from Upton take A4104 and turn left opposite Tunnel Hill P.O. Area: 2ha (5 acres). Altitude: 20m (65ft). Soil: about neutral. Rainfall: 660mm (26in). Labour employed: one plus owners. Open for NGS.

This is a fine modern house in brick of a beautiful soft red. It was completed in 1953 but a start was made on the garden in 1951-2.

In some respects this garden is almost unique among all others in this book. The whole project — house and garden — was planned as an integral unit in the first place and has been subjected to little alteration

Above: Dinmore Manor. The cloisters are an attractive background to the rock garden which is well planted with forms of *Acer palmatum,* dwarf rhododendrons, ericas and conifers.

Below: Duckswich House. Millstones, used as steps down from the main terrace, give a touch of distinction to this modern garden.

since. Most gardens are modified and restyled over the years and retain features of different periods. This one was created on open farmland and has just matured over thirty years.

The garden is large by modern standards and the original design and planting was by Jefferies of Cirencester. It has a professional stamp on it but the owner's contribution must not be underestimated.

From the terrace in the south front we look over a very large expanse of open lawn. Informal beds of shrubs are around the margins and at the southern end we can see a pool of fair size. To the west some four to five miles away is the Hereford Beacon at the southern tip of the Malverns.

The terrace edge is curved — almost semicircular — and the level is maintained by a retaining wall of red sandstone, specially brought from the Forest of Dean to match the brick of the house. In the spring it is colourful with alyssum and aubrieta. Leading down to the lawn below are two sets of steps, to the south-east and south-west respectively, made of millstones laid flat. In the middle, at lawn level is a small semicircular formal pond with a wrought iron background bearing the date, just in case future generations forget when the house was built.

On the west side of the main lawn a low branched multi-stemmed *Catalpa bignonioides* flowers well but has not, so far, fruited and a medlar is producing its usual dense umbrella head with branches to lawn level. It is grafted on hawthorn and suckers freely.

As we approach the pool a very fine *Amelanchier canadensis* is a feature in April. Beyond the pool is a natural woodland garden with the native *Anemona nemorosa* and the introduced *A. blanda* naturalised. Also naturalised are some of the older types of narcissus — especially those dainty little things that used to be called 'Leedsii' before the modern classification came into being.

Rhododendrons can be grown here but are not completely happy. A vigorous young *Eucryphia* 'Nymansay' however is quite at home.

On the west side is an herbaceous garden, rectangular in shape and enclosed in clipped yew hedges with access points on all sides. The planting is in two large elliptical beds down the middle with a central sundial between them. This garden has been somewhat modified since the original plan when there were borders in front of the hedge. Lawn now goes up to the hedge and makes for easier clipping as well as a better proportioned layout.

To the south-east of the house is an orchard type planting of fruit trees with a few ornamentals such as almond and cherries also included. The fruit trees are grown as much for their flowers as for their fruit.

The entrance drive comes in from the east to the north front. South of this, screening the tennis court, are more shrubs among which were noted *Ribes aureum,* the North American 'Buffalo Currant' with yellow flowers

Dunley Hall. John Lea, Britain's foremost daffodil breeder, recording his new seedlings and making more crosses.

and glossy leaves, the fine foliaged *Viburnum davidii* and *Buddleia alternifolia.*

East of the main terrace is a large *Garrya elliptica* and nearby, free fruiting sea buckthorns, *Hippophae rhamnoides.* An attractive wistaria covered pergola screens the tennis court on this side.

This must be counted as a fine modern garden. It has a good range of interesting plants. The formal and informal do not clash and the whole layout shows excellent good taste.

Dunley Hall
J.S.B. Lea Esq.

Stourport-on-Severn, 2.4km (1½ miles) SW of Stourport on A451. Area: 2.5ha (6¼ acres). Altitude: 60m (200ft). Soil: sandy loam, lime free. Rainfall: 700mm (27.5in). Open for NGS.

The house dates from about 1540 and was probably a farm house for some centuries. The present owner has lived there all his life but for most of that time the garden was comparatively small — consisting of drive, kitchen garden and a small area immediately adjoining the house. Most of the present garden was a field until 1962 when the planting of choice trees and shrubs seriously commenced.

The short entrance drive leads into a courtyard the surrounding walls of which are well covered in climbers, notably wisteria, *Vitis coignetiae,* and *V. vinifera purpurea.* In the drive itself a specimen of *Garrya elliptica* faces one as one enters.

On the opposite side of the house, facing south west lies the garden proper. There is a large central expanse of lawn around which trees and shrubs are grouped in irregular borders, especially on the south west side. An old half-timbered barn forms an attractive feature on the east side of the lawn.

It is fortunate that when the field was taken over some mature trees went with it. Two beech, one oak and a lime form a dominant group near the centre and give the sense of maturity which cannot be obtained with new plantings. There are also numerous birch planted just before the last war and are now handsome elegant trees. A few scots pines and other trees complete the pre 1962 picture and give height and character.

Planting since 1962 consists of a large collection of choice and interesting trees and shrubs but in the planting the overall design has not been lost. One feels that items were chosen because they suited that particular position rather than because the owner wanted to grow that shrub anyway and had to find room for it. The design nevertheless is simple and amounts to little more than keeping the centre open and paying attention to associations and contrasts.

Magnolias abound in this garden. *M. X loebneri* 'Merrill' is already a small tree and flowers freely. The very beautiful *M. hypoleuca (obovata)* is happily established as are the two fine forms of *M. campbellii*, 'Charles Raffil' and *mollicomata*. Other notables are *M. X veitchii*, *M. soulangeana alba* and *M. salicifolia*. *M. wilsonii* is now recovering from the drought of 1976 in which it suffered badly.

A standard of *Cladastris sinensis* forms a pleasant little umbrella as does *Gleditsia japonica*, as yet almost spineless.

A tree of which Mr. Lea is particularly proud is a healthy young specimen of *Sorbus domestica*, the true service tree, which was clonally propagated from the old tree at Arley which was itself a direct descendant of the truly wild tree in the Wyre Forest which disappeared last century. *Metasequoia glyptostroboides* from the original seed importations in 1948 is doing quite well but not as large as some others in the south of England.

That very fine rambling evergreen rose, *Rosa lucens*, which now seems to be more correctly known as *R. longicuspis* sprawls about happily near the south west corner. Mr. Lea tells me that it is now attracting the attention of the rose breeders which is not surprising for its huge panicles of large white highly scented flowers suggest that it has a contribution to make, especially if, as I believe it is resistant to black spot and mildew.

Some seedling *Malus toringoides* show considerable variation in fruit size and shape but are brilliant in autumn colour both of fruit and foliage. *Prunus sargentii* has made good growth and there are now some sizeable trees of this excellent cherry.

If that were all that is of horticultural interest at Dunley it would be an interesting garden but it is in another field that John Lea has attained fame. He is today our foremost breeder of exhibition daffodils.

The Royal Horticultural Society awards the Engleheart Cup each year for the best exhibit of twelve cultivars raised by the exhibitor. Mr Lea has won this cup nine times in the period 1971-81 and for the last seven years on the run. He has also had the best bloom in the show twenty times. An impressive record.

To visit Dunley at daffodil time is a pleasure that should not be missed. Perfection in any field is always worth looking for and this is perfection indeed.

Eastnor Castle

The Hon. Mrs Hervey-Bathurst

Ledbury, 4km (2½ miles) from Ledbury on A438 Tewkesbury road. Area: approx. 32ha (80 acres) plus 10ha (25 acres) Lake. Altitude: 90m (300ft). Rainfall: 840mm (33in). Open frequently from Easter to end of September. See H.H.C.G.

This is a mock mediaeval castle built early in the nineteenth century. The garden proper is not open to the public and it is the arboretum which is the attraction. This contains a large conifer collection and includes specimens as fine as any to be seen in Britain. Many of these were planted by Lord Somers in the period 1840-60.

The main drive enters the arboretum from the north and on the right hand or western side one is immediately confronted with what is claimed to be the largest *Cedrus atlantica*, the Atlas cedar, in Britain. Nearby is a fine Redwood, *Sequoia sempervirens*. Further west is a Noble Fir, *Abies procera* and a particularly pleasing *Chamaecyparis nootkatensis*. This is broadly conical with an attenuated apex and is a tree of distinction.

Poplars are an important tree in the large commercial woodlands on the estate and a representative collection of the varieties used is to be seen on the east side of the entrance gate along the roadside.

Continuing along the drive we find a group of large Wellingtonias on the left hand side. There are numerous Lebanon and Deodar cedars.

Just before the drive turns left to lead to the castle courtyard car park one sees ahead a superb Bishop's Pine, *Pinus muricata* from California. This is broadly domed with blunt pointed top and massive lower branches which are typical of this species. A little to the south of this is a large specimen of the uncommon Lucombe Oak *Quercus x lucombeana*, a hybrid between *Q. cerris* and *Q. suber*. The first named parent is the Turkey oak and is deciduous, the second is the Cork oak and is evergreen. The cross appears to have arisen in several places and occurs naturally in Southern Europe. Our form is credited to a nurseryman named Lucombe of Exeter where it arose in 1762. It is semi-evergreen and the bark is somewhat corky. In fact it is as one would expect intermediate between its parents.

Travelling south west from here we pass many more fine trees. Incense cedars, western hemlocks, pines in variety, douglas fir and others. There are broadleaved deciduous trees also. Many fine oaks are obviously older than the conifers. The rare hop hornbeam *Ostrya carpinifolia* is here. This never makes a very big tree. It is a relative of the true hornbeam and our common hazel.

An old Grecian fir *Abies cephalonica* is slowly wearing out but it has been a fine specimen.

We can continue southwards to a little summer house and turning east we arrive at the southern end of the lake. The outlet runs noisily over a weir and forms a stream which is crossed by a narrow footbridge. From here we can reach the eastern bank of the lake and get a fine view of the castle on steeply rising ground on the opposite bank.

Returning via the west side of the lake we find yet another group of Wellingtonias.

Eastnor is a place where all can find pleasure. Merely to walk among fine trees is a delight even if one knows little about them. The connoisseur or knowledgeable tree specialist could spend many days here and still make exciting discoveries.

Fawley Court

Mr and Mrs J.P.F. Clay

12km (7½ miles) from Ross on Wye, west of B4224 Ross — Hereford road. Turn off for How Caple about 5 miles from Ross. Area: 1ha (2.5ac). Altitude: 90m (300ft). Soil: free draining sand. Alkaline.One full time gardener. Opens occasionally under the National Garden Scheme.

Although the house was built in 1610 there is no surviving evidence of a garden prior to the present one which is only about fifteen years old. Prior to that time there was a small kitchen garden behind the house and very little more. That kitchen garden has now been planted with roses and herbaceous plants with a central lawn. A hedge of rose 'Nevada' forms a roadside boundary and, on the terrace below, the hedge is continued with the hybrid musk 'Penelope'. The garden at this point is some five or six feet above road level and is supported by a retaining wall. The exceptionally free drainage presents drought problems in dry weather.

There are made up beds of azaleas and on the side and front of the house are more roses in rectangular beds.

Daffodils and other bulbs are planted in grass on both sides of the road in front of the house and on the side opposite the house a water garden has been developed over the last eight years from farm land. This is based on three pools. One of these by the roadside is really an ancient horsepond. The second has been dredged and is now the main feature. The third is still beyond the garden boundary but one suspects that it may one day be incorporated into the garden.

The first two pools are surrounded by mown grass with large areas including shrub roses and many other choice shrubs. There is a row of weeping willows along the lower side of the second pool.

The garden is still developing and is very well managed by the gardener, Mr Edwards.

Garnons
Sir John Cotterill

11km (7 miles) W of Hereford on N side of A438. Area: 7ha (17 acres). Altitude: 120m (400ft). Soil: lime free. Rainfall: 750mm (29.5in). Labour employed: one, plus one part-time. Open for NGS.

The house faces south and looks over lawns to the Repton parkland beyond. The lawn level is about eight feet above the park and is supported by a retaining wall. A very large neatly trimmed pyracantha covers part of the house.

The so-called 'old garden' on the west side consists of lawn on lowerppart and a sloping bank above with many new tree plantings. *Betula jacquemontii* was doing well and two *Sorbus aucuparia* 'Beissneri' planted in 1965 had reached a height of 25 feet. Their bright orange bark was most striking. Also worth noting was *S. hupenhense* planted in 1972.

A holm oak 'tunnel' leads to 'The Pleasance' where rhododendrons and other shrubs have been established in open woodland. The familiar *Rhododendron* 'Praecox' was in flower in early April. On a grander scale is *R. calophytum* one of the finest of the large leaved species. The pretty little *Forsythia ovata* looked well on this occasion. Why is this not grown more widely in small gardens?

Some very good young specimens of *Acer hersii* were noted and the uncommon *Quercus imbricaria* making a particularly erect tree with thinner lower branches than is usual for oaks. The elliptic, entire leaves are not very oak-like.

Access to the east garden from the south lawn is through a tunnel under the entrance drive. There are several good Lebanon Cedars, *Cedrus libani* on the east side and numerous large oaks in grass with daffodils underneath. This grass is now mown once a year only which means that the daffodil foliage is able to die off completely. How often one finds it cut prematurely in the interests of tidiness. In this part of the garden yews are prominent, some quite large. Groups of rhododendrons have been planted and the bold leaved *R. rex* was quite happy in a sheltered spot.

Sorbus aria 'Majestica' has reached 40 feet in 15 years from planting, *Liquidamber styraciflua* 35 feet in 19 years and *Sorbus scalaris* quite a big tree in 15 years. This latter species is one of the most interesting of E.H. Wilson's introductions and is rarely seen.

Clipped yew and box hedges indicate our approach to more formal gardening as the walled garden is reached. As with most walled gardens things have changed but here good standards still apply. A hard tennis court has taken one sector out of cultivation and a large block of poplar cutting beds has meant a change of use.

A line of old bothies against the outside of the garden wall remind one of the grand old days.

Gatley Park, Leinthall Earls

Capt and Mrs Thomas Dunne

9 miles NW of Leominster. Turn E off A4110 between Aymestry and Wigmore. Area: 0.8ha (2ac). Altitude: 165m (550ft). Soil: medium loam, neutral to slightly alkaline. Rainfall: 750mm (29.5in). Open for NGS.

The house was originally a black and white structure of Tudor period. In 1634 it was bricked over by Samson Eure and this is the Jacobean house we have today. Philip Dunne purchased the estate in 1679 and it has remained in the family ever since.

The house is approached by a mile long drive through well wooded parkland from the village of Leinthall Earls. The entrance drive is on the north side of the house. On the south side the land falls away steeply giving fine views over woodlands. It has one of the most beautiful settings in the West Midlands.

The garden seems to have been essentially a Victorian creation. Most of the layout was completed around 1870 and no substantial changes in design have been made since.

There is an area of lawn on each side of the entrance drive. To the west of this are double hedges of clipped yew with domes on top. On the east side there is a retaining wall supporting a raised border. The north and east sides are enclosed by walls, the south by the house itself. The west facing border under the east wall is a mixed planting of shrubs and herbaceous plants with a preponderance of shrub roses. A particularly floriferous group of *Agapanthus* is noteworthy.

On the west side of the house is a small lawn with a clipped yew balustrade, beyond which, still further west is a swimming pool and north of this a hard tennis court. Both of these are discretely tucked away and are not seen by casual garden visitors as they regretably are in so many gardens.

South of the house are a series of four terraces set on the steep slope. The top terrace consists of lawn with climbers and shrubs on the wall of the house. *Magnolia grandiflora, Jasminum nudiflorum, Chaenomeles*, and roses were noted here. The second terrace is mainly grass with a border under the wall. The purple leaved vine *Vitis vinifera purpurea* is particularly effective. Terrace number three consists of formal rose beds in grass. This terrace is itself on four levels being stepped down to the west. On one of these sub-terraces is a central bird-path. The lowest terrace, merging into woodland, has a border of shrub roses.

Spring bulbs are a feature of an area at the end of the approach drive, east of the house. The old walled kitchen garden deep down the hillside has now been abandoned but a small kitchen garden has been established to the east of the terraces.

Haffield

Mr and Mrs Alan Cadbury

4.8km (3 miles) S of Ledbury on A417, 3.2 km (3 miles) from junction 2 of M50 on road to Ledbury. Area: 2.4ha (6 acres). Altitude: 60m (200ft). Soil: netural. Rainfall: 840mm (33in). Labour employed: one plus part-time man. Open for NGS.

The principal horticultural feature of Haffield today is a garden in an old quarry which has been developed by the present owners during the last twenty seven years. There are many fine trees, some dating from the early nineteenth century, when the house was built, some much earlier. But before talking about these present day features we will dwell for a moment on an earlier period.

Some years ago Miles Hadfield sent to Mrs Cadbury an extract from The Gardener's Magazine of 1836. The article, by D. Beaton, then Head Gardener at Haffield, describes a vineyard purchased about 1720 by Jacob Tonson, a London bookseller and publisher. This appears to have been part of a total purchase of twenty five acres. It is thought that the main grape grown was White Muscadine and from the evidence of wine making equipment including a wine press purchased with the property it would seem that wine making was well established. The superb tulip tree on the main lawn was also probably planted around the middle of the eighteenth century.

By 1815 the property and two other estates passed to William Gordon who engaged Sir Robert Smirke to design the house. This is a typical Regency style small mansion facing almost due south and looking straight at May Hill eight miles away. Doubtless many trees belong to this period including Cedars of Lebanon and possibly a very fine Holm Oak although this may be older.

Gordon died in 1837 and the next owner Dr W.C. Henry continued tree planting. Most notable is an avenue of Wellingtonias *Sequoiadendron giganteum* lining what is now a farm road but which once was doubtless the main access drive. These were planted in 1868 and there is little doubt that the numerous coast redwoods (*Sequoia sempervirens*) and other American conifers belong also to the Dr. Henry period. Henry died in 1892 and after three more owners and two world wars Haffield was purchased by the present owners in 1954.

The garden today is an excellent compromise between the elaborate and detailed management of earlier years and the modern labour saving garden. The wide expanse of open lawn still gives uninterrupted views over May Hill. The ancient tulip tree, once struck by lightening, which destroyed the main trunk, has produced such vigorous regrowth as to make it one of the finest in Britain, is on the west side of the open lawn. Paired with it but about two centuries younger is a cedar of Lebanon planted in the late 1950s. Further back but wider apart are a pair of *Cryptomeria japonica* of nineteenth century origin. A high retaining wall level with the lawn forms the southern boundary of the garden.

Further east the lawn is planted with several trees of interest including a *Ginkgo biloba*. This leads round to the entrance drive flanked with tall rhodo-dendrons against a background of woodland with azaleas underplanted.

Opposite the east front of the house with the woodland behind it is the quarry garden. This consists of massive exposures of Haffield Breccia rising in amphitheatre fashion above the floor of neatly mown lawn. A plant of ivy 'Gold Heart' is covering a vertical face. A prostrate cotoneaster tumbles down some twenty feet. Camellias, well budded and very healthy occupy areas at the base along with fuchsias. There are masses of *Polypodium vulgare* and clumps of *Phyllitis scolopendrium*, two common native ferns but welcome none the less. There are many of the usual rock plants and spring bulbs.

Moving round to the west of the house we find a large sloping grass bank in which the native daffodil is naturalised in quantity. Numerous trees are growing here including an attractive silver birch, a youngish *Cedrus atlantica glauca, Picea pungens glauca*, a rather columnar Wellingtonia and yet another *Sequoia sempervirens.* Near the foot of the bank we merge with the western end of the main lawn. Here is an elderly specimen of the cucumber tree *Magnolia acuminata* now more or less lying down and *M. virginiana (glauca)* still in the flush of youth. Wedged in the SW corner of two walls of the house is a particularly robust and well furnished *M. grandiflora.* Many other recent plantings are to be found in this area.

A mysterious short tunnel connects the west lawn with the walled garden. Its origin is unknown and its function not obvious. Most people will enter the walled garden by the more conventional route through the door. There is really a walled garden within a walled garden. The main garden has been abandoned but is kept tidy and consists of mown grass. A few old fruit trees remain on the walls. The smaller garden is well managed and cropped. A range of old pits that no doubt have seen pineapples and melons in years gone by, now produce inefficiently a few tomatoes and the old lean-to vineries struggle on to the end. It is quite uneconomic to repair them and they remain as does the bothy behind the wall a reminder of days past.

Hagley Hall

Viscount and Viscountess Cobham

Stourbridge, 13km (8 miles) from Birmingham on S side of A456 Birmingham to Kidderminster road. Area: 800ha (2,000 acres). Altitude: (450-750ft). Soil: lime free. Rainfall: 700mm (27.5in). In 1981 open daily 1.30pm — 5.0pm from 23 May to 6 September.

Hagley is interesting in that it was one of the first of the 'picturesque' landscape gardens of the mid-eighteenth century. The first Lord Lyttelton, influenced by the poet William Shenstone and the poet and writer Alexander Pope among others conceived the idea of a vast landscape with eye catching columns, temples and mock ruins. The steeply undulating slopes of the Clent Hills provided an ideal site for such an enterprise and during the 1750's the work was carried out.

The house itself was built in 1760, replacing an Elizabethan manor. Sanderson Miller of Radway, on the Edge Hills in Warwickshire, was the architect of both house and ruined castle and probably other features.

What makes Hagley unusual among the landscape gardens of the period is the absence of subsequent 'Victorianisation' such as occurred with so many. Gardening in the strict sense seems to have been confined to the large walled garden, as it still is.

The Church is near the north east front of the house and north of this point on a distant hill is the obelisk. The needs of agriculture prevent public access to this feature but it was meant to be viewed from a distance anyway. The route the public must follow includes the Prince of Wales monument north east from the church. Lord Lyttelton was secretary to Frederick Prince of Wales, hence the tribute.

The pools and cascades, once, no doubt, a notable feature, have become somewhat silted up and Pope's Urn now consists only of its plinth bearing the date 1714. Plans for the restoration of many features however are in hand. Sanderson Miller's mock castle ruin is the most distant point of the official route.

Fine trees abound in the park. There are Lebanon Cedars, horse chestnuts, limes and beech but the trees that impressed me most were the sycamores. The sycamore is so often regarded as a weed among trees, competing with buddleias on bombsites and even establishing itself in gaps between paving slabs. Here at Hagley they have been planted with room to develop and been given some measure of care. They are quite majestic.

Anyone looking for a one and a half mile walk in beautiful country could do worse than visit Hagley.

Hergest Croft

W.L. Banks Esq. and R.A. Banks Esq.

About 1.6km (1 mile) W of Kington. Turn L off A44. Area: 20ha (50 acres). Altitude: 240m (800in). Soil: Fairly light, stony, acid. Rainfall: 89cm (35in). Labour employed: five plus Mr R.A. Banks. Open daily from May to September and on some days earlier and later. See Yellow Book (NGS).

Hergest Croft as a home for trees and other plants has slowly evolved over the past century. No famous garden designers have been concerned with its development. No master plan seems to have existed at any time.

The garden designer will decide on his scheme. He will require his plants to have certain characteristics of colour, form and texture and will select those plants accordingly.

The plantsman decides that he would like to grow certain plants and then proceeds to find somewhere to put them. This presupposes that there are sites suitable for the plants in question. The owners of Hergest Croft have always been plantsmen but this must not be taken as implying a lack of appreciation of grouping and siting for effect, but it does mean that the well being of the plant came first. The part is greater than the whole.

The history of Hergest Croft goes back to the mid nineteenth century when R.W. Banks (1820-1891) purchased Ridgebourne. His son W.H. Banks (1867-1930) was a garden enthusiast and on his marriage in 1895 started building Hergest Croft which he altered and extended until the First World War. He laid the garden out much as it is today and planted the conifer avenue on the west of the garden.

In 1910 Park Wood was purchased and he planted masses of rhododendrons, especially on the south west sloping bank, now known as the Flower Fall. These rhododendrons were the ordinary garden hybrids of the time. W.H. Banks was greatly assisted by his head gardener George Bampfield whose high standards of work matched those of his employer.

After the war rhododendrons continued to be planted both at Park Wood and Hergest Croft. Several thousand were planted in the first ten years. By now species and first crosses were occupying his attention and he sought far and wide for supplies. Around 200 different species were obtained from some 40 sources at this period.

It was shortly after the First World War that George James came as head gardener. He had had his early training at Overbury Court and was thus well versed in the highest standards of private gardening but the large scale tree and shrub collection was a new experience and a new responsibility which he accepted readily.

W.H. Banks died in 1930 and his widow carried on as best she could with the help of George James. Our present Mr R.A. Banks (son of W.H.) was unable to spend much time at Hergest Croft and some decline set in until after the Second World War. By 1953 he was able to do more. George James retired after 34 years service and Bill Cowdell who had been in the garden since he was 14 took over. When he retired at the end of 1974 he had served 51 years.

Mr R.A. Banks had retired in 1964 and devoted most of his time to the garden. The recovery of wartime neglect was now under way.

During the years that have elapsed since the original plantings much overcrowding has occured and it has been necessary to do a great deal of careful thinning. New plantings have gone on all the time.

Although the trees and woodland plantings are the most important part of Hergest Croft we must not overlook the numerous attractive features of the garden proper.

One enters the garden with the house on the right or west side past some beds of daffodils to a small rock and water garden with two informal pools providing a natural feature against a background of trees and shrubs. In addition to water lilies in the pools there are the usual marginals *Peltiphyllum peltatum, Lysichitum americanum,* candelabra primulas; in fact most of the plants one expects to find in such a situation in a good garden. The earlier mention of daffodils is a reminder that in the spring the garden abounds in bulbs. There is a considerable snowdrop collection with forms of *Galanthus nivalis* and *G. plicatum* present in quantity. *Scilla bifolia* has naturalised in the mown grass and *S. siberica* is abundant in the rock and bog garden. *Crocus vernus,* the first crocus to get on the British list as a naturalised alien, is an early feature followed by daffodils and *Anemone appenina.* Under an old hornbeam at the northern entrance to the rock garden we find an area of *Fritillaria meleagris* and *Erythronium revolutum* 'Johnsonii', a good pink form of the species. These early bulbs are rarely seen by garden visitors but the garden is often opened for a few days extra to the advertised times for those who wish to come.

The path from the rock garden leads on to the lawn over which the south front of the house looks. Westwards of this is further lawn, and further west from this is the conifer avenue planted at the turn of the century. North from here is the main collection of deciduous azaleas.

The layout of the western area comprises a group of trees and shrubs in rough mown grass with pockets of interest and the occasional larger vista.

A catalogue of all the species represented would convey little of the character of this garden. Items which I noted include a massive *Pinus nigra* supporting *Vitis coignettiae,* many birches, some of dubious identity. Birches look so much alike. *Betula jacquemontii, B. albo-sinensis, B. papyrifera* and the large leaved multi-stemmed *B. medwediewii* however, are not subject to much dispute. *B. davurica* is less certain. The rare Japanese *Zelkova serrata* is interesting and a hybrid walnut *Juglans nigra x regia* planted at the start of the century must be uncommon. *Cedrella sinensis,* the so-called Chinese cedar but not even a conifer, in fact more like ailanthus, was another tree of interest.

Acers are an important genus at Hergest Croft. A fine specimen of *A. griseum* near the gate to Park Wood has a clear trunk just over a metre high and a girth of over one and a half metres (5½ft) in 1971 when its height was 15m (50ft). It was planted in 1910, and is one of the oldest in the country. *A palmatum* 'Senaki' is about of the same age and had a height of nine metres (30ft) and a branch spread of seven and a half metres (25ft) in 1971. This is a very pleasing tree with its bright red young branches and bright pale green leaves, turning rich gold in the autumn. This was at one time quite rare but it is now more widely planted but there can be few specimens to equal this one.

Possibly the rarest maple here is in Park Wood. This is *A. giraldii.* The young shoots carry a white bloom and the leaves are white felted underneath. It is otherwise a little like sycamore. Other acers I made notes of as being of interest were *A nikoense* with its glorious autumn colour and the unusual fastigiate *A. palmatum* 'Ribesifolium'.

The gutta-percha tree *Eucommia ulmoides,* otherwise the hardy rubber tree is recognised by its latex which when drawn out into strands hardens and has considerable tensile strength. This is a Chinese species and is rarely seen.

Davidia involucrata always attracts attention and is now commonly planted but as it takes a long time to reach flowering size leaves are more common than flowers in most gardens. Two fine specimens flowering very freely in 1979 are here. These are believed to have been planted in 1903 and are of the var. *vilmoriniana* which came here via France in 1901. Wilson's introduction of the type species was not until 1904. The larger of the two trees at Hergest Croft measured 16½m (55ft) x one metre (3½ft) in 1961.

Park Wood is a natural coomb with a pool made by damming the stream which flows through in a southwesterly direction. A bridge crosses at the dammed end. Looking south west from the bridge in rhododendron time one looks over the magnificent 'Flower Fall' earlier mentioned. This is a double bank of considerable size the flowers seeming to tumble in cascades into the stream below.

With a collection of rhododendrons of this size it is impossible to mention all but a few by name. The hybrid 'Loderi' must, however, not be passed over. This superb cultivar of tree size and exquisite perfume is one of the outstanding features of Park Wood.

Whereas the earlier rhododendron plantings at Park Wood were at the lower levels with garden hybrids the later plantings at higher levels were mainly with species. This is a feature which adds interest to the walk through this fascinating woodland.

A few items that I noted in Park Wood may be mentioned. I was impressed by the elegance of *Carpinus turczaninowii* with its small leaves and delicate growth. A good stand of that fine Chinese poplar, *Populus lasiocarpa* has produced fertile seed. A fine specimen of *Abies bracteata*, with long bracts to the cones and sharp spiny points to its very large leaves, catches the eye. A collection of larches has recently been planted. *Thuja koraiensis* measuring 9.3m (31ft) x 0.6m (2ft) in 1961, and now obviously much bigger is an attractive species. A tall, narrow, columnar tree with tips of branches sweeping upwards and a silver reverse to the shoots, this could be a good tree for small gardens. It was apparently introduced by E.H. Wilson in 1917. The trees in Park Wood were planted in 1925. *Lomatia ferruginea*, an interesting small shrubby tree from Chile, had lost its top in recent snow but enough remained to show the beauty of its rusty brown young shoots and much divided leaves. The California Bay

Above: Hergest Croft. Usually thought of as a place for trees and rhododendrons, it is a surprise to many to find a considerable herbaceous collection. These borders in the old kitchen garden are very fine.

Below: Loen. A garden on the edge of the Wyre Forest showing transition from natural woodland to modern informal garden.

Umbellularia californica is noted for its strongly aromatic foliage when crushed. It is not common and although not a very distinguished plant it adds variety.

The pond at Park Wood has margins heavily planted with osmundas, rodgersias, lysichitums, and other moisture lovers and clumps of bamboos add grace to the scene.

Returning to the main Hergest Croft garden we must visit the walled garden, containing, in addition to soft fruit and vegetables, herbaceous borders and other features. There is a small bird bath which forms the central feature surrounded by formal beds in a lawn. It was interesting to see the perennial wallflower Wenlock Beauty used as a bedding plant and left in for several years. It is hardly ever out of flower.

Herbaceous borders with wide grass paths were well planted with a good range of plants. Bearded iris were a feature in June and an exceptionally fine clump of *Dictamnus albus*, the purple form, was outstanding.

Other herbaceous plants of interest noted in various places were *Senecio smithii*, *Bulbinella hookeri* and cimicifugas.

Loen

Mr and Mrs S.K. Quayle

Long Bank, Bewdley, 3km (2 miles) W of Bewdley on A456. Turn left beside red brick church into small lane. Area: 2.4ha (6.0 acres). Altitude: 120m (400ft). Soil: sandy loam. Acid. Rainfall: 700m (27.5in). Labour employed: one man. Open for NGS.

To start off with a piece of Wyre Forest is a good step towards a fine garden. When this site is then handled so that its original character is not lost but the garden is fitted into it a fine garden has been achieved. This is what has happened at Loen.

Mr and Mrs Quayle built their attractive modern house in 1935 on the Wyre Forest margin. The site contained some mature oaks and birch but had been coppiced over a very long period so that much immature birch was present also and some clearing was necessary.

The war halted work but afterwards development steadily went on and most of the main features were established by 1970.

The site slopes quite steeply in places and the natural levels were maintained. A semi-formal area was created around the house and this gradually passes into natural wild garden and light woodland.

A water garden is an important central feature. There is no natural stream and the flow is maintained by a circulating pump. On level ground one can have a static pool but on sloping ground one expects to see the water running down from pool to pool and this it does. Planting is well done. *Iris laevigata* was noted as were double white caltha, *Primula florindae*, *P. bulleyana*, *Ranunculus lingua*, ferns including the attractive but not common oak fern, *Theylipteris dryopteris* and others.

Shrubs in great diversity are planted in modern style informal beds so arranged that they fit easily into the natural woodland. Berberis, hebes, hydrangeas, azaleas, and euonymus are found in variety. There are also *Kolkwitzia amabilis*, *Stewartia pseudocamellia*, with its lovely bark, and *Magnolia stellata*

The whole effect is one of gentle beauty and one feels it is an easy garden to maintain. It is certainly an easy garden to look at.

Madresfield Court

The Dowager Countess Beauchamp

Malvern, about 1.6km (1 mile) from Malvern Link. Turn SE off A449 Malvern — Worcester. Area: 28ha (70 acres). Altitude: 36m (120ft). Soil: medium to heavy loam, neutral to slightly alkaline. Rainfall: 660mm (26in). Labour employed: three full-time. Three part-time plus forestry staff. Open one day a year for Madresfield Show in early September.

To the older, and now nearly extinct, race of professional gardeners the name Madresfield Court means a delicious purple/black grape, rather difficult to manage and inclined to split. It is, I would think, still the highest quality black grape in cultivation in Britain, though there are probably few gardens where it is to be found.

The grape, however, was but one of the many claims for distinction of these fine gardens in the nineteenth and early twentieth centuries. The limited opening times and lack of publicity on a national scale has led to Madresfield becoming a forgotten garden which is a pity for it ranks with the best as a survival of nineteenth century gardening.

Our story might well begin with Sir William Lygon who died in 1584 after building a moated mansion on the present site. His descendant was created Earl Beauchamp in 1815 but died a year later. He was succeeded by three sons and two grandsons so that the sixth Earl was reached in only

Whitfield. The apple arches date from 1850.

Beaucastle. *Lilium regale* against the background of the ivy-clad house.

Above: Madresfield Court. The east terrace is divided from the house by the moat.

Below: Madresfield Court. Part of one of the vineries wholly planted with the Madresfield Court grape. The vine at the far end is said to be the original and dates from the mid 1860's.

three generations.

The fifth Earl succeeded to the title in 1863 and commenced reconstruction of the present house in 1865, but he died in 1866 and the work continued for another ten years. This was the period which saw the real beginning of the present garden. Some time in the 1840s a Mr Cox was appointed head gardener. He was obviously a man of considerable ability which matched the enlightened ambitions of his employers. He was, however, a gardener not a garden designer, landscape consultant or any of the other professions which have often been involved in the layout of great estates. His job was to carry out the wishes of his employer which he certainly did. No nationally known garden designer has ever worked at Madresfield.

In 1866 an avenue of Abies procera glauca was planted by the Worcester nurseryman Richard Smith. They were said to have been grafted on to Abies alba and to have reached a height of 50ft by 1889 and in a fine healthy condition. They were still there in 1912 but by then an avenue of oaks, Quercus cerris and Q. borealis had been planted behind 'to take over when the firs are past their prime'. Something must have gone wrong with the abies.

At about the same time as the abies were planted an avenue of cedars Cedrus atlantica was also put in. A third avenue of elms probably existed earlier and the three formed a triangle. This latter avenue was replaced by lombardy poplars around the turn of the century. Today this triangle of cedar, oak and poplar is one of the features of Madresfield.

It was in the 1866-68 period that the present four acre walled garden was constructed and a large range of glass erected. This was much farther from the house than the old kitchen garden. Here were grown the Madresfield Court grapes that were awarded a First Class Certificate in 1868. This was raised by Cox and was said to be a cross between Black Morocco and Muscat of Alexandria. Lee of Hammersmith introduced it to commerce.

In 1883 Cox died and was succeeded by one of Britain's great gardeners. William Crump had been head gardener at Blenheim Palace for seven years and had raised the Blenheim Orange Melon. He had achieved distinction as an exhibitor at RHS shows but the scope at Blenheim was too limited for his wide ranging talents and ambitions. At Madresfield he found an employer who was actively interested in all aspects of work on the estate.

Fruit growing under glass and outdoors became a special feature. Crump no longer exhibited as he had done at Blenheim but concentrated on promoting fruit growing in the area. He became a lecturer for the Worcestershire County Council and organised pruning competitions. He ran a small nursery near the walled garden producing 2,000 fruit trees per annum which his lordship gave away to tenants on the estate. When the trees were neglected by the tenants and poor Crump despaired of educating them a scheme was devised whereby the garden staff carried out pruning and spraying for an annual charge of three pence per plum tree and six pence per apple tree. The estate almost covered its costs and the tenants made a profit.

In 1897 the Victoria Medal of Honour was instituted and Wm Crump was one of the original 60 recipients.

The relationship between employer and gardener was a happy one and when the sixth Earl died in 1891 and was succeeded by the young Viscount Elmley the bond even strengthened. On his engagement in 1902 he did not want Crump to hear of it through an intermediary but wrote 'I must tell you myself of my great happiness. Lady Lettice Grosvenor has promised to be my wife and live at Madresfield. Am most lucky. Beauchamp'.

The fine late dessert apple Wm. Crump which was at one time planted commercially in the West Midlands received an RHS Award of Merit in December 1908 and a First Class Certificate in January 1910. Opinions differ as to the origin of this apple. It is agreed that it was a cross between Cox's Orange and Worcester Pearmain. Some authorities say it was raised by Crump himself, others that it was raised by Rowe, the Worcester nurseryman and named Wm. Crump in his honour. The latter seems the more likely. Crump retired in 1919 and died in 1932 aged 89. Cox and Crump between them had served the Beauchamps for a little short of 80 years.

As they stand today the gardens have lost some of their former glory but at no period have they suffered real neglect. In the 1880s it was said 'there was no hardy tree, shrub, bulb or herbaceous plant of merit, introduced of late years that has not found a home in these gardens'. This policy did not continue long into the twentieth century otherwise we would have had just another modern garden. There are a few Japanese maples but most of the garden is a nineteenth century survival.

The garden on the east of the house consists of a small lower terrace at moat level above which is the main east terrace formal garden with a central fountain and beds partly enclosed in bays of clipped yew.

North of this is Caesars' lawn, which has been known as the bowling green lawn or croquet lawn over the years. The north side of this is a gently curving yew hedge. Here are busts of the 12 Caesars, each occupying a neatly clipped niche in the hedge. The busts were brought from Italy by the sixth Earl.

On the south of the house two L shaped pools form a sort of outer moat enclosing an area of lawn. On this is an oldish mulberry and a very old *Catalpa bignonioides* leaning into the pool and annually leaning further. Its branches now form a nesting site for moorhens. This was referred to as a grand specimen in 1885.

Some distance to the south east a row of ginkgos borders a tennis court on the site of the c 1865 kitchen garden. One female fruits freely.

The main house entrance is on the south side over an attractive brick bridge. Opposite is an avenue of Leyland Cypress replacing an elm avenue lost through Dutch elm disease. From the west side of the house the cedar avenue runs straight and slightly east of north for about a quarter of a mile. It then intersects the end of the oak avenue, which runs slightly south of west to form two sides of an equilateral triangle, the third being the poplars. The ground under these trees is full of naturalised bulbs, mostly smaller kinds such as *Fritillaria meleagris, Erythronium dens-canis, crocus spp, narcissus spp*, snowdrops, muscari, scillas, all by the hundreds of thousands. In the autumn one finds large areas of naturalised *Cyclamen neapolitanum* and *Crocus speciosus*, colchicums and others.

About half way along the cedar avenue within the triangle is a semicircular arbor of limes forming a tunnel. Within this semi-circle was once a children's play area and later a rose garden with fan shaped beds of hybrid perpetuals. Now it is just mown grass with bulbs.

The sundial garden is almost exactly as it was created, probably late last century. The central sundial feature is by James Gibb. The garden is a long rectangle surrounded by a holly hedge. A central path of red tiles is flanked on each side by grass strips. The borders contain herbaceous plants. Nearby is a maze in yew. Other gardens in this area have disappeared and fine trees have taken over.

North of the oak avenue is an extensive stream-side wild garden, no longer maintained as it once was and no longer containing the immense range of plants listed in early reports but here is to be found a superb relic of nineteenth century garden history.

Before the modern rock garden fashion became established with the works of Reginald Farrer and others there had been an interest in the use of massive rocks as spectacles. There was no attempt to imitate natural strata or to create sites for choice alpine plants. These were really a sort of Victorian folly rather than a rock garden of today. The name 'Rock Follies' seems appropriate.

The leading exponent in this field was Pulham of Broxbourne, Herts. The 'rocks' were synthetic, having a core of bricks and rubble and an outer facing of cement. This sounds horrible today but the craftsmanship that went into creating these features was considerable and the imitation of wind erosion was remarkably good. The 'rocks' at Madresfield still carry the signature of their creator. 'B.M.J. Pulham. Broxbourne A.D. 1878-79' and then follows the names of the workmen.

There are probably few really good examples of this old art form left today and this must rank among the finest. It is to be hoped that it will long be preserved as the museum piece that it is.

Fine trees abound in this garden. An *Abies grandis* near the rocks was once said to be the tallest tree in Worcestershire. Its vital statistics in 1931 were 114ft x 11ft 11in and at one time was recorded as 135ft high but has since lost its top. Alan Mitchell's figures for 1975 were 124ft x 13ft 7in. Another specimen was 126ft x 12ft 4in at that time. Other notable trees (1975 figures) are *Calocedrus decurrens* 92ft x 11ft 6in, *Cedrus atlantica* 102ft x 10ft 10in, *Cupressus macrocarpa* planted 1898 74ft x 9ft 9in, *Picea breweriana* 48ft x 4ft 2in, a fine specimen, *P. orientalis* 75ft x 7ft 11in, very attractive, *P. smithiana* 70ft x 5ft 5in, the uncommon *Pinus sylvestris* 'fastigiata' 48ft x 3ft 10in, *Pinus jeffreyi* 77ft x 6ft 8in *Sequoia sempervirens* 109ft x 17ft 4in, *Sequoiadendron giganteum* 102ft x 19ft 4in, *Juglans cinerea* 56ft x 5ft 6in, *Carya laciniosa* 65ft x 4ft 6in and *Tilia petiolaris* 83ft x 8ft 9in.

The largest avenue of all in this garden of avenues was the three quarter mile one of mature elms, two rows on each side, a victim of Dutch elm disease in the early days of the outbreak.

Moccas Court

Richard Chester-Master Esq.

21km (13 miles) west of Hereford. One mile north of B4352 on south of River Wye. Area: 4ha (10 acres). Altitude: 60m (200 ft). Rainfall: 750mm (29.5in).

The Moccas Estate has been in the possession of only four families since the end of the thirteenth century. Hugh de Fresne was licensed to fortify his manor house in 1294 but the resulting Moccas Castle was about one mile away from the present house, near the deer park.

The next two owners were the Vaughans and the Cornewalls. Velters Cornewall, who died in 1768, was MP for Herefordshire for 46 years. He achieved local acclaim by successfully opposing the tax on cider and perry.

By 1771 Catherine Cornewall was the sole heiress to the estate and the building of the present house began around 1775 to plans prepared by Robert and James Adam and supervised by Gloucestershire architect Anthony Keck.

'Capability' Brown prepared plans for which he was paid £100 in 1778.

Humphrey Repton seems also to have been involved personally. In his 'Observations on the Theory and Practice of Landscape Gardening' he writes:

'Where a ridge of ground very near to the eye intercepts the view of a valley below, it is wonderful how great an effect may be produced by a very trifling removal of the ridge only; thus at Moccas Court a very small quantity of earth concealed from the house the view of that beautiful reach of the river Wye, which has since been opened'.

Considerable records exist of this early period. In 1786 the 'Sunk fence was finished, bridge to garden made, north east side of garden paled and planted'. Trees were planted on a large scale in garden and park. In 1793 there is an entry 'Began the wall by Repton's advice from the house above the river and moved the rails further from the house'. The wall was finished the following year and a shrubbery planted. The same year they 'made a melon pit'. Tree planting continued well into the nineteenth century.

Since its creation the garden of Moccas doubtless changed with the changing fashions of the time. After the Brown/Repton era formal Victorian gardens were created.

After World War II the estate fell into decline but restoration, with a simplified garden layout has been undertaken since 1968.

Most of the area around the Court is now under grass. The River Wye is very close and forms the north north east boundary of the garden. There are some good trees, especially a notable plane.

Some distance east of the Court a stream flows through a ravine into the river. This was originally bridged in 1786 and after World War I it was made into a rock and water garden. This has now largely been restored and contains many plants of interest including *Iris kaempferi, I. siberica, Ligularia, Hosta, Lysichytum, Gunnera, Peltiphyllum peltatum* and others including many ferns. It is a fine piece of natural gardening.

But it is the gentle tree clad slopes above the Wye that give Moccas its real character. It would have been so easy to have planted beds of bright flowers and to have cheapened the place by so doing. Moccas is growing old gracefully. It is very beautiful.

Monnington Court
Angela Connor and John Bulmer

Monnington on Wye, 14km (9 miles) W of Hereford via A438. 2.4km (1½ miles) S of Main Road. Area: 1.2ha (3 acres). Altitude: 70m (230ft). Soil: Medium loam. Acid. Rainfall: 750mm (29.5in). Labour employed: casual. Open for NGS.

This is a garden in the making, most of the work having been done since 1974.

The house is in part c 1100 but the main part is 1650 built by a Thomas Tompkins and was purchased by the present owners in 1965. The church adjoins the garden and the churchyard is said to contain the grave of Owain Glendwr.

A large pool occupies most of the garden area. There are resident swans, mallard, coot and little grebe and visiting Canada geese. Trees, shrubs and waterside plants are becoming established. A new avenue is planned to reach down to the river.

The situation is a pleasant one with Moccas Court just across the river.

The Old Post Office
Mrs J. Loughery

Abbey Dore, 4km (2.5 miles) NW of A465 at point midway between Hereford and Abergavenny. Area: 0.2ha (0.5 acres). Altitude: 75m (250ft). Soil: neutral to alkaline. Rainfall: 750mm (29.5in). Open occasionally for NGS.

This is an old style cottage garden made from a piece of bramble infested field during the last ten years. The garden slopes gently upwards from the cottage and faces more or less south west.

There are two large herbaceous borders and some island beds set in lawn. The herbaceous plant range is considerable. Planting is close and staking is rarely done.

A hedge of *Rosa gallica* 'versicolor' ('Rosa Mundi') is a notable feature and a useful range of shrubs is well established.

The Old Rectory

Prof. J.M. Malins

Elmley Lovett, five miles north west of Droitwich. Approach via A442 Droitwich to Kidderminster road or A449 Worcester to Kidderminster road. Signposted Elmley Lovett. Area: 0.8ha (2 acres). Altitude: 45m (150ft). Soil: sandy loam. Lime free. Rainfall: 700mm (27.5in). Open for NGS and local functions.

The house dates from 1709 and was a Rectory until the present owner took over in 1946.

The garden is roughly rectangular. It falls away steeply to a lane beyond the north west boundary.

The entrance drive leading to the front of the house has a large specimen of *Magnolia stellata* which must be of considerable age. Other shrubs noted here were *Hoheria lyalli* and a pleasantly sprawling specimen of *Fatshedera lizei* — how much better this plant looks lying down than tied upright to supports. *Hamamelis mollis*, although it suffered considerably from the dry years of 1975/6 is recovering slowly. Also in the drive is a fine twenty three year old specimen of the Algerian oak *Quercus canariensis*.

A large lawn surrounds the house on rather more than two sides and on it are two fine specimen trees — one beech and one oak — which dominate the garden. The oak is ageing but it will see a good many more years yet.

In this garden there has been little effort to create vistas. The aim has been to find space for growing a large variety of interesting and rare trees and shrubs. Design gives way to function.

On the north west of the main lawn is an area of shrubs, and beyond this vegetables compete for the steadily shrinking space. Grass paths divide cultivated areas. In this part of the garden I noted a young *Idesia polycarpa* and a sizeable specimen of *Cornus controversa*. *Quercus phellos*, looking so un-oak-like with its willowy leaves, although still small is growing well. A specimen of *Eucryphia glutinosa* 'Rostrevor' bears abundant flowers.

I was surprised to see *Salia matsudana tortuosa* growing so freely on this dry sandy soil. One must suppose that the soil provides conditions suitable for a very deep root run.

Losses through dutch elm disease have made available an area at the north-west end of the garden and replanting has been going on here for some years. *Fraxinus velutina* planted in 1971 is already making a sizeable tree and other recent plantings noted are *Fagus engleriana, Betula ermanii,*

Notofagus antarctica, Parottia persica, numerous magnolias, *Tilia japonica, Davidia vilmoriniana, Alnus imperialis* and *Crataegus laciniata. Zelkova serrata* has already reached a substantial size. A standard *Stransvaesia davidii* is a reminder of how good this would be in a small garden.

This recently planted 'arboretum' is broken up with short lengths of informal hedges of shrub roses, *Berberis darwinii* and *Berberis stenophylla.*

Returning to the main lawn, there is a Ha-Ha on the south west boundary behind the house and beyond the south east of the lawn are herbaceous borders. Behind these is a small block of apples on dwarfing rootstocks. A south west facing wall has a large collection of somewhat tender shrubs. Among many others were noted *Sophora tetraptera, Abutilon megapotamicum, A. milleri variegatum, Fabiana imbricata, Cistus corbarensis, Myrtus luma, Abelia grandiflora,* and prostanthera.

There is a fine young specimen of *Arbutus Arachnoides,* now 1½ metres high and looking particularly happy. In the corner behind the garage is a small formal rose garden and in this area are *Drimys winteri, Griselinia littoralis, Mahonia lomarifolia,* and *Magnolia grandiflora* 'Goliath'.

Many other uncommon and choice trees, shrubs and conifers are being planted and in years to come the collection will become an important one.

Orchard Farm
The Misses M. & S. Barrie

On A44 in Broadway on S side of road near foot of Broadway Hill. Area: 2.8ha (7 acres). Altitude: 114m (380ft). Soil: clay loam but with much imported soil. Rainfall: 660mm (26in). Labour employed: two full-time. Open for NGS.

Previous owners of this property have included Lady Maud Bowes-Lyon and Sir Gerald Nabarro but when the present owners came in 1974 there was little to excite interest in the garden. Bedding plants had been put in and the place kept tidy but little more.

The efforts of the last seven years have been directed at creating a mature modern garden in the shortest possible time. It has, in part, succeeded. Broad sweeping borders have been created with an immense range of modern shrubs and ground cover plants. However there seem to be establishment problems possibly connected with the use of imported soil or perhaps lack of, or more likely, over-preparation. Hedges seem to have been particularly prone to trouble.

However, it would be wrong to give the impression that this is not a very fine garden. One enters on the west side of the house and west of the

Above: Broadfield Court. Yew hedges enclose the rose garden and the terrace with well head.

Below: Orchard Farm. The west front. There are just enough climbers to break the hard lines without concealing too much of the beautiful Cotswold stone.

drive is a lawn with two rows of flowering cherries across the north end and at the south end the garden's most distinguished, and probably oldest inhabitant, a massive perry pear tree, low branched and expertly braced, whose origins must go back to the beginning of last century. With the care it is getting it looks good for many more years. An old mulberry is nearby and a new Leyland cypress hedge forms the west boundary.

The garden proper lies east of the drive and south of the house. Near the house clipped yew hedges and topiaries remain from an earlier period.

The west facing front door looks out over a sunken garden with many ericas in corner beds and soft toned grey foliage much used. West of the sunken garden enclosed by tall yew hedges against the entrance drive is a lawn area with a round pool in the middle and roses in beds around the outside. The two form intimate little gardens in contrast with the larger scale of most of the remainder.

The chief newly designed area, south of the house consists of extensive lawn with informal borders on each side. The east border consists of deep lobes balanced by similar lobes of lawn. The border is backed by newly planted yew hedges which, when mature, will add to the character of the garden.

A full list of shrubs used would amount to the same as a catalogue from an average modern nursery. Prostrate junipers, berberis, dogwoods, maples, senecio, cotinus, *Prunus cistena* and others are all here and are well grouped for effect.

On the east side at a higher level is the swimming pool. South of this a wide cross path runs across the garden east to west. Beyond that a large lawn area with many recently planted trees and a few older ones. Patches of daffodils brighten the scene in the spring.

The south boundary consists of a north facing bank with a few birches, beeches and pines and daffodils underneath. At the foot of the bank is a large rectangular pool constructed in the course of a stream which flows down from Broadway Hill.

There is an attractive low branched beech and a Wellingtonia on the lawn near the garage block which add welcome height to the garden.

Overbury Court

Mrs Edward Holland-Martin

8km (5 miles) NE of Tewkesbury. Area: 7.5ha (18¾ acres). Altitude: 60m (220ft). Soil: clay loam, calcareous. Rainfall: 700mm (27.5in). Open for NGS.

The setting of this garden is as near perfect as one could wish. Lying on the lower southern slopes of Bredon Hill in a village of Cotswold stone, maintained at a standard of perfection that can hardly be surpassed anywhere else in Britain, one obviously gets off to a good start. Here the favoured climate of the Vale of Evesham is combined with architectural standards not found in the workaday market gardening villages in the centre of the Vale.

The association of the Holland-Martin family with Overbury dates from 1723. In 1735 the old house was burnt down and the present house was built on the same site in 1740. There have been Victorian and Edwardian additions.

Although there is no evidence of Capability Brown having worked at Overbury there is a strong Brownian style in the parkland. The pools, fed by a diverted stream, on the west side of the house also seem to have a touch of Brown, though hardly of his size. They certainly date from the mid-eighteenth century. The superb planes, *Platanus acerifolia*, nearby are probably of about the same age.

During the nineteenth century the usual Victorian formal gardens were created. In 1900 Sir Richard Biddulph Martin modified and enlarged the conservatory on the west side of the house. This was later pulled down by the present owner.

In the 1920s several garden designers had a hand in various work. Geoffrey Jellicoe and Guy Dauber remodelled certain areas and Aubrey Waterfield co-operated in creating a sunken garden with formal flower beds.

The need to reduce labour requirements led to Russell Page being engaged in 1968. He brought in the park railing on the north and west side, created shrub borders and made use of modern ground cover plants.

The main drive leads to the east side of the house. South of the drive is a shrub border of recent origin and now well established. On the opposite side is a lawn with two lombardy poplars and a Judas tree *Cercis siliquastrum*.

The churchyard was at one time part of the garden but a dividing wall has since been built. A row of very fine, low spreading cherries *Prunus*

Above: Madresfield Court. Part of Pulham's rock garden. The archway is above head height. The 'rocks' are synthetic. This is among the finest surviving examples of this firm's early work.

Below: Overbury Court. The south front with the flask shaped Irish yews and on the left the sunken garden, once with an elaborate pattern of beds, now a croquet lawn. On the churchyard boundary is a row of *Juniperus chinensis*.

serrulata 'Shirotae' runs from the curve of the drive across into the churchyard as a reminder of the former state. In the churchyard too is a locally famous *Magnolia soulangeana*, which attracts many visitors in the spring and a row of *Juniperus chinensis* on the west boundary.

The formal garden south of the house runs down to the public road but is supported by an eight feet high retaining wall so that the road is hidden and the vista is one of open parkland. A yew hedge provides a screen to prying eyes without spoiling the view from the garden. An area between the hedge and roadside wall was planted with *Hypericum calycinum* by Russell Page. This is an example of excellent use of this rather invasive plant. It has difficulty in penetrating the yew hedge and an eight feet drop on to a paved footpath could hardly be survived!

In the south east corner of this garden is a gazebo built in 1923 and is a copy of one at Westhall Manor, Burford. Running north from this and forming the east boundary of the south garden is a wide herbaceous border which is a feature of the garden.

Eight pairs of Irish yews border a wide path running north and south through the middle of the south garden. On the east of this is the swimming pool. To be in such a central position may seem unusual. These things are usually in some secluded corner where their blue tiles and garish ambience will not appear incongruous. But this swimming pool is different. It was constructed on the site of an old lily pool and it was intended to be an area of unplanted water that would reflect its surroundings. It is not the modern ornate swimming pool but just a rectangular area of still water.

Matching the swimming pool on the west of the central path is the sunken garden. Once filled with an elaborate design of formal beds it now has a mixed shrub and herbaceous border under its west facing wall and is otherwise a croquet lawn.

Further west is the Kemerton Walk. This runs north and south down to the Kemerton road. It is flanked by two wide borders, mainly of shrub roses and edged with *Vinca major variegata*.

West of the house is the main lawn with its pools and cascade. Here are the previously mentioned planes. South of this is the kitchen garden and tennis court.

The management of this garden is to the highest of standards. The head gardener, Mr Michael Tyas, is Kew trained and all of the work has a professional stamp.

Pershore College of Horticulture

Principal. W.J. Simpson Esq
Superintendent of Gardens. R.J. Hares Esq.

On A44 1.6km (1 mile) east of Pershore. Area: 4ha (10 acres) amenity area and grounds, plus commercial fruit, vegetable, glass and nursery areas, totalling 72ha (180 acres) in all. Altitude: c 30 (100ft). Soil: very variable. Rainfall: 660mm (26in). Open days are held annually.

The Avonbank Estate which forms the hub of the College was taken over in 1951 for development as a Horticultural Institute and the first intake of students was in the autumn of 1954. The original farm contained large areas of the most intractable Lower Lias clay, quite unsuitable for horticulture but over the years much of this has been sold off and new river terrace land at Pensham has been added. There is now plenty of land suitable for intensive crop production and enough of the heavier soil to give students a wider experience.

Originally the main emphasis was with commercial fruit, vegetable and glasshouse crops but the link with the Department of Landscape Architecture of the Gloucester College of Art and Design in the early 1960's gave impetus to studies in amenity horticulture and this was further emphasised by the development of a course in Hardy Nursery Stock Production.

Marriotts Bank, an area of about 4-5 acres at the north west corner of the estate with variable soil and, in places, steeply sloping was developed as an arboretum mainly under the direction of Miss Muriel Blore. Here are to be found a wide range of conifers, a substantial *Sorbus* collection, *Acer, Eucalyptus*, and most of the common genera of deciduous trees. A picnic area has been made near the far end. Some parts are now being opened up a little to provide vistas, notably one looking over Pershore Abbey which, unfortunately, also includes the particularly offensive gasholder. No distant view of Pershore seems to be able to avoid it.

The areas nearer the College are laid out with a good range of shrubs and ground cover plants, mostly well labelled. The quadrangle contains a white mulberry, *Morus alba*, planted in 1956 and now making a good tree after early struggles with an offensive builder's 'top soil'. Other notable trees in this area with planting dates are *Paulownia tomentosa* (1957), *Liquidamber styraciflua* (1966), *Acer capillipes* (1966), *Mespilus germanica* (1965) and *Betula nigra* (1965).

Hedges and screens include x *Cupressocyparis leylandii*, *Chamaecyparis lawsoniana*, *Thuja plicata*, and *Taxus baccata*.

A large shrub belt forms the east boundary of the playing field. Beds of herbaceous plants are in a lawn north of the drive and a large herb collection is in a border south west of the house.

Student plots and demonstration areas provide much of interest for those visitors who want to probe more deeply into modern horticulture. Otherwise it is quite enjoyable just to wander about and look.

Pontrillas Court

G. Keown-Boyd Esq.

17.6km (11 miles) SW of Hereford. Just off A465 Hereford — Abergavenny road. Area: 1.25ha (3 acres). Altitude: 66m (220ft). Soil: clay loam. Acid. Rainfall: 750mm (29.5in).

The house was built in 1630 and has been in the present owner's family since 1934. At one time it was occupied by Geo. Bentham but when, and for how long seems uncertain. Tradition has it that some of the trees, notably a large tulip tree *Liriodendron tulipifera* were planted by Bentham.

Today the garden consists mainly of lawn with a woodland area leading down to the River Monnow. There are some very good trees including a copper beech and three planes near the riverside. A small spruce woodland twenty years old is looking quite happy.

At one time Pontrilas was noted for its herbaceous borders but some have now been eliminated and roses have taken their place. They are still, however, quite a feature and there is no shortage of colour for much of the year.

The kitchen garden is well cropped and well managed and contains some traditional espalier fruit trees.

The Priory

Mr and Hon. Mrs Peter Healing

Kemeston, 8 km (5 miles) NE of Tewkesbury. Area: 1.25ha (3 acres). Altitude: 90m (300ft). Soil: clay loam, neutral. Rainfall: 660mm (26in). Labour employed: one man 3 days per week. Open for NGS.

The name 'Priory' is strictly a misnomer so far as the present house is concerned. It is a fine Georgian house with no record of religious connections. However, the name seems to have been associated with the property as far as records go. There is a sixteenth century ruin which adds character and distinction but again no evidence of its earlier functions.

The present owner has been here since 1938 when the garden was essentially a Victorian survival with no trees of consequence and little to inspire. Obviously little was done in the war years but in 1946 with RAF service over the development of the present fine garden commenced.

Mr Healing is first and foremost a grower of plants. In the early days his exhibition vegetables were to be seen at local shows. Now vegetables are grown only to eat. The perfectionism however, has not been lost. Everything has to be grown as well as possible.

The garden today consists of an entrance drive to the left of which, as one enters is a large expanse of lawn on which are a walnut, a weeping hornbeam and a weeping purple beech. The weeping elm has gone the way of all elms in this part of Britain.

Shrub roses and herbaceous plants are grown in borders with strong emphasis on colour grouping. The red border in front of the old ruin and adjoining a large, dome clipped yew is particularly fine. Phlox, *Lobelia fulgens*, penstemons, Bishop of Llandaf dahlias, tobacco plants, cannas and many others, annual and perennial, hardy and tender combine to produce maximum effect from midsummer onwards.

Silver and white borders are also a feature and *Eucalyptus coccifera, E. niphophila* and *E. gunnii* give height to these. Some eight or nine eucalyptus species are grown.

An enclosed area, behind clipped yew hedges is the 'New Garden'. This was a kitchen garden until 1974 and is now an informal garden with a stepping stone central path. This is at its best in June and July. Plants are mostly of soft tones of silver, pinks and lavender.

A stream forms the western boundary and here we find the least formal part of the garden. Ligularias, primulas, gunneras and other moisture

The Priory, Kemerton. *Datura suaveolens*, a typical example of the high standard of cultivation found in this garden where perfection is the norm.

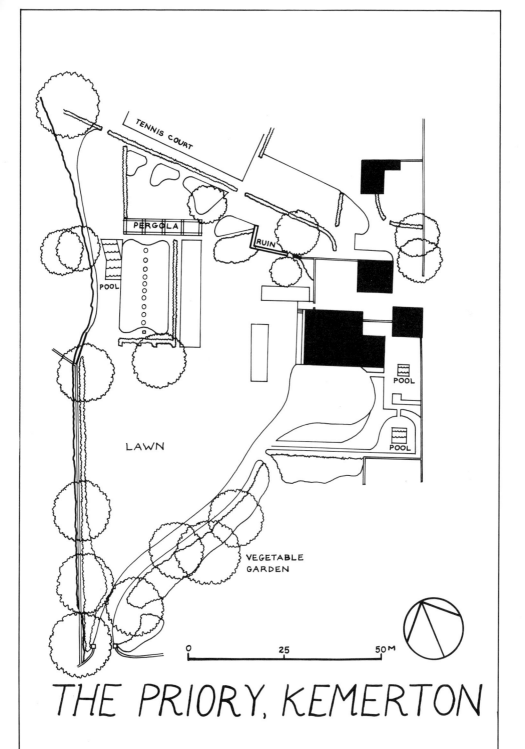

TENNIS COURT

PERGOLA

POOL

RUIN

POOL

POOL

LAWN

VEGETABLE
GARDEN

0   25   50 M

THE PRIORY, KEMERTON

lovers are quite happy here. Rose species are prominent on the higher ground above water level. There are some 30 or 40 rose species and a good collection of hybrid musks.

North of the New Garden is a pergola with roses and clematis and north of this, on the boundary an area of recently planted trees.

In the north west corner near to the house is the small Pool Garden with shaded borders containing ferns, hostas and lilies.

There is still a sizeable kitchen garden and in it are greenhouses, well equipped with mist propagation units and automatic temperature and ventilation control. Pride of place in this area goes to the orchid collection. Mr Healing is one of the best cymbidium growers we have.

Some years ago I wrote of this garden that it was not too fussily tidy yet not unkempt. Tidy it certainly is but the impression one is left with is that the plants are cared for rather than constrained.

St. Catherine's Farm

D.S. Jackson Esq.

Bredon's Norton, on Woollashill (part of Bredon Hill) N of Bredon's Norton. Area: 1.6ha (4 acres). Altitude: 105m (350ft). Soil: calcareous. Rainfall: 660mm (26in). Open occasionally for NGS.

When approaching St Catherines Farm from Bredon's Norton one has the impression that one is getting near the top of Bredon Hill. It is surprising to find that it is only 350 feet up and that the top of the hill is another 600 feet climb, but it must be appreciated that the River Avon, a mile or so away, is below 50 feet. One is starting from near zero.

This garden is, in many ways, a typical country garden but it has features that give it a little extra character and interest.

When the present owner came here in 1937 the property had fallen into a state of dilapidation but it had known much grander days and links with that earlier period remained and have been restored. A lengthy illustrated article in 'Garden Life' July 20 1912 describes the garden and its owner Fred Davis J.P. Mr Davis was apparently a highly successful raiser and exhibitor of tuberous begonias at a national level. He also created a garden with some typical Victorian features. He died in 1935 aged 87, having spent his whole life here.

A central lawn has on its south west side a large pool with an island reached by a rustic bridge which has doubtless been repaired a few times since Davis' day. In places around the margin are large Sarsen stones which were brought down from the hill by Davis when man and horse were the only source of power.

A typical small Victorian rockery survives on the far side of the lawn from the house. This has a natural waterfall in it from a spring above. It is now somewhat overgrown but Hart's Tongue and other ferns, hostas, and many other plants, some native, make a pleasant assortment. The little annual yellow saxifrage *S. cymbalaria* (or *S. sibthorpii?*), is happy in the splash of the waterfall.

On the east side the present owner has created a vista with island beds of low plants and a few trees including silver birch and *Pyrus salicifolia*. Below the pool outlet on the south west the garden has recently been extended with an overflow channel to create a new water garden and a substantial area of lawn.

There are some good trees here, notably Atlas Cedars and Austrian Pines.

Spetchley Park
R.J. Berkeley Esq.

5km (3 miles) E of Worcester on A422. Area: 25 acres. Altitude: 54m (180ft). Soil: Variable Keuper Marl to sandy loam. Neutral. Rainfall: 660mm (26in). Open regularly.

The Spetchley Estate was purchased by Rowland Berkeley in 1605 and has been in the family ever since. This is quite a long time by ordinary standards but Berkeley standards are not ordinary. They have occupied Berkeley Castle continually since the twelfth century.

Little seems to have been recorded of the garden at Spetchley in the early days. A fine Cedar of Lebanon which went in the gales of January 1976 was said to be the one mentioned by John Evelyn in the late seventeenth century. This author certainly refers to the owner of Spetchley in 1683 as '. . .grandson to the honest judge. A most ingenious, virtuous, and religious gentleman, seated neere Worcester, and very curious in gardening'. The 'honest judge' was Sir Robert Berkeley a very distinguished judge of the reign of James I.

The park with its red and fallow deer has probably changed little in two hundred or more years but the garden as we see it today is substantially a product of the late nineteenth and early twentieth century. It was on 20th August 1891 that Rose Willmott of Warley Place, Essex married Robert Berkeley of Spetchley. By the time she died in 1922 the garden had been created. In those thirty one years Rose Berkeley built up one of the finest collections of plants in the country.

It would, however, be wrong to give all the credit to Rose. Her younger sister, Ellen Willmott, who continued at Warley until her death in 1934, aged seventy four, was of course one of the most famous gardeners of her time. The Fountain Garden is regarded as being Miss Willmott's especial creation. This consists of a central fountain and pool surrounded by four gardens, each enclosed with clipped yew hedges. Within the enclosures are a series of beds with paved paths separating them, thirty six beds in all. It was, apparently, the original plan that each bed should contain plants of a different family. The approach was thus strictly botanical. The arrangement of the plants in families has long been discontinued but the botanical interest at Spetchley has never wavered. Most of the plants grown are natural species.

On the death of his mother in 1922 the responsibility for the garden was taken over by the late Capt. R.G.W. Berkeley who added continually to the plant collection. Those of us who were fortunate enough to know him and to be escorted round the garden by him personally marvelled at his astounding plant knowledge. His encyclopaedic memory continued even when in his later years he was confined to a wheelchair.

The second world war did not deal kindly with Spetchley. Labour problems afterwards meant that many of Miss Willmott's little gems were lost. But the emphasis changed. A fine collection of sorbus species was planted alongside the lake. Many other trees and shrubs, some of great rarity, add dignity and interest.

The present owner is devoting much of his time to maintaining and further developing the garden in spite of difficulties. Spring bulbs have always been a great feature of Spetchley. These are being increasingly planted and a particularly fine collection of small bulbous plants now exists.

We enter the garden through the Melon Yard, an old frameyard with glasshouses. The walls contain many plants of rarity and interest. At one time *Rosa hardii* and *Clematis texensis* both flourished but, alas, are now gone. One can, however, still find *Pileostegia viburnoides*, *Trachelospermum jasminoides*, *Mahonia lomarifolia*, *Feijoa selloana*, *Lippia citriodora*, *Bignonia capreolata*, *Tecoma radicans* and *Cytisus battandieri* among many others. Keeping them company is a gnarled and venerable Keswick Codlin.

From the Melon Yard we pass southwards into a large rectangular enclosed garden with a central round pond and cross paths lined with espalier fruit trees. Within this area is the walled kitchen garden now used as a plant sales department.

South of this is Ellen Willmott's Fountain Garden and beyond this areas of lawn and ultimately, forming the southern boundary, the lake. The garden is one of great variety, Woodland walks, open vistas, fine trees all combine to make this a fine garden but it is to the immense plant collection that Spetchley owes its claim to fame.

The tree paeony *P. x lemoinei* 'Souvenier de Maxime Cornu' was obtained by Ellen Willmott from the Royal Gardens at Peking. The hydrangea collection is considerable and includes *H. aspera, sargentiana, villosa, quercifolia* as well as a good range of the usual lacecaps.

Seeing *Dipelta floribunda* here makes one wish it were more readily available but it is not the easiest to propagate. The sorbus collection is quite large. *S. megalocarpa* has sticky red buds rather like horse chestnut and in that respect bears some resemblance to *S. sarjentiana* but the latter has pinnate leaves.

Almost every visit reveals something new and if Spetchley is not the tidiest of gardens it is certainly one of the richest in plant content.

Stone House Cottage
Major and the Hon. Mrs Arbuthnot

Stone, 2m SE of Kidderminster on A448 Kidderminster — Bromsgrove. Area: 0.4ha (one acre). Altitude: 6.6m (220ft). Soil: sand. Acid. Rainfall: 700mm (27.5in). Open for NGS.

This was the walled garden belonging to the big house but by 1973 had become totally derelict. The gardener's cottage was modernised and extended into the garden. The garden slopes to the south and the slope was retained apart from a level terrace which was made around the house.

The walls enclose the garden on the east, north and north west. To the south one has views of the Malvern Hills twenty miles away and southerly and south western gales have free access. A hedge has been planted as a windbreak. It is planned to reach a height of eight feet with windows at intervals.

Of the original garden all that remains is a fig tree and part of a greenhouse. The main paths form a T and the garden is divided into units of special interest. A white and yellow garden is bounded by a box hedge and a small, rather intimate garden is surrounded by a yew hedge recently planted.

There is a large herbaceous garden leading to an elliptic garden designed to conform to the curve in the wall.

The south facing wall has its brick buttresses supplemented with living buttresses of pittorporum. This provides separate pockets, and planting has been designed to give each a distinctive character. Here are to be found many of the tender shrubs and climbers that are a feature of this garden.

A small winter garden is mainly stocked with plants flowering very early in the year.

The success of tender plants in this garden is quite surprising. Lapagerias came through the 1978/9 winter and were growing well in the summer following. Other shrubs and climbers usually associated with the favoured west of Scotland or Cornish gardens are surviving and flourishing. Of particular interest are *Acacia pravissima, Bignonia capreolata, Desmodium praestans, Paederia scandens, Lonicera etrusca, Oxylobus arbutifolius, Mitraria coccinea, Drimys winteri*, but the full plant list is very large. It will be interesting to see what the next twenty years will being to this unique garden.

A small commercial nursery is attached to the garden and stocks of high quality pants are available throughout the year.

Summerway
Mr and Mrs Graeme Anton

Torton, 3m S of Kidderminster A449 turn W signpost Wilden Top. Area: 1.2ha (3 acres). Altitude: 60m (200ft). Soil: sand acid. Rainfall: 700mm (27.5in). Labour employed: one full-time. Open for NGS.

A modern garden made out of a derelict plum orchard during the last 19 years, mostly in fact during the last ten.

Trees under grass are a main feature but there is also a pool and rock garden with a good range of appropriate plants. There are mixed shrub and herbaceous borders and a particularly attractive silver border which presents a pleasing aspect for most of the year.

Shrub roses are being planted and it will be interesting to see how they behave on this very light soil.

Lilies have been raised from seed in large quantities and should soon be a feature of great interest. Spring bulbs are here in quantity. The garden is usually open for a whole week in April when they are at their best.

Returning to the trees I was particularly impressed with a fine young silver maple *(Acer saccharinum laciniatum)* which in sixteen years has a girth of two feet. Its pendulous branches and cut leaves make it one of the most beautiful of trees.

Altogether some 300 trees have been planted and there has been emphasis on cultivars and varieties of standard species. There are, for instance, five or six forms of the common beech and similarly of birch. Sorbus species and cultivars include the large leaved *S. mitchellii*.

Maples include *Acer hersii, A. circinatum, Pseudoplatanus* 'Brilliantissimum'. There is the inevitable *Robinia pseudacacia* 'Friesia' and several forms of horse chestnut. A variegated tulip tree, still small, has ambitions to be a big tree one day.

This is a pleasant garden to walk around, although I must confess, my visit coincided with a deluge of rain that limited one's appreciation.

The Weir
National Trust

Swainshill, 5 miles west of Hereford on A438. Area: 4.4ha (11 acres). Altitude: 60m (200ft). Soil: medium loam, lime free. Rainfall: 750mm (30in). See NT publications for opening times.

The most striking feature of this garden is the steeply sloping bank above the River Wye bearing in the spring masses of daffodils and bluebells.

The property was acquired by the National Trust in 1959 under the will of Mr R.C. Parr who had owned it since 1922.

There are some nice specimen trees and a small rock garden of Cheddar limestone.

Whitfield

G.M. Clive Esq.

Wormbridge, Hereford, 12.8km (8 miles) SW Hereford A465. Drive 1½ miles long NW side of main road. Area: 10.4ha (26 acres). Woodlands: 400ha (1,000 acres). Altitude: 126m (420ft). Soil: medium to heavy loam. Lime free in places. Rainfall: 750mm (30in). Labour employed: two, full-time. Open occasionally for NGS.

This pleasantly situated estate in the south west corner of Herefordshire is about five miles from the Welsh border to the south with the Black Mountains ten miles to the west. The deep clay loam has proved particularly suited to trees and many fine specimens are to be found here.

The house was built mainly between 1750-1770. Lady Katherine Stanhope was the owner until 1797 when the estate passed to the Clive family who have remained here ever since. Parkland planting was carried out in typical mid-eighteenth century fashion in the early days and two notable matching groups of oaks undoubtedly date from this period.

The camellia house or conservatory was built, probably as an orangery, in 1775. The glass roof was a nineteenth century modification. Today there are some very large Camellias probably planted last century, tree Ferns, *Dicksonia antarctica, Iris wattii* and many other items of interest. In front of the conservatory, planted in 1778, is one of the oldest and largest *Ginkgo biloba* in Britain — probably ranking number three in each category. In 1963 Alan Mitchell recorded it as 20m x 3.75m (68ft x 12ft. 5½ins). The beech walk was planted in 1775 and still contains some superb original trees.

The walled garden seems to date from the early nineteenth century and incorporates the conservatory on its north side. There are paths enclosed in apple arches planted in 1850. Some of the trees are probably original but some are replacements. These and numerous espaliers are all well maintained in traditional manner and have now become museum pieces of considerable interest.

The terraces on the south side of the house were constructed in 1880. The main terrace consists of a large expanse of lawn with a central fountain brought from Copt Hall, Epping since the last war. The lawn is surrounded by clipped yew hedges with topiary specimens on top. The yew hedges were planted in 1914 but not clipped until 1920. South of this is a lower terrace with a Ha-Ha/retaining wall forming the ultimate boundary. On the west the lower terrace continues with another yew topiary hedge on its west side. Peacocks add colour and character to the scene. Between the house and main lawn is a terrace with several double rows of pleached limes recently planted and not yet fulfilling their intended role.

Early in the nineteenth century Uvedale Price was involved in giving advice. Some superb Cedars of Lebanon are of this period and one specimen — 25.5m x 6.7m (85ft x 22ft 4ins) in 1963 — is a magnificent tree.

On the north side of the house is a chain of pools recently created from earlier ones. On the bank of the main pool is a fine specimen of the uncommon *Zelkova serrata* which in 1963 was 12m x 2m (40ft x 6ft 10ins) and was at that time the largest girth recorded by Alan Mitchell for the species.

One of Whitfield's proudest claims is that of having the tallest oak of any species in Britain. It is the Sessile Oak *Quercus petraea*, and was recorded as being 40m x 4.3m (135ft x 14ft 3ins) in 1963. It is probably not adding much to its height now but is still getting fatter. For sheer grandeur I choose the grove of Redwoods *Sequoia sempervirens* as the high spot of Whitfield. The twenty odd trees were planted in 1851 and are now among the finest in Britain. Standing among them one can imagine what David Douglas must have felt when seeing them for the first time. The tallest in 1963 measured 39m x 4.8m (130ft x 16ft). As the tallest in California is 112m high they still have a long way to go but they are young by comparison and look in excellent health. The grove is being greatly extended and trees planted in 1966 are now 12m (40ft) high. A group of *Cryptomeria japonica* adjoins them.

A fine Wellingtonia, *Sequoiadendron giganteum*, from the original importation of seed from Calaveras Grove in 1853, planted in 1856 was 38m x 5.8m (126ft x 19ft 1in) in 1963.

There is a Pendulous Oak, a form of *Quercus robur*, very rare and probably a seedling from a tree formerly at Moccas Court. Other trees of note include a Deodar Cedar 33m x 4.3m (110ft x 14ft 4in) (1963), limes, planes, liquidambars, liriodendrons and the rare Himalayan *Alnus nitida*. New plantings in the woodlands include *Notofagus procera* and a few *N. antarctica*.

A pleasant walk of about 1½ miles has been laid out to include the main features of Whitfield for the benefit of visitors.

Winds Point
Winds Point Trust

On N side of A449, Malvern — Ledbury Road at highest point and just opposite the large car park. Area: 2.4ha (6 acres). Altitude: 300m (100ft). Rainfall: 750mm (29.5in). Open regularly for NGS.

Just north of the Hereford Beacon towards the southern end of the Malvern ridge lies Winds Point, the home of Jenny Lind for the last fifteen years of her life. I can hear younger readers saying 'Who was Jenny Lind?' I will say briefly that Jenny Lind, Swedish by birth, international by reputation was one of the greatest of nineteenth century singers and I hope that the knowledgeable will forgive me.

After the singer's death in 1887 the property was purchased by the Cadbury family who now administer the Trust.

This garden is the nearest approach to the truly wild or natural garden we have in this book. The site was a quarry with some old cottages when Jenny Lind bought it and built the present house. Now the high and precipitous quarry face with masses of ivy tumbling over it forms the background to the main part of the garden which lies to the left of the drive as one enters on the west side of the house.

A rock garden has been constructed near the foot of the quarry face and this merges into the natural strata of the rocks. Mown lawn occupies much of the level ground at the bottom and a few random boulders are scattered over the grass.

The effect is very much that of a natural alpine scene. Coloured primroses, *Anemone blanda, Scilla siberica, Cyclamen neapolitanum* and *C. coum*, were noted as being naturalised and flourishing.

Around and above are many Scots Pines, birches, beeches, yews and a few introduced conifers such as Lawson's cypress. There is a large *Robinia pseudoacacia* in the drive. A steep walk leads up to a little summer house above the quarry and views of the Worcester and Hereford Beacons can be obtained through the trees.

The south front of the house looks over a wide lawn to the countryside far below.

Witley Park House

Mr and Mrs W.A.M. Edwards

On A443 Worcester — Tenbury road. On the left hand side, ½ mile past Little Witley Post Office. Area: 7.2ha (18 acres). Altitude: 60m (200ft). Soil: sand to sandy loam acid. Drainage free except below pool outlet. Rainfall: 750mm (29.5in). Labour employed: owner and one part-time man. Open for NGS.

The house is quite modern (1961) and was bought by the present owner in 1965. It is situated on what was once part of the park of Witley Court, a nearby semi-derelict mansion, once among the grandest of the stately homes.

Included in the 18 acres of garden is the nine acre Warford Pool which is the fifth and last of a chain of pools in the original park. The pool naturally dominates the garden.

Most of the land area was farmed at the time the house was built and only a few mature trees existed, mostly near the pool outlet.

The present owner embarked on a tree planting programme at the start and has now planted 2,800 trees of more than 100 species.

From the house one looks down a gently sloping lawn to the pool below. An island in the middle, with trees and shrubs is an 'eye catcher' and relieves the bareness of the water. A row of well spaced *Tsuga heterophylla* runs down the western edge of the main lawn. This tree is growing well wherever it is planted here and they are already becoming a feature.

The entrance drive runs nearly parallel to the road leaving a grass strip between. Down the middle of this is a row of mixed conifers, including *Abies grandis*, *Pinus wallichiana*, *Tsuga heterophylla*, chamaecyparis and others. They have nearly all grown well and many are around five metres high and almost touching in the row. A decision will obviously have to be made. Should they be thinned to allow the remainder to become specimens? At present they are an attractive feature.

The area east of the entrance gate forms a gully leading down to the outlet end of the pool. Here there are some mature trees. A conifer screen continuous with the one on the drive runs near the roadside boundary. A beech hedge has recently been planted on the road boundary itself to replace a hedge of *Thuja plicata* which does not appear to have grown very well.

Spring bulbs are a prominent feature of this lower grass area, and numerous interesting trees are here also. The inevitable *Metasequoia glyptostroboides* is growing fairly well but doing rather better is a redwood *Sequoia sempervirens* which has a place of special affection for Mr. Edwards as he grew it from a bark bud cutting he collected in California. Young trees of *Liquidambar styraciflua* and *L. formosana* are growing well.

Below the pool outlet is a moist area with shade from trees. A collection of ferns is being established as well as Rhododendrons and Camellias. This is still rather a wild area and when slightly tamed it will be an attractive feature.

A path along the south side of the pool provides a pleasant boundary walk. A variety of trees, recently planted along the boundary fence will become interesting in future years. There are numerous oaks among which may be noted *Quercus phellos, Q x. kewensis,* and *Q. palustris* as well as *Sorbus hupehensis* and *Crataegus jackii.* The pool margin along this boundary provides potential planting sites for moisture loving perennials which, one hopes, may one day be filled — but the owner wisely avoids schemes involving too much labour and he is proceeding with caution where much hard work is involved.

Beyond the west end of the pool is a 4½ acre block which for many years was planted with commercial gooseberries. In 1972 these were cleared and planted with woodland, the main species used were Japanese larch, sweet chestnut and *Thuja plicata.* This already forms an effective backcloth especially when viewing the garden from the outlet end of the pool.

On one of my visits I was fortunate to witness from this point the arrival of about forty Canada Geese, an impressive sight indeed.

The Gardens of
Shropshire

Clwyd

Cheshire

ELLESMERE ■
• **The Lythe**

MARKET DRAYTON ■

■OSWESTRY

• Hodnet Hall

Staffordshire

Peplow Hall •

• Sansaw Hall

Acote School
The Grove
• Magnolias

Oak Cottage Herb Farm

SHREWSBURY ■
• Attingham Park

■ TELFORD

Weston Park •

Swallow Hayes

Limeburners •
• Hatton Grange

Pitchford Hall •
Golding Manor •

Benthall Hall •
Beckbury Hall •

MUCH WENLOCK ■ • Wenlock Abbey

Astley Abbots House •
Dunval Hall •
• Stanley Hall

Henley •
Morville Hall ■
Meadow House •
BRIDGNORTH ■
• Lower Hall

• Ludstone Hall
Dairy House

The Morleys •
CHURCH STRETTON ■

• Gatacre Park

Millichope Park •
Old Rectory •
Dudmaston •

The Old Parsonage •
• Broncroft Castle

Burwarton House

Powys

Upper Shelderton House •

Mawley Hall •

■LUDLOW ■

Ashford Court •
Burford House •

Ashford Manor
Hereford and Worcester

The Gardens of

Shropshire

Scale: 0 5 10 15 20 25 30 kilometres

0 5 10 15 miles

Upton House. Terrace below top lawn.

New Place, Stratford-upon-Avon. The recreated Tudor Knot Garden in Shakespeare's last home.

Adcote School

Adcote School Educational Trust Ltd
Head Mistress Mrs Susan Cecchet.

At Little Ness 13km (8 miles) NW of Shrewsbury. Turn N off A5 at Montford Bridge. Area: 10ha (25 acres). Altitude: 70m (230ft). Soil: sandy loam, lime free. Rainfall: 760mm (30in). Open for NGS.

Historic houses often lead a precarious existence. Neglect, decay and even total demolition is the doom of many. One of the happiest fates is to become a school, as many do. Adcote, a girls school, is a good example. Built in 1876-9 for Mrs Rebecca Darby of the ironmaster dynasty of Coalbrookdale by the architect Norman Shaw the house is an A1 listed building and the garden provides an appropriate setting. The school was established here in 1927.

Obviously some of the frills have gone. Some of the parkland has been sold off. This still contains some fine trees much older than the house. Few of the trees in the garden would have been there at the time the house was built but many including Austrian Pines, yews, copper beeches, a large plane, a very fine Wellingtonia, two red oaks, a fine three stemmed tulip tree and some good Lebanon Cedars are all probably of about that period.

The drive comes into a walled courtyard on the west front. The south front has a broad terrace consisting of a wide gravel path and a strip of lawn enclosed in a clipped yew hedge. Steps lead down to the main lawn. Under the terrace wall is a long herbaceous border with a stone kerb separating it from the gravel path. How much easier this is to maintain than those silly grass strips beloved by Victorians and how much more attractive!

The main lawn is very large and consists of several bays with groups of trees between. A fine, and still youngish, copper beech is in a prominent position near the boundary and opposite the steps leading down from the terrace.

Above: Adcote School. Norman Shaw's fine stonework in a garden setting that has remained typically Victorian.

Below: Attingham Park. The River Tern flows through the Repton parkland. Birch and beech frame the group of Lebanon Cedars beyond.

Rhododendrons including *R. ponticum* and large flowered hybrids form bold groups and perfume is provided by numbers of Ghent Azaleas.

East of the house is the walled garden, now entirely grassed down and used for lacrosse. The south boundary of this area is a holly hedge, not a wall, and this forms the north side of a long vista on the east front. A yew hedge forms the south side. A central gravel path flanked by lawn strips with two rows of Portugal laurels, once clipped as stalked hemispheres but now less formal are all in keeping with the atmosphere of the place.

In a corner west of the south terrace is a Victorian style rock garden which is in process of restoration.

Ashford Court

Brigadier and Mrs R.C. Windsor Clive

Ashford Carbonel, 4.8km (3 miles) S of Ludlow just E of A49 Ludlow — Leominster. Area: 0.8ha (2 acres). Altitude: 90m (300ft). Soil: clay loam. Rainfall: 840mm (33in). Labour employed: family labour only. Open occasionally for NGS.

The present house was built about 1830 and is on the site of an earlier one. The entrance drive is on the north side of the house and north of this is a belt of newly planted trees including pines, birch, larch, prunus, sorbus and other small trees.

South and west of the house lies the main garden. There is a large area of lawn. Three things strike one instantly as one enters. There is a good specimen of Cedar of Lebanon, a magnificent Tulip Tree, *Liriodendron tulipifera*, and a superb stretch of the R. Teme just beyond the south boundary.

A modern mixed shrub and herbaceous border is backed by a hedge of *Chamaecyparis lawsoniana* 'Fletcheri'. *Acer griseum, Cotinus coggygria*, and a double Philadelphus, probably 'Manteau d'Hermine' were noted in particular.

The kitchen garden is well stocked and very well managed. There is nothing pretentious about this garden. it reflects simple good taste.

Ashford Manor

Kit Hall Esq.

Ashford Carbonel, 2¾ miles S of Ludlow. E of A49 Ludlow — Leominster road. Area: 1ha (2½ acres). Altitude: 90m (300ft). Soil: clay loam slightly alkaline. Rainfall: 840mm (33in). Open for NGS.

Ashford Manor is an attractive stone built house dating from 1600. In the early nineteenth century the then owner, a certain Mr. Downs, built on in brick and plastered the whole facade in Regency style.

The present owner inherited the property from his father around 1926 and in 1930 pulled down the Regency extensions and re-established the original Tudor character. The house is in perfect accord with the garden around it.

Kit Hall is a professional flower arranger and at one time lectured extensively. The plants reflect this interest. 'Flower' is perhaps hardly the right word for his interest lies mainly with foliage.

A large area of lawn flanks the south side of the entrance drive. The house looks out over this and much of the planting, all informal, is around the house and under a serpentine wall of beautiful old brick twelve feet or more high in places. This planted area is not large.

There is a fine specimen of *Vitis coignetiae* on the house and also a flourishing *Clematis armandii*. The climbing polyantha rose Phyllis Bide is not often seen nowadays but a flourishing specimen eight to ten feet high occupies part of the west facing wall. For the rest the garden consists of hostas, euphorbias, ivies and other plants of attractive form and gentle colours. There is nothing blatant and nothing vulgar. This is to be expected in a garden created by a man who is also a painter of considerable talent.

Astley Abbotts House

H.E. Hodgson Esq.

5km (3 miles) NW of Bridgnorth via B4373; turn R at Crosslanehead. Area: 2.2ha (5½ acres). Altitude: 105m (350ft). Soil: heavy clay lime free. Rainfall: 700mm (27.5in). Labour employed: owner and a little casual. Open for NGS.

The north eastern slope of this intractable clay garden does not encourage one to do much cultivation and it is probably true to say that the less one sees of the soil the better. But these heavy clays will grow trees and shrubs very well and this garden shows how best to deal with the difficult conditions.

We approach this beautiful half-timbered house from the south side and the garden lies on our right opposite the east front. The house dates from 1605 and may at one time have been a staging post. Mr and Mrs Hodgson have been here since 1954.

On the west of the drive is a fine Wellingtonia and an even finer one a little way down the slope to the east. Nearby are many other trees including specimens of Cedar of Lebanon, Austrian Pines, Douglas Fir, Coast Redwood and others. An old *Araucaria araucana* is looking its age and a gnarled Oriental Plane has not much longer to live. There are some very fine copper beeches.

A paved terrace along the east front of the house was laid with London paving slabs when it was decided to replace this beautiful York stone with man-made synthetics. Fortunate are those gardens that were able to take advantage of this change over, or should we say foresighted were the garden owners who did so? Among notable items on the terrace is a particularly vigorous and flourishing *Magnolia grandiflora* 'Exmouth'.

Below the paved terrace is a grass terrace with formal rose beds and a small lily pool. Below this the open lawn slopes gently away. A *Calocedrus decurrens* occupies a central position bold and upright.

On the north side of the main lawn is an herbaceous border with a path separating it from a shrub border on the north boundary. Here were noted *Paeonia lutea ludlowii*, *Viburnum plicatum*, *Berberis darwinii* and *Hibiscus syriacus* among others. The path dips steeply down to the extreme east point and from there we can climb back along the south boundary through a deep coomb with a stream at the bottom. Rhododendrons flourish on the banks and bluebells are in abundance among some very fine oaks. The native *Polygonum bistorta* intermingles with the bluebells and sometimes forms large patches. Three bridges constructed by Mr Hodgson cross the stream. A young *Rhododendron hodgsonii* is looking quite happy. This is one of the very large leaved species from the Himalayas and is, of course, named after another Mr Hodgson.

The path up the coomb brings us eventually back to the southern edge of the lawn with its fine trees but in the meantime we will have passed through one of the most attractive of wild gardens.

There are some very good ornamental cherries including the very large white flowered 'Tai-haku'. Erica arborea is particularly happy. Although frost damaged in 1979 it seems to cope quite well with normal winters.

A little east of the entrance gate is a kitchen garden, surrounded and internally divided with beech hedges and further screened by a multi-arch line of climbing roses.

Attingham Park
The National Trust

On N side of A5 at Atcham Bridge. 6.4km (4 miles) SE of Shrewsbury. Area: 8ha 920 acres). Altitude: 30m (100ft). Soil: lime free. Rainfall: 760mm (30in). Open regularly. See N.T. Publication.

The house was built between 1783 and 1785 for the first Lord Beswick. Repton worked here in 1797-98 and suggested among other things moving the main entrance to its present position at Atcham. There are many fine trees, some planted by Repton. In particular a grove of Lebanon Cedars on the north east side should be mentioned.

A little to the east of the house is the River Tern flowing south under the A5 to join the Severn. An attractive shrub lined walk follows the course of the Tern for about half a mile. There are displays of azaleas and rhododendrons and daffodils in the spring. Sumachs, Red Oaks and Dogwoods provide autumn colour.

Beckbury Hall

Sir Humphrey Browne

6.5km (4 miles) S of Shifnal in triangle formed by Wolverhampton — Shifnal — Bridgnorth. Area: 1.2ha (3 acres). Altitude: 90m (300ft). Soil: medium loam. Lime free. Rainfall: 700mm (27.5in). Labour employed: one full-time, one part-time. Open for NGS.

Although the house dates from early sixteenth century, alterations in eighteenth and nineteenth centuries have concealed much of the original.

A large expanse of lawn lies in front of the house which faces south. On the eastern lawn boundary is a wide herbaceous border backed by a yew hedge with a sensible path between to facilitate cutting. Why do some people make work by planting right up to the hedge and adding to the problems of hedge cutting?

Well grown bedding plants add seasonal colour and on the western boundary is a shrub border. East of the yew hedge is a long border of old shrub roses which are a notable feature of this garden. There are some very good Tree Paeonies and bulbs are abundant in the spring.

The kitchen garden is exceptionally well managed and the standard of plant raising generally is high.

Most intriging of all the features at Beckbury is the old cockpit. The stone edged central dais has become filled up with the passage of time but it must surely be one of the best preserved examples in existence. The amphitheatre has become overgrown with trees and scrub but the atmosphere remains. What a wonderful site for an open air theatre in the round!

Benthall Hall

The National Trust

Broseley, 2.4km (1.5m) SW of Ironbridge. 6.4km (4 miles) NE of Much Wenlock via B4375. Area: 1.2ha (3 acres). Altitude: 190m (620ft). Soil: limey. Rainfall: 700mm (27.5in). Open regularly. See NT Publication.

The roots of the Benthall family go back at least as far as the eleventh or twelfth century but the present house is mid to late sixteenth century. Descendents of the Benthalls owned the estate until around the end of the eighteenth century. In 1844 it was purchased by Lord Forester owner of the Willey estate nearby.

It is from a little later than this that the story of the garden at Benthall begins. About 1860 the brothers George and Arthur Maw, local tile manufacturers, rented the property and during the next thirty years George gave Benthall a permanent place in the history of British horticulture.

Maw was a keen amateur botanist, and above all, an authority on the petaloid monocotyledons. In 1886 he completed his masterly work *The Genus Crocus*, one of the great classics of horticultural literature and now very rare. He was responsible for introducing many species of bulbous plants into cultivation. These were raised in sunken pits covered with frames in conventional Victorian style, hence the name 'pit light'. These pits now a mere depression in the ground, are still to be seen. Many small bulbous species survive at Benthall from Maw's time, notably *Chionodoxa luciliae* as well as many crocus species.

From 1890 to 1906 the tenants were Robert Bateman and his wife and they were probably responsible for much of the garden as it is today. The semi-formal terraced rockery, known as the Pixie Garden is one of Bateman's legacies.

In 1934 the Benthalls came back to their ancestral home and in 1958 gave the property to the National Trust but continued to live here. The present occupiers, Sir Paul and Lady Benthall have done much to restore the garden to its former state after a period of enforced neglect during the Second World War. The most pleasing feature of Sir Paul's efforts has been his reluctance to alter any of the existing features. It would have been so easy to sweep away weed infested Victorian rockeries which, after all, had no great artistic merit. And how many people would have preserved a mere hollow in the ground just because George Maw originally made it? We must be grateful to Sir Paul. In this philistine age so much gets destroyed.

So much for the past. What is the garden like today? As indicated above the atmosphere is essentially Victorian.

The abovementioned Pixie Garden of Bateman's on the west side of the house consists of a rectangular pool with stone wall terracing beyond and formally clipped yew and box specimens. The terraces contain a large range of interesting plants, notable among them are *Tropaeolum polyphyllum, Cardamine septuaphylla*, the latter like a giant white flowered ladies' smock, and a yellow anemone from Kashmir. Incorporated in the high north wall is a dovecote of eighteenth century construction and on it is the Grecian Silk Vine, (*Periploca graeca*) one of the Asclepiads all of which bear silky hairs on their seeds.

South of the house is the main lawn and still further south a very healthy specimen of the Colorado Blue Spruce (*Picea pungens glauca*). It is a comparatively young tree — perhaps twenty years old — and is well furnished to ground level. The dense, glaucous blue young growths completely hide the inner browning leaves.

Flanking the lawn are more rock banks where we find an Acanthus said to be a rare species from the Balkans.

On the east side is an interesting wild garden area near the site of Maw's old frame pits. *Lathraea squamaria*, the native toothwort is parasitic on the roots of hazel. This plant is devoid of chlorophyll; its white toothlike fleshy leaves are wholly underground and it is attached to the shallow roots of the host plant by its modified root system. Only its flowers appear above ground. Here also we find an interesting thistle (*Cirsium oleraceum*) and *Valeriana pyrenaica*.

The geraniums G. *phaeum* and G. *nodosum* are naturalised as are many other items of interest to botanists.

There is a typical walled kitchen garden and an expanse of grass known as the Bowling Green and thought to be part of a Tudor Garden.

I have left until last mention of the great problem of Benthall. *Petasites fragrans*, the Winter Heliotrope, with its delicious perfume in the early days of spring is one of the most pernicious of weeds and it has obtained a stranglehold of much of the rock garden and some other places. One feels that nothing short of an intensive herbicide programme could eradicate it. Such treatment would, of course, eradicate everything else, which, I am sure, is what everyone wants to avoid. I would like to try painting the leaves with glyphosate or aminotriazole just to see if selective destruction was possible.

Broncroft Castle

Mr and Mrs C.T.C. Brinton

Craven Arms, 2.5km (1½ *miles*) E of B4368 Bridgnorth — Craven Arms, at point 11km (7 *miles) from Craven Arms. Area: 1.2ha (3 acres). Altitude: 135m (450ft). Soil: medium loam. Almost lime free. Rainfall: 840mm (33in). Labour employed: one full-time. Open for NGS.*

Broncroft Castle is pleasantly situated four miles west of Brown Clee (1790ft) with Corve Dale running away to the south west and Wenlock Edge on the far side of the valley.

Much of the garden has been developed since the last war but the lawns and trees in front of the castle are of a much earlier period. A weeping ash, *Fraxinus excelsior* 'Pendula' with its usual twisting canopy and a naturally grown box, *Buxus sempervirens,* are prominent. Box makes a very attractive small tree grown thus yet how rarely gardeners resist the temptation to get the shears to work to produce hemispheres, pyramids or peacocks. There is an arch of Portugal Laurel and, on the west boundary of the lawn a shrub border of recent origin in which I noted *Hamamelis mollis, Mahonia japonica, Elaegnus pungens* and many ericas.

The stream garden behind the castle is a development of the last twenty years and includes an area recently cleared of dead elms. This is a delightful example of natural stream-side gardening with a good shrub collection and a wide range of waterside herbaceous plants. There is a paved path near the stream edge and a raised grass path at a higher level. The banks are covered with snowdrops and other bulbs in the spring.

An old orchard has, in part, been planted with ornamental trees which are already becoming a feature of note. A young Davidia seemed particularly happy. There is a tidily maintained kitchen garden.

Burford House
John Treasure Esq

1.6km (1 mile) W of Tenbury Wells on A456. Area: 1.6ha (4 acres). Altitude: 60m (200ft). Soil: about neutral. Rainfall: 840mm (33in). Open in afternoons April to October.

John Treasure purchased Burford House in 1954 and immediately set about creating a modern garden in keeping with the fine early eighteenth century house. As the garden he then found had little of consequence in it except a few mature trees he was able to start from the beginning without wondering what could be destroyed and what left. Naturally, the mature trees were left. They now add character to what would otherwise be a 'new looking' garden.

The plan has been to blend formality with informality. Formal pools, steps, terraces, vases and urns give way to broad curving stretches of lawn with large planted areas of shrubs and herbaceous plants among which annuals are freely used. Mr Treasure is a clematis specialist and it is not surprising to find that most of the species and cultivars in cultivation in Britain are to be found in this garden.

Above: Burford House. This is the garden that has about everything in outdoor ornamental gardening. The small patio area with formal pool and prostrate junipers is one of the many facets.

Below: Gatacre Park. The west front of the mid nineteenth century house looks out over a large lawn with many trees and shrubs. The large clump of *Yucca gloriosa* to the left of the picture is thought to be contemporary with the house.

On the north side of the house is a formal rectangular pool with water lilies. West of this is an informal water garden in which that interesting free floater, the Water Soldier, *Stratiotes aloides* was noted. This plant sinks to the bottom in the winter, returning to the top again when the weather warms up. Moisture loving plants in this area include *Rheum palmatum, Peltiphyllum peltatum, Rodgersia sp.* and *Iris laevigata*. The neatly edged grass paths are sometimes straight and formal, sometimes they wander about.

The main part of the garden lies south and west of the house and the River Teme forms the boundary. Great care is taken in grouping plants. Bold foliage groups of hostas, rodgersias and the like contrast with the dainty elegance of dieramas. Astilbes are used effectively along the streamside where Iris kaempferi, ligularias, sedges and grasses keep them company.

Mr Treasure is a plantsman and he has a preference for natural species. This, however, is not applied too rigidly. If it were most of the clematis would be left out. He is always ready to accept improved forms of most plant species but with roses he rules out the modern hybrid teas and floribundas whilst accepting the older shrub roses and rose species provided they can be kept up to his standard of tidiness. This is achieved by training on special supports.

Weed control is so near perfect at Burford that it has been described as the tidest garden in Britain. Certainly I know of no tidier one. One has the feeling that no weeds have seeded here since Mr Treasure came. No seeds — no weeds. Once perfection in weed control has been attained it is not difficult to maintain it but there must be no 'letting up' and constant vigilance here maintains the high standard of perfection.

Mr Treasure is always looking for new plants and has a watchful eye for natural seedlings. Some years ago three seedlings of *Rosa filipes* 'Kiftsgate' arose. One of these 'Treasure Trove', was put on the market a year or two ago. It is a soft apricot colour with a pink flush and has the vigour of its parent. The second has now been named 'Pink Bouquet' and the third, white in colour, is attempting to smother the willow tree that supports it. Other roses that have been very successful are *R. sinowilsonii*, and 'La Mortola'.

An interesting clematis is *C. kochii*, a more or less herbaceous American species related to *C. viorna*. The hybrids of *C. texensis* are greatly admired and are very successful at Burford.

I had almost forgotten the double delphinium 'Alice Artindale' which was quite often seen in the 1930's but rarely nowadays and *Penstemon* 'Rubicunda' which Graham Thomas says was raised at Lyme Park in 1906 is another old cultivar of merit. Numerous other herbaceous species and cultivars of note find a place in this garden. The double pink primrose 'Sue Jervis' was almost lost to cultivation but is here preserved. *Cardiocrinum giganteum* does well and all the meconopsis are successful especially *M. sheldonii* and the hybrid 'Branklyn' form. *Eryngium alpinum* is well known but the hybrid *E.x zabellii* seems rare but is a plant of note.

Melianthus major has wintered out successfully and *Rehmannia angulata* is being tried out but it is doubtful if it would survive any but the mildest winters. *Nierembergia frutescens* is another plant that has proved hardier than is usually thought.

Burwarton House
The Viscount Boyne

Bridgnorth, 10 miles from both Bridgnorth and Ludlow on B4364. Area: 14ha (35 acres). Altitude: 300m (1000ft). Soil: medium loam. Lime free. Rainfall: 840mm (33in). Open for NGS.

This fine estate on the east side of Brown Clee has inevitably seen changes over the last two centuries. The house was built around 1780–1800. The terrace on the south side of the house at one time had a more elaborate formal layout than that at present existing. In the 1920s Brenda Colvin was involved, possibly with others, in extending the terrace and creating an enclosed rose garden behind yew hedges with peep holes. The hedges still exist but now enclose hard and grass tennis courts. Groups of Rhododendrons occupy the middle terrace above the yew hedges.

The main interest in this garden is in the trees. There are many fine specimens and particularly effective groupings and vistas. A Deodar Cedar is among the largest in the country. Noteworthy conifers include *Cryptomeria japonica*, *Pseudotsuga menziesii*, *Tsuga heterophylla*, *Chamaecyparis nootkatensis*. Some of the finest specimens are to be found among the broadleaved species. The beeches both green and purple are as good as any likely to be found anywhere. Sycamores are outstanding and there is a particularly good variegated one.

There are banks of rhododendrons under the trees. This is a pleasant place to wander about in. One passes from garden to parkland to woodland without ever being quite sure which one is in.

Dairy House
Miss N.E. Wood

Ludstone, 11km (7 miles) W of Wolverhampton just S of A454 Wolverhampton — Bridgnorth. Area: 1.2ha (3 acres). Altitude: 60m (200ft). Soil: sandy gravel. Rainfall: 19mm (27.5 in). Labour employed: one full-time. Open on numerous occasions annually under NGS and for local charities etc. Party bookings by clubs and societies welcomed.

This was originally part of the Ludstone Estate and is on the opposite side of the road to Ludstone Hall. In the seventeenth century it was a two up, two down dairy cottage with farm buildings. It was enlarged in 1854 and given a north facing Georgian style facade. South facing windows were added in the 1920s and the present owner carried out major reconstruction before coming to live here in 1956.

About one acre around the house had previously been cultivated. The further two acres was decrepit semi-woodland on the site of an old gravel quarry and had long been used as an unofficial refuse tip

Progress in clearing has been steady and continuous. By 1960 the general layout of the north west end of the garden near the house had been completed. Lawns were established, the main heather bed planted, the rockery, in red sandstone, constructed, and clearance of the main bank on the east side of the garden begun. The basic layout was suggested by Percy Cane who was also responsible for the terrace and paving. The winter of 1962/3, when temperatures down to 2°F were recorded, took heavy toll of newly planted shrubs but work continued.

The poor hungry soil proved difficult in dry summer spells and an underground mains irrigation system was installed for the summer of 1969 with sprinkler points that enabled the whole garden to be watered.

In the dry summers of 1975/76 this was to make the difference between life and death for many of the plants.

The garden was first opened to the public in 1971 and has proved very popular as it demonstrates what can be done with a difficult site with care and perseverence.

The Pool forms the north east boundary and is linked to the moat system of Ludstone Hall. The main lawn leads down to the pool edge. Running south from the main lawn is the High Level grass walk from which can be seen attractive views of the garden and the countryside beyond with Claverley Church as a landmark.

Facing west and leading down to the lawn below is the Main Bank crossed in places by steps. Planting is almost entirely with drought

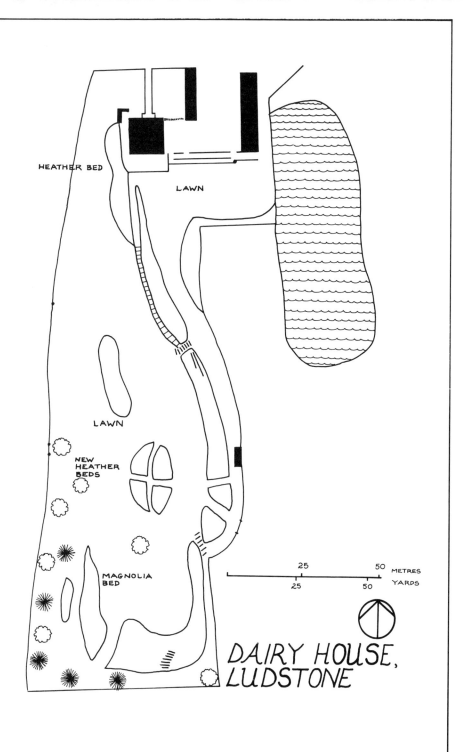

HEATHER BED

LAWN

LAWN

NEW
HEATHER
BEDS

MAGNOLIA
BED

25   50 METRES
25   50 YARDS

DAIRY HOUSE,
LUDSTONE

resistant plants with special emphasis on silvers and greys of 'Mediterranean Maquis' type.

In the glade below are groups of heather beds, a viburnum bed and a magnolia bed. Some of the larches, spruces and pines are original occupants but new plantings of Scots pine and silver birch have been made and there is a good young Norway Maple. Hostas, ferns, hellebores, lilies, crinums, agapanthas and nerines all flourish and spring bulbs are a feature in their season.

Dudmaston
The National Trust

At Quatt 5.6km (3.5 miles) SE of Bridgnorth on W side of A442. Area: 3.2ha (8 acres). Altitude: 75m (250ft). Soil: lime free. Open Wednesdays and Thursdays during summer.

The property was inherited by Lady Labouchere from her uncle Geoffrey Wolryche-Whitmore in 1952 and given by her to the National Trust in 1978. Sir George and Lady Labouchere continue to live in the house.

The house dates from the end of the seventeenth century and is attributed to Francis Smith of Warwick. Some modifications took place during the nineteenth century.

The parkland and garden have evolved over many centuries but much of the present garden has been created since the middle of last century when a chain of pools were combined to form the present lake which now forms the south west boundary below a large terraced lawn. Looking down from the lawn we see on our right a steep bank above the north west corner of the lake where retaining walls supplement the natural outcrop of Old Red Sandstone to create a terraced rock garden in which are planted heathers, many shrubs and the smaller conifers.

On the opposite side of the lawn in the north east corner of the pool is an interesting bog garden in which are found numerous candelabra primulas, *Rheum palmatum*, *Iris siberica* and others liking this habitat. I noted a very effective group of *Primula viallii* in full bloom at the time of my visit. Ferns occupy cool niches nearby.

To the south the ground rises and in this area a long rectangular border was planted in last century with American shrubs including kalmias, azaleas, and such like. We still find a preponderance of American plants with *Garrya elliptica* and *Calycanthus floridus* among them but Asian immigrants have crept in without doing harm.

The border below the terrace in front of the house contains a good collection of shrub roses and the steps leading up to the terrace itself are covered with that delightful but invasive little daisy, *Erigeron mucronatum*. Mention might also be made of an ancient mulberry — how often mulberry trees are 'ancient' — on the outside of the wall of the old walled garden. This one is a fine specimen.

We must not overlook another feature of Dudmaston — a fine collection of botanical paintings, drawings and prints representing most of the important artists. Lady Labouchere herself is an accomplished artist and has devoted much time to building up this exhibition.

Dunval Hall

G.P.A. Thompson Esq.

3.6km (2¼ miles) NW of Bridgnorth on B4373. Area: 0.8ha (2 acres). Altitude: 105m (350ft). Soil: heavy clay loam, slightly calcareous. Rainfall: 700mm (27.5in). Labour employed: part-time plus owner. Open for NGS.

The present owners have been at Dunval since 1945 and the garden has been almost wholly created since that time. The house however is Tudor being built in 1598. Great care has been taken in any necessary restoration work and we have today one of the best preserved smaller manor houses of its period. Making a garden around such a house calls for care. There is no point in trying to recreate a Tudor garden. Tudor gardens were never very satisfactory even in their own day. Recreations tend to be rather gimmicky.

As it is the garden seems to complement the house almost perfectly as it proceeds from semi-formal to informal in design. The drive comes in on the impressive north east front and forms a small courtyard in which are three raised beds edged with aubrietia, arabis etc. and filled with bedding plants, thus providing seasonal colour. The scale is just about right.

The garden slopes from north east to south west and is on three sides of the house — all that is except the north west which is an old farmyard. Above the entrance drive is a lawn with simple rectangular rose beds on three sides. Two topiary figures of birds flank the steps leading to the lawn and at the top boundary are some fine cherries with daffodils beneath. Nearby is a healthy young copper beech. A gateway on the south east boundary leads into a field used as a car park when the garden is open.

A semi-wild woodland area extends along the south east boundary with a screen of spruce, some silver birches, poplars and shrubs with daffodils underneath. There is a fine old yew. Nearer to the house on the south east side is a lawn with herbaceous borders. A purple nut hedge, *Corylus maxima purpurea*, forms a boundary with the wild garden beyond. Steps lead down to a little secret garden with yew hedges and borders around a central strip of lawn.

The level of the secret garden is maintained with a high retaining wall in front of which is a wide herbaceous border and the extensive lower lawn. A brick retaining wall forms the south west boundary. The field below has a few old fruit trees suriviving from the days when it was obviously an orchard. A pair of horse chestnuts have been planted axial with the gateway leading down from the lawn.

The lower lawn continues to the north west as a wide parallel strip with the field below on one side and the rear wall of farm buildings on the other. This has been christened 'The Deck' from its resemblance to the deck of a ship. Along this is a row of *Sorbus grandiflora*, a species of which I have no knowledge. The buds were just bursting at the time of my visit and the inflorescences are said to hang very like small wistaria racemes. It would seem to be an impressive small tree and requires further investigation as to nomenclature.

At the far end of 'The Deck' and occupying the west corner of the garden is an Italian style patio garden with swimming pool, screened and secluded so that it is detached and unrelated to the rest of the garden. One has to be in it before one sees it.

This feature was started in 1964 and finished in 1965 and is the personal work of Mr. Thompson. The pool is cleverly designed with a ten feet 'sump' to accommodate the deepest of divers and a shelf all round so that a child can swim to the side anywhere and stand. Four *Chamaecyparis lawsoniana* 'Fletcheri' are on each side. These, although with obvious 'Fletcheri' foliage are broad and blunt and quite unfletcherlike in form. Close examination reveals that the top half has been cut off and the branches tied in to create a distinct shape without resorting to clipping. It is very competently done. It will be interesting to see what the next twenty years will produce. *Vitis coignettiae* sprawls over the fence on the field boundary. Its large leaves with brilliant autumn colour are a notable feature.

Gatacre Park

Sir Edward and Lady Thompson

At Six Ashes 10km (6 miles) SE of Bridgnorth on A458. Area: 3.2ha (8 acres). Altitude: 150m (500ft). Soil: Lime free. Rainfall: 840mm (33in). Open for NGS.

The present house was built in 1850 replacing an Elizabethan house. Like so many old estates it has a place in history for shelter was given to Royalist troops after the Battle of Worcester and it is well authenticated that the Earl of Derby stayed here *en route* to Boscabel.

Sir Edward's father bought the property in 1923 and the garden has developed continually since that time. Some fine trees exist from earlier periods and are certainly older than the house. An 80 feet *Liriodendron tulipifera*, the Tulip Tree is probably contemporary with the house as is a multistemmed Western Hemlock, *Tsuga heterophylla*. A large sprawling clump of *Yucca gloriosa* is also thought to be about the same age. These are all on the lawn on the west front of the house left of the drive as one enters. This is a large area with shrub beds and borders against a background of trees. The vista from the house is very pleasing. A wide range of shrubs is here and there are notably large specimens of *Ozothamnus rosmarinifolius* and *O. ledifolius*. These two shrubs have an ericaceous look about them but they are really composites and highly tolerant of lime. Yet they look as though they belong among the rhododendrons. Among the younger trees in this area are a particularly good Manna Ash, a *Magnolia kobus* and an attractive mulberry elegant and upright with its lower branches sweeping down to the lawn. This tree was planted in 1933 so is now around half a century old. A mere youngster.

In the north east corner of this west lawn is an intriguing sunken garden made on the site of an old potting shed. A central narrow rectangular pool is flanked by three columnar clipped *Cupressus macrocarpa* on each side. The surrounding banks are planted with ferns and other shade tolerant plants. A wrought iron gateway and steps lead along a woodland path and across the back drive to the woodland garden proper to which we will return. Before leaving the west garden we must note the rather uncommon *Hydrangea strigosa* with coarse bristly adpressed hairs on leaves and young shoots. I mistook it for *H. aspera*.

South of the house is a lawn with an effective grey border and borders of shrub roses. Steps lead down to the terrace below with its topiary walk. Topiaries are usually Victorian survivals. These have been created by Sir

Edward and Lady Thompson themselves since around 1950. There are fifteen in number and they range from corkscrews to teapots (with lid) and from monsters of uncertain identity to aeroplanes. I thought that there was a very good Spitfire.

The south facing wall above the topiaries has an immense wistaria and two uncommon shrubs of great interest *Azara serrata* with broadly oval evergreen leaves and scented flowers in the summer. The second is *Abelia triflora*, a large deciduous shrub with masses of highly perfumed flowers at the time of one of my visits in early July. A large lawn occupies the east front.

It is the three acre woodland garden with its large rhododendron collection that is perhaps the main feature of interest at Gatacre. The woodland itself was created by the Thompsons for Sir Edward helped his father plant larch, pines and oaks here in 1935 and the earliest rhododendrons followed soon after.

Wind damage often occurs on the large leaved rhododendrons. Nevertheless *R. rex* and *R. macabeanum* are reasonably successful. Sir Edward has raised many seedlings. Some of his best are from *R. wardii*. I was impressed with the almost blue young leaves of a seedling of *R. cinnabarinum*. Also of interest for its young foliage which is silvery is *R. yakushimanum*. The older leaves are rusty brown underneath. Among the later flowering hybrids worth noting are the Goldsworth seedlings 'Tortoiseshell Champagne' and 'Tortoiseshell Orange'.

A fine group of *Pieris* is near the entrance to the woodland garden. Of special note are the 'Wakehurst form' and 'Flower of the Forest'.

A copy of the famous Warwick Vase, about half size, is a focal point at the end of the main ride.

Glazeley Old Rectory
Mrs C.H. Taylor

3½ miles S of Bridgnorth on B4363 Bridgnorth — Cleobury Mortimer Road. Altitude: 90m (300ft). Rainfall: 700mm (27.5in). Open under NGS or by appointment.

For many years a nursery, well known among hardy plant specialists, with an interesting collection of unusual plants. The nursery has recently discontinued but the attached garden remains. It consists of a number of informal beds of varying character and plant content. There is a pleasant cottage garden atmosphere in an attractive natural setting.

Golding Manor
Mr and Mrs H.A. Hartley

11km (7 miles) SE of Shrewsbury between A49 and A458. Area: 0.6ha (1½ acres). Altitude: 100m (328ft). Soil: neutral to slightly limey. Rainfall: 700mm (27.5in). Open occasionally for NGS.

At first glance this seems a conventional farm garden. The farmyard is on the east side of the house. Rectangular lawns surround the other three sides with straight edged borders around the boundaries. Nothing could be simpler or more ordinary. Closer acquaintance soon shows that this is a rather exceptional garden.

The house itself is a good example of a mid–seventeenth century (1668) manor house and provides an excellent starting point for the garden. Even the lawn is a little different. The first impression is that of a fine close mown lawn but tread on it and it is like a deep pile carpet. It is, in fact, mown quite high but the turf is fine and close.

The borders around the lawn show a standard of cultivation not commonly seen. This applies particularly to the lilies of which there is a large collection. Auriculas do well here and there is a good selection of spring flowering bulbs. An uncommon shrub I noted in this area was *Raphiolepis x delacourii* which is not particularly hardy but seems to be surviving under a south facing wall.

Tropaeolum polyphyllum is now well established and is even becoming rampant. *Anacyclus depressus*, that attractive prostrate white daisy with pink backs to the florets, was once thought of as a choice plant for the alpine house. Here it flourishes as a front of the border herbaceous plant.

We now come to the feature that makes Golding really different. As we walk to the southern edge of the lawn we see twenty feet below a rectangular bowl or saucer kitchen garden. Two ten feet high walls with a well planted border on the middle terrace maintain the levels. Mrs Hartley is certain that the depression is natural. The retaining walls are of the same period as the house. The wall of the middle terrace gives protection to *Carpentaria californica, Azara lanceolata, Passiflora coerulea* and many other shrubs. The border contains an immense stock of herbaceous plants including a bold eight feet high group of *Eremurus robustus* self sown and left where they put themselves.

Development is still going on and with such a unique site all sorts of things are possible.

The Grove

Mr and Mrs Philip Radcliffe Evans

Kinton, near Nesscliff, 16km (10 miles) NW of Shrewsbury, just W of A5. Area: 0.2ha (0.5 acres). Altitude: 90m (295ft). Rainfall: 760mm (30in). Open for NGS.

This attractive garden has been created by the present owners since 1972/3 without paid help. The main part of the garden is on the south side of the house. A paved area along the south front is heavily planted with herbs and old 'cottagey' plants. The sun lounge/greenhouse contains some more tender subjects such as *Lippia citriodora* and *Salvia grahamii*.

A box hedge, surviving from an earlier period, screens the kitchen garden on the east side. *Juniperus confertus* sprawls around the base of a sundial in front of the house and a large hazel stump, suckering freely, is a central feature, blocking the view of the more distant garden. This consists of a broad central lawn with a wide border on the west side planted with a good selection of shrubs and ground cover.

At the south end the lawn broadens out and shrub roses form the southern boundary. A little fruit plantation occupies the south east corner. Recently planted trees include purple leaved birch, tortuous willow, and eucalyptus.

On the west and north of the house are more shrubs and shrub roses in borders and lawn beds.

Hatton Grange

R.J. Kenyon-Slaney Esq

---

2 miles SE of Shifnal on S side of A464. 1 mile drive through lodge gate entrance. Soil: sandy loam, lime free. Labour employed: 1 full-time, 1 part-time in kitchen garden. Open once or twice a year for NGS.

The house was built for Plowden Slaney, a direct ancestor of the present owner over the period 1764–68. There were some Victorian alterations and other additions removed by the present owner.

The garden area around the house is somewhere in excess of five acres, with extensive areas of lawn. A ha-ha separates the garden from parkland on the south side. There are two formal gardens surrounded by clipped yew hedges in front of the house. One of these is a rose garden the other of mixed planting. These were constructed in the 1930's by the present owner's father.

An outstanding specimen of *Hydrangea petiolaris* keeps company with a Kiftsgate rose on a high wall and there are large specimens of *Magnolia kobus*.

By far the greatest attraction of Hatton is the chain of pools in a deep ravine some 400 yards from the house. This ravine is said to have been caused by a geological fault.

At the time the house was built a small brook running through the ravine was dammed (or possibly re-dammed as there is some evidence that pools existed at an earlier date) to create a series of pools.

There are now four pools ranging in size from one to four acres with a total length of half a mile and with paths on both sides. The banks were originally planted with beech and oak to form natural English woodland but the present owner's father widened the range of plants in the 1930's with extensive plantings of rhododendrons, azaleas, magnolias and many other things to create a natural style woodland garden of great merit.

The rhododendrons suffered badly in the drought of 1976 and many of the rare species were lost but enough remain together with some fine specimen trees of the original planting to make this one of the best examples of woodland waterside planting in the West Midlands.

Henley

Mr and Mrs J. Long

Tasley, Nr. Bridgnorth, 2.4km (1½ miles) NW of Bridgnorth on N side of A458 Bridgnorth — Shrewsbury road. Area: 1ha (2½ acres). Altitude: 105m (350ft). Soil: medium clay loam, lime free. Rainfall: 700mm (27.5in). Open by appointment for NGS. (Tel. Morville 240).

The garden at Henley Farm is a recent creation on an exposed site with few mature trees apart from the odd old fruit tree remaining from a farm orchard. The enthusiasm with which the venture has been accompanied is, however, quite exceptional and one awaits the maturing of the plantings with great interest.

Since 1971/2 more than one thousand species, varieties and cultivars of trees and shrubs have been planted along with a large collection of bulbs, ground cover and herbaceous plants. Many items are quite rare and are a delight to the keen plantsman.

The approach to Henley off the A458 is via a road over open farm land. The entrance drive proper is bordered by rockwork with a large collection of appropriate plants including many bulbs, especially colourful in the spring.

Occupying a central position in the garden is a large pool with a steep bank on the SE side planted with many shrubs including rhododendrons. The inevitable *Metasequoia glyptostroboides* and *Picea breweriana* are here and many other conifers. There is a good collection of shrub roses.

On the NW side of the pool is a very large collection of trees and shrubs planted in grass with cultivated and heavily mulched areas around. It is worth noting that it is not always the rarest that are most interesting; *Sambucus nigra pulverulenta*, one of the variegated forms of common elder was most effective and it was pleasing to find the oleaster, *Elaegnus angustifolius*, a shrub with centuries of cultivation behind it yet too often neglected nowadays. It ranks among the most deliciously scented of all shrubs and can even reach tree size.

With almost thirty different kinds of sorbus it is not easy to pick out a few for special mention. Mr Long is very pleased with *S. aucuparia* 'Xanthocarpa' which he prefers to Joseph Rock. *S. pohuashanensis* a tall, upright growing Chinese species belonging to the Mountain Ash section is also doing well. *S. discolor*, related to the more familiar *S. hupehensis* is also worth noting.

A large collection of young birches is being established from seed imported from N. America. Taxonomy and nomenclature in this group is rather confused. When one hears of large new planting one wonders whether it will add to our knowledge or confusion!! But all birches are beautiful and the more kinds we can try out the better.

The snowdrop collection runs into forty to fifty species, varieties and cultivars. At the time of my visit an interesting item was a group of the uncommon *Bulbocodium vernum*. A large collection of *Erythronium spp* is becoming naturalised as are many of the smaller daffodils, species and cultivars.

Epimediums are becoming a feature and there are many fine hellebores.

Hodnet Hall

Mr and Hon. Mrs A. Heber-Percy

In Hodnet Village on A442 Whitchurch — Telford road. Area: 28ha (70 acres). Altitude: 90m (300ft). Soil: clay to loam overlying Bunter Sandstone. Lime free. Rainfall: 760mm (30in). Labour employed: four. Open most of summer. See HHCG.

Hodnet is a modern garden that is old enough to have matured and fortunate enough to have had, apart from some inevitable dropping of standards during the Second World War, continual skilled care since the time of its inception.

The Hebers have owned the Hodnet estate for over 900 years but little has survived from the earlier occupations. The present house dates from about 1870 and is of red brick in the later Elizabethan style. It replaces the original Elizabethan Hodnet Hall of which only the stable block now remains. The garden of the old Hall was in the north west corner of the present garden near the Magnolia Walk.

In 1870 the garden was that immediately around the house. The top terrace on the south front and the present enclosed private garden would have been the extent of the garden, in other words the areas to which the public do not have access today. The walled kitchen garden was probably laid out about 1860.

It was in 1922 that the late Brigadier A.G.W. Heber-Percy started an ambitious programme of garden construction on a scale that has rarely been attempted in the last 60 years. The house stands on a plateau looking over a valley to the south. A small stream flowed through a marshy swamp into a small pond known as the Horse Wash Pond and it would

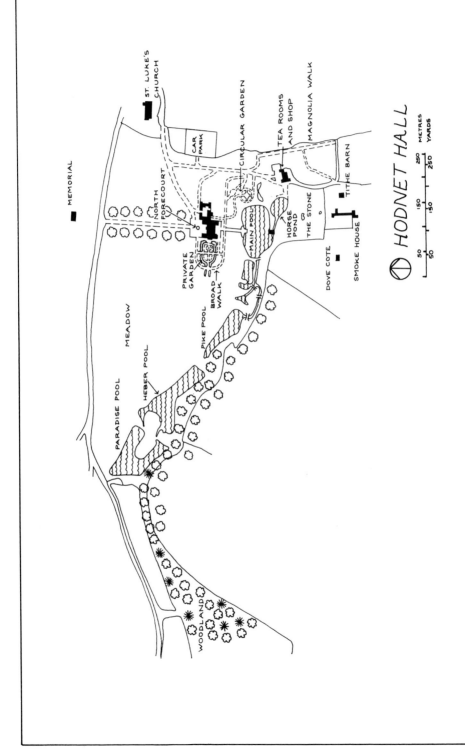

HODNET HALL

ST. LUKE'S CHURCH

MEMORIAL

CAR PARK

NORTH FORECOURT

CIRCULAR GARDEN

TEA ROOMS AND SHOP

MAGNOLIA WALK

PRIVATE GARDEN

MAIN POOL

HORSE POND

THE STONE

TITHE BARN

BROAD WALK

DOVE COTE

SMOKE HOUSE

PIKE POOL

HEBER POOL

PARADISE POOL

MEADOW

WOODLAND

METRES

YARDS

50   150   250
50   150   250

obviously have been used for watering horses after a day's work in the fields. The sloping banks above the marsh had some fine oaks which still remain as outstanding features in the present garden.

By building a series of dams up the valley the Brigadier constructed a chain of seven pools plus some minor ones extending upstream through a belt of natural woodland. People have dammed valleys before. Capability Brown created larger lakes but when Brown made a lake a few trees were planted and that was the end of it. With Hodnet it was only the beginning for development of this fine water garden is still going on.

Broadly speaking we may say that up to 1930 work was confined to producing the outline scheme. Planting on a limited scale took place until the outbreak of war when for obvious reasons development discontinued. From 1950 onwards the main planting of the Water Garden took place. A little later the Shrub Rose Garden or Stone Garden was created. The Stone is a large granite boulder which was removed from the Horse Wash Pond in 1960. It now forms a feature of interest. The shrub borders north of the stables date from about 1957-9.

The Brigadier died in 1962 and development since that time has been in the hands of the present owner. This has amounted to further planting in the Water Garden and development generally. In 1977 a borehole was sunk in order to obtain an improved water supply. This led to considerable opening up of the pools and providing sites for additional planting. So the garden today represents over 50 years continued development.

In a garden of this size it is impossible to take everything in on a single visit. Interest changes with the seasons, for this is a garden planned to have something to show every season of the year.

Visitors will enter through the gateway by St Luke's church. The car park is just off the beech avenue to the left. In the car park is a notable weeping beech and two *Metasequoia glyptostroboides* which are making fine trees. A good starting point for a walk through the garden is the North Forecourt. Looking northwards from the house across the A442 road one sees a semi — ruined erection of stone columns. This is a folly erected as a memorial to the late Brigadier. It is, in fact, a portico from Apley Castle, near Wellington which was acquired by the Brigadier himself when the castle was demolished in 1956.

If we go westwards from the forecourt through a woodland path under larches and other trees with rhododendrons underneath and note some groups of *Cardiocrinum giganteum* in passing we reach the meadow above the pools. Turn left and we are on the Broad Walk. This is a wide gravel path which runs along the south front of the house below the top. or private terrace. From this point we may see, looking due south, a mid-seventeenth century dovecote standing in the field beyond the garden boundary. Flights of stone steps connected with sandstone paving run down to the main pool. If we continue along the Broad Walk we can go down a twisting path against a sandstone cliff face to the Circular Garden which consists of a circular bed with a central statue around which are planted *Hydrangea paniculata, Caryopteris* and lavender. There are three concentric grass strips joined by cross paths of grass so that two rings each of four beds are created. The inner ring is planted with the H.T. Rose 'King's Ransom', the outer ring with herbaceous paeonies. This formal garden in an informal setting appears a little odd at first but it is large enough to stand on its own as a feature and need not be considered as part of a larger scheme. Above the Circular Garden is the Camellia Garden which is particularly attractive in the spring when in addition to Camellias we will find rhododendrons, flowering cherries and other things.

Turning back through the Circular Garden we cross over to the Main Pool. On our left below the pool outlet is a line of small pools linked by the stream.

There are *Lysichytums* in the stream. Their broad bold leaves following yellow spathes in the spring always have distinct character. In broad irregular areas around the pools there are *Matteuchia struthiopteris*, the Shuttlecock Fern which has shortly creeping rhizomes so that each tuft of leaves stands separate from its neighbours and the shuttlecock form is clearly seen, *Rodgersia aesculifolia* with leaves like the Horse Chestnut as its specific name suggests; *Iris siberica, Astilbes, Primula japonica, Smilacina racemosa* and other waterside plants. Above, and around are rhododendrons, hydrangeas and laburnum. In the mown grass of this area is a Monkey Puzzle *Araucaria araucana* and a *Davidia* as well as some fine specimen oaks and other trees.

Going westwards with the Main Pool on our left and the terraced bank on our right we follow a mown grass drift past a little summer house in red sandstone with stone tiles. The bank on our right is a mass of maples, especially forms of *Acer palmatum,* azaleas, ericas in variety, *Chaenomeles* and *Pyracantha. Yucca filamentosa* is prominent by the main steps to the top terrace. We reach the Main Pool inlet by passing along the gently sloping bank with its fine oaks and we are now in the water garden proper.

This is a complicated pattern of streams and pools with wooden bridges, water lilies in the pools, masses of *Astilbes, Filipendulas, Primula florindae,* numerous ferns, most prominent of which is the Royal Fern, *Osmunda regalis.* There are *Ligularias* and *Hostas* in abundance. An odd little incongruity is a circular, raised brick bed of *Agapanthus,* Headbourne Hybrids. There are some low growing conifers, notably *Juniperus x media pfitzeriana* and other shrubs.

We now reach Pike Pool where marginal planting is much more natural and there are no water lilies. There are, however, some fine gunneras near the dam at the pool inlet. The pool above, Heber Pool, is even more natural with flanking woodland to the south and open meadow to the north. A most attractive feature of the Hodnet Water Garden is the way the transition is made from the highly 'gardened' eastern end to the wholly wild western end. Instead of asiatic filipendulas we have native meadow sweet. The woodlands are filled with bluebells and floating on the water is *Potamogeton natans*.

Turning south and crossing between Heber Pool and Paradise Pool we return on the south side of the water garden. On the south bank of the Main Pool are colourful red twigged dogwoods and weeping willows. There is also a collection of cherries including 'Okame', 'Accolade', 'Hisakura', 'Kursar', 'Amanogawa', 'Ojochin', and 'Ukon'.

On the right, above the cherries is the Stone Garden which, as stated above, gets its name from the boulder which is a central feature. The ground rises steeply at this point and one gets a good view of the house and terraced banks beyond the main pool.

Above the Stone Garden is a small woodland area of scots pines, oaks and sycamores. Here there is an odd little summer house sort of structure, said to be an old smoke house. One has visions of sides of bacon or, perhaps, pike and carp hanging there above smouldering logs.

Further to the south is a fine old half-timbered tithe barn of 1619 and beyond it the Walled Garden where a full range of vegetables, soft fruits and plants under glass are grown. A fastigiate tulip tree has been planted at the road junction and recent woodland plantings nearby are intended to provide a windbreak in years to come.

Below here, to the north east is the shrub area laid out in 1957-9 and now after over twenty years fully established. Mature oaks provide the light shade so loved by rhododendrons, camellias and hydrangeas. The latter include *H. villosa*, *H. aspera* and *H. xanthoneura wilsonii*.

North east from here we reach an open rectangular lawn. One assumes that it was a tennis court at some time in the past. On its edge is a summer house and below on the north many interesting trees including the large flowered form of the snowdrop tree *Halesia monticola vestita* and *Davidia involucrata*.

East of this running north and south and forming the garden boundary is the Magnolia Walk, planted in 1956-7. Here will be found many of the deciduous magnolias including *M. mollicomata*, *M. sinensis* and *M. lennei*. Behind the magnolias are many more trees, *Parottia persica*, fastigiate hornbeam and a twisted hazel among others. This walk leads down to the beech avenue and the car park.

Limeburners
Mr and Mrs J.E. Derry

On outskirts of Ironbridge, Telford. Take B4380 from Ironbridge up Lincoln Hill. Turn L at top of hill. Garden is just beyond the Beeches Hospital. Area: 3.8ha (9.5 acres). Altitude: around 45m (150ft). Soil: mostly introduced but some original limestone area on margin. Rainfall: 760mm (30in). Family labour only. Open for NGS.

It has been the present writer's policy, in a long career in horticulture to choose a place to live by the quality of the soil. This is not always possible, there may be no choice but whenever there is, soil is the factor that tips the scales.

To come across an old refuse tip on the edge of an area of once beautiful country now being devastated by new town development and to find that the site has been chosen deliberately for a garden and a place to build a house is at first surprising. But the Derrys are surprising people. They were so distressed at the destruction of wild life in the new town that they felt they must do what they could to create a refuge as near as possible to the centre of devastation.

The story begins in last century or even earlier when digging of limestone started. By 1900 when these operations finished a deep ravine had been created and some of the workings could have been described as mines rather than quarries. If such a site could have been left alone a nature reserve would have resulted spontaneously but these places have a fatal attraction to local authority refuse departments and so over the years rubbish of all kinds was tipped in until it had reached a depth of 50ft or more. Such was the beginning of Limeburners.

It was in 1927 that the present owners started reclamation work. Bulky items such as old cars were beaten flat, the site roughly levelled and thousands of tons of top soil was imported. The dry summers of 1975/6 did not help the establishment of the newly planted material but slowly the garden evolved.

We now have a more or less level lawn area with informal shrub beds, an artificial pool and a naturally moist area below. Many plants are chosen because of their attraction to insects.

Steep banks still exist. The original limestone quarry face forms the boundary on one side. A Scots pine once grew on the top of this. A landslide brought it down to the bottom where it still is, vertical and reasonably happy. One misleading thing about steep slopes is their area.

The 9½ acres given as the area here is in horizontal equivalent. The true surface area is much greater.

The hardest work has been completed but development will continue. Already the results are very gratifying. It will soon become a fine garden.

Lower Hall
Mr and Mrs C.F. Dumbell

Worfield, 1 mile N of A454 Wolverhampton — Bridgnorth road. 3½ NE of Bridgnorth. Area: 1.8ha (4.5 acres). Altitude: 54m (180ft). Soil: partly lime free, partly limey. Rainfall: 700mm (27.5in). Open under NGS or by appointment.

This must rank among the finest modern gardens of its size with much of great interest. Although the house is of mid sixteenth century the garden has largely been created by the present owners since their purchase of the property in 1964. Fortunately there are sufficient mature trees and other established features to take away any feeling of 'newness' which one finds with gardens recently created on a bare site.

The River Worfe divides the garden into two roughly equal halves. The original garden is on the house side of the river and the soil is somewhat alkaline. Beyond the river is the more recently developed woodland garden which is lime free. A small lake provides the central point of a large water garden with excellent marginal planting.

A new courtyard with fountain has recently been made on the south west front of the house. The old turf has been removed and replaced with gravel. This has been planted with a range of green foliage plants. Colour planning is a feature important to Mrs Dumbell.

The old walled garden is on the south east side of the house. The walls are mostly of the local red sandstone but parts are of beautiful old matured brick. Paths are also in brick.

Lanning Roper has designed a small formal garden within the walled garden. Four conically clipped box with lavender and santolina surround a central lead statue and create an atmosphere in keeping with the house itself. There is also a red and pink border, and a white border in which the rose 'Iceberg' is prominent. All strong colours are avoided.

A swimming pool is partly screened by a yew hedge and nearby is a wide spreading specimen of the cherry 'Kanzan'. This is a reminder that this cherry does eventually lose the funnel shape of its youth. One

Above: Lower Hall, Worfield. The pergola within the old walled garden. *Clematis armandii* has just shed its blossom.

Below: Lower Hall, Worfield. Streamside planting in which *Rheum palmatum, Lysichytum americanum,* hostas and other such subjects are flourishing.

Above: Bredon Springs. Closely packed herbaceous plants are colourful weed suppressors.

Below: Birmingham University Botanical Garden. The Wild Garden. *Gunnera manicata* emerging in late spring.

Above: Burford House. *Meconopsis sheldonii* is but one of the many fine plants in this garden.

Below: Golding Manor. Eremurus against the seventeenth century wall of the middle terrace.

wonders how many of those planted as street trees or in small gardens could be allowed to attain mature form if they wanted to.

Another feature is an apothecaries garden in which is to be found a large collection of plants mentioned in the old herbals. A pergola supported by brick pillars is planted with white or pale coloured roses, *Clematis armandii*, Wistaria and a grape vine.

A cage with soft fruit and a block of apples occupies the south west side of the walled garden.

On leaving the walled garden one passes into an entirely different style of modern informal planting. A large lawn with specimen trees leads to the lake and stream garden. There are two weirs. 'Lake' is perhaps a misnomer by Capability Brown's standards but it is an attractive stretch of water. Around the margin we find *Caltha palustris*, the taller *C. polypetala* and a white species, probably *C. leptosepala*. A strip of lawn of varying width separates the lake from a broad border on the banks of a little stream, an offshoot from the main watercourse. Here the waterside plants grow in great luxury. *Rheum palmatum*, *Hosta*, *Lysichitum*, *Smilacina*, *Rodgersia* and others of that habitat group flourish particularly well.

One goes over a stone footbridge and then crosses the main stream by a wooden bridge to arrive at the woodland garden or wild garden. Here the emphasis is on natural species. A substantial collection of rhododendrons is a feature of this area. Planting is in informal beds and borders separated by mown grass. The stream runs along one side. Native alders and birches present a homely touch.

Attractive bark is displayed by snake bark maples, *Prunus serrula*, mahogany red bark, even on small twigs, and *Betula albo-sinensis*, orange red trunk. One expects to find *Metasequoia glyptostroboides* and *Cercidiphyllum japonicum* in the best modern gardens and one is not disappointed.

It is, however, the herbaceous plants that give this garden its most distinctive character. Many of these are North American woodlanders such as *Sanguinaria canadensis*, the Bloodroot, with its pink or white flowers on six inch stems and heart shaped leaves. *Tiarella cordifolia* with foamy white flowers above low foliage, surely one of the best of our woodland ground coverers. There is *Viola cucculata* with white, blue veined flowers and foliage that disappears in winter, and another little yellow violet from Virginia. *Trilliums* are here in variety and *Dodecatheons* bearing their cyclamen — like flowers.

Not all of the herbaceous plants are of such low stature as the above for there are *Gunnera*, *Ligularia*, *Heracleum*, *Peltiphyllum*, etc. all showing exceptional vigour. Notable ferns are *Onoclea sensibilis* and *Matteuchia struthiopteris*. One could fill a good sized catalogue with the plants grown here but the above gives an idea of the range covered.

What cannot be over emphasised is the high standard of management and cultivation throughout.

Ludstone Hall

Mr and Mrs Geo. Ferguson

Claverley, 7 miles W of Wolverhampton, S of A454. Area: 4ha (10 acres). Altitude: 87m (290ft). Soil: sandy loam, lime free. Rainfall: 700mm (27.5in). Labour employed: two. Open for NGS.

Ludstone Hall has some delightful features. There are fine trees, a mediaeval moat, a so-called knot garden and a Jacobean house of great beauty, as well as a good range of modern shrubs and a woodland garden. The main entrance drive bordered by grass strips leads straight to the south front. Tall hedges hide everything to left or right and concentrate attention on the house itself. When we do get past the hedges and turn right we can enter the garden east of the drive. This has always been called the knot garden but it is not quite typical of those depicted in works of Tudor or seventeenth century period.

Prior to 1870 the house was just a farmhouse for more than a century but in that year it was bought by Joseph R. Cartwright who proceeded to restore the house, create a lake, now part of the Dairy House, opposite, build the stable block, the lodge at the entrance gate, and lay out the garden. In the forty years before his death in 1910 he completed the broad plan of the garden as it is today, and constructed the knot garden.

As this last feature is probably unique in the whole of Britain a detailed description may not be out of place. It is rectangular in shape and slightly sunken. Tall hedges of mixed green and variegated holly screen it from the road and drive. A privet hedge separates it from the kitchen garden and a retaining wall with a low parapet borders the fourth side and allows it to be seen from the house.

Wide lawn cross paths divide it into four sectors. Opposite diagonal sectors are now planted with roses. The other two sectors are as originally laid out. Each has a central corkscrew topiary some six to seven feet high surrounded by a low box hedge. Playing card pips, spades, clubs, hearts and diamonds are arranged around the centre in four blocks, each pip itself being surrounded by a low box hedge of the same level so that the top if flat. There are four clipped domes rising above the general level. The

Above: Ludstone Hall. The huge 'knot garden' with its playing card motif was laid out towards the end of the last century.

Below: Morville Hall. The crossing and interlacing of trunks and branches of the yew walk rival anything that can be achieved by modern sculpture.

pattern is complicated and its original formation must have required skill
and patience. Although it is suffering a little from old age — it is probably
about ninety years old — it remains an interesting museum piece.

To the west of the entrance drive behind a tall hedge of holly and yew is
a large expanse of lawn. A long curving bed of herbaceous plants is two or
more yards from the hedge, allowing hedgeclipping to take place in
comfort. The south and west borders of the lawn are planted with trees
and shrubs. A fine old cherry is near the end of the drive.

The moat is crossed by a wide bridge on the south front and by a little
hump-backed stone bridge on the west side. This leads to a paved terrace
which runs along the west side of the house.

On the north of the house a large lawn forms a peninsula with the moat
on two sides and a large pool beyond. The pool dates from the thirteenth
century. Still further to the north is the woodland wild garden with a
stream running through it and which has been the centre of activity over
the last thirty years. The last owner, Mr M.H. Rollason was responsible
for this work.

There are some superb silver birches, good beeches, a few oaks and a
large common alder at the head of the pool. Newer plantings making
good growth are two *Ginkgo biloba* and two *Liquidamber styraciflua* in a sunken
grassed area. On the extreme north boundary is a screen of larch, spruce
and poplar. And just to emphasise the age of the site two of the most
massive sweet chestnut trunks I can recall seeing. They must be about as
old as the house.

There are, of course, both evergreen and deciduous rhododendrons,
mahonias, viburnums, and a good range of shrubs. Bulbs are abundant in
the spring. *Lysichitum ameircanum* and other plants of moist shade grow
along the stream side. At the north end of the west lawn is a small terraced
garden with formal beds and a pergola against the wall dividing it from
the woodland garden. On the pergola are wistaria, roses and *Hydrangea
petiolaris*.

The Lythe
Mr and Mrs L.R. Jebb

*About 1 mile SE of Ellesmere on A528. Area: 1.6ha (4 acres). Altitude: 100m (330ft). Soil:
light sand, acid. Rainfall: 760mm (30in). Labour employed: casual. Opens from time to time
NGS.*

The house is Regency but the garden dates mainly from the beginning of the present century with modification since the last war.

A ha-ha forms the boundary with parkland to the south. Wide gravel paths separate areas of lawn in which are informally planted beds of shrubs. Rhododendrons, azaleas, heaths and maples are prominent. A specimen of the rare *Taxodium ascendens* was planted in 1930 and there is a fine Westfelton Yew *Taxus baccata dovastoniana*. Other trees include Blue cedars, *Ailanthus* and I noted a particularly good specimen of silver birch near the main drive. There are some especially fine variegated hollies.

The walled garden is now partly tennis court but the remainder is well maintained. A border on the outside of the walled garden is stocked with a good range of plants among which are *Rosa moyesii, Hydrangea petiolaris, Clematis orientalis, Paeonia lutea ludlowii, Buddleia alternifolia, Cytisus battandierii, Piptanthus laburnifolius, Choisya ternata, Staphyllea colchica, Eucryphia* sp.

There is an interesting collection of herbaceous plants and in the autumn of 1979 colchicums were notably attractive.

The Magnolias
Mr and Mrs Percy Thrower

Merrington, Bomere Heath. 6 miles NW of Shrewsbury between B5067 and A528. Area 0.6ha (1½ acre). Altitude: 100m (330ft). Soil: variable, lime free. Rainfall: 760mm (30in). Labour: owner plus part-time help. Open for Gardeners Sunday. (See Green Book).

The garden has been created in less than 20 years by one of Britain's best known gardeners. In 1962 the site was an open field sloping to the south with views of the rolling Shropshire countryside. In this year 1½ acres was fenced off at the top and preparations for the garden began.

Amateurs can learn much from the manner in which this garden has developed. Ease of maintenance has been the main aim throughout. Some bulldozing was carried out to fill in low places and top soil was removed and returned. This has resulted in about three inches of top soil over gravel at the top end, a good medium loam about half-way down and clay at the bottom.

A three year ley was sown and kept mown. Island beds and pools were made and the grass area improved by herbicide treatment and management to produce an acceptable grass area — not a first class lawn. The area around the house was reseeded but native grasses have come in.

The house was sited to give best possible views and the approach drive was made at the back or north side to prevent obstruction by cars. A retaining wall of local red sandstone was built along the roadside. This matches nearby buildings. Beech hedges were planted on the roadside and on the left hand side of the drive as one enters to screen a kitchen garden. On the field side a quickthorn boundary hedge was planted and this was layed when it was eight feet high — a reminder that hedgelaying is still carried out in Shropshire, although regretably a dying art over much of Britain.

Apart from a few small areas annual bedding is avoided. Almost all planting was permanent but inevitably as the plants grew thinning became necessary. The absence of free lime made possible the growing of calcifuge plants.

In the rock garden around the pools the most vigorous plants have taken over and much of the stone has disappeared from view. Rhododendrons and ericas predominate.

Scots pines were planted in NE corner with silver birches in foreground. Conifers include *Chamaecyparis lawsoniana* Golden form, *Cupressocyparis leylandii*, *Metasequoia glyptostroboides*, *Thuja plicata*, *Cedrus libani*, *C. atlantica glauca*, Weeping form, and *Picea pungens glauca*. Other trees of note are *Liriodendron tulipifera*, *Liquidamber styraciflua*, *Betula papyrifera*, *B. youngii*, *Eucalyptus gunnii*. *Cercidiphyllum*, various acers, cherries and ornamental crabs. As these trees grow the character of the garden will inevitably change. Some, one suspects, may never reach maturity.

There is no attempt at specialisation but an all the year round interest is assured with *Prunus subbirtella autumnalis, Jasminum nudiflorum, Mahonia japonica, Viburnum fragrans. V. xbodnantense* and *Erica carnea* for the winter months, daffodils and numerous shrubs in the spring and, of course roses, clematis and other things in the summer. Autumn colour, both foliage and fruit is plentiful.

Along the top of the bank is a pergola with *Clematis florida bicolor*, Wistaria and climbing roses, including Zephyrin Droughin, Mme Alfred Carriere, and Pauls Lemon Pillar.

Although the garden may seem to be somewhat exposed it was pleasing to hear that *Embothrium* survived the 1979 winter and that *Carpentaria californica* was only slightly scorched.

A feature of considerable interest to many is the kitchen garden. Cordon fruit trees form a boundary along the top side. Tomatoes are grown to a high state of perfection in the greenhouse and a great variety of vegetables of equally high standard produced.

Mawley Hall

Mr and Mrs Anthony Galliers-Pratt

3km (2 miles) SE of Cleobury Mortimer. S of A4117. Altitude: 120m (400ft). Soil: lime free. Rainfall: 700mm (27.5in). Open for NGS and GS.

To be situated on the western edge of the Wyre Forest and six miles east of Clee Hill is a good start in making a garden. To have a fine eighteenth century house as a centre piece is an added advantage. The property had, however, been badly neglected when the present owners purchased it in the early 1960's and the garden, except for many fine trees was non-existent.

Many people creating a garden on such a site would have concentrated on beds and borders of shrubs and shrub roses in the modern manner. Not so Mrs Galliers-Pratt. The house dates from 1730 — just before the eighteenth century landscape movement swept away formal parterres. Formal parterres have returned to Mawley and they have great charm.

On the west front are two matching parterres edged and divided with dwarf box. A white rhododendron forms a centre piece surrounded by *Hebe pagei* and a dwarf lavender. The beds are mostly filled with silver foliage plants and there are four pillars of *Hedera colchica*. Several of the plants used are quite modern introductions and the feature is best described as a twentieth century variation on an early eighteenth century theme.

Equally intriguing is the herb garden, north-east of the house. It has a central path with five upright junipers a side. The garden consists of beds edged with boards and separated by narrow gravel paths. The effect is Tudor or even almost mediaeval. The range of herbs is immense and the atmosphere delightful. Adjoining the herb garden on the east side is a wide brick path with large square beds down the middle. These are planted with chamomile, pennyroyal and other such things but we are brought back to the present day with a jerk when we see numerous plants of *Hebe hulkeana* along the edge.

White flowers are used extensively at Mawley. This is particularly so in plantings around the swimming pool. This is approached through a wrought iron gate from the herb garden and is quite one of the most attractive swimming pools I have seen. Another formal feature is the rose garden beside the coach house.

Nevertheless the total area of these formal gardens is not large and much of the garden consists of rough mown grass under trees with informal shrub planting. Pleasant walks and pleasing vistas have been created and this is the line on which future development is planned. But it is the formal gardens that make Mawley a little bit different.

Meadow House

Mr and Mrs Ronald Sidaway

Oldbury, Bridgnorth, 1.6km (1 mile) SW of Bridgnorth on Cleobury Mortimer road B4363. Area: 1.2ha (3 acres). Altitude: 90m (300ft). Soil: loam to clay loam, lime free. Rainfall: 700mm (27.5in). Open regularly for NGS.

This is a modern house with a modern garden but although it dates only from 1962 it gains some measure of greater maturity from trees that were present on the original site. Some fine old beeches on the roadside are actually passing their best and in such a situation are not likely to remain long if they threaten to become dangerous. There is also another boundary belt of larch and birch, a pleasant combination of light foliage. A large walnut is on the north west boundary.

A chamaecyparis hedge gives protection from north and north west and there are beech hedges along the entrance drive. Newly planted trees include many interesting items. A seventeen year old *Catalpa bignonioides* looks particularly well and *Ginkgo biloba*, is making nine inches extension growth per annum although I have seen better foliage on other trees. No modern garden of reasonable size is without *Metasequoia glyptostroboides*. This and the ginkgo are both survivors of an ancient flora, both from China and both very beautiful trees.

The cedars, *Cedrus diodara* and *C. atlantica glauca* are making good trees and *Liriodendron tulipifera* should, one day, be one of the tallest of the garden's occupants.

Trees, however, are not the garden's main interest at the moment. Formal rose beds in grass are an important feature and there are informal beds of shrubs and herbaceous plants. Lilies are grown in cultivated areas under trees. Living trees are used to support climbing roses and clematis. This is a garden with many interesting plants and is very well managed.

Millichope Park

Mr and Mrs Lindsay Bury

Munslow, on A4368 13km (8 miles) NE of Craven Arms 22km (14 miles) SW of Bridgnorth.
Area: 5ha (13 acres). Altitude: 180m (600ft). Soil: variable, partly lime free. Rainfall: 840mm
(33in). Labour employed: one man and one boy. Open usually once a year in aid of NGS.

It is often a hair's breadth decision that determines whether a fine house
survives or is obliterated. Such is the case with Millichope and we must be
grateful that the survival lobby won.

The present house was built in the late 1830's (completed in 1840) by the
Rev. Robert Norgrave Pemberton, the architect being Edward Haycock
of Shrewsbury. For centuries the estate had been in the More family and
the Rev. Pemberton's grandfather inherited it from his cousin Catherine
More. At that time there was a black and white house further down the
hill.

The Mores left their mark in the form of an Ionic Temple designed by
Geo. Steuart in 1770. This stands on a Wenlock limestone cliff on the
opposite side of the lake when viewed from the house. The landscape
designer Eames appears to have worked with Steuart at this time.

The Pemberton's descendents sold Millichope to H.J. Beckwith, the
present owner's great grandfather, in 1891. After some years of indecision
restoration was eventually carried out around 1968-70 and Mr and Mrs
Bury moved in 1971. The garden had been virtually untouched since 1930.

The setting of the house is superb — on the lower slopes of Wenlock
Edge just above Corvedale with Brown Clee some ten miles to the south
east. The entrance drive is cut through the limestone giving high vertical
faces on each side. High above is Steuart's Ionic Temple.

One of the changes made in the restoration was to bring the drive to the
north east side of the house instead of the south east front. This meant
creating a new courtyard. The lawn was carried right up to the south east
front. From this point one looks down over the sloping lawn, on which is
a particularly fine specimen of *Abies procera*, to the main lake below. We
also see a black walnut, *Juglans nigra*, a *Magnolia acuminata*, and a superb
sweet chestnut.

The lake, together with another one below was made at the time the
house was built and many of the trees, especially the American conifers
would date from that period or shortly after.

To the south west of the front lawn is a new formal garden, or, more

accurately, three formal gardens. Swimming pools always create a
problem in siting. Whether they be rectangular or circular or a
combination of both they always seem out of place. Here the problem has
been handled very successfully. The site was a grass tennis court. At the
house end a water garden with two rectangular lily ponds has been made.
Beyond that is a garden with herbaceous plant beds and at the far end the
swimming pool fitting neatly and unobtrusively into the general pattern.
When the boundary hedges have grown a little more the picture will be
complete.

The lower pool is a large area of new development with enormous possibilities. Clearing is going ahead as fast as labour permits. Dogwoods and
willows are being planted and as these and other plantings mature it will
be an outstanding feature. Fine trees abound on this estate and large
woodlands provide a background to the garden and parkland.

There are few pleasures to equal that of restoring neglected houses and
gardens. At Millichope this is illustrated almost to perfection. The
possibilities are infinite. Deep down one wishes one could return to the
days when a dozen or more gardeners would have been employed but that
was the nineteenth century. This is the twentieth. We must be thankful
that so much is being done.

The Morleys

Mr and Mrs J. Knight

---

*Wallsbank, 5.6km (3.5m) E of Church Stretton on B4371. Take left fork for Stone Acton and
Cardington. Garden is 400yds on right. Area: 1.2ha (3 acres). Altitude: 186m (620ft). Soil:
lime free. Rainfall: 840mm (33in). Labour employed: no employed labour. Open under NGS.*

This was a neglected smallholding with the usual 'pig and poultry' out-
buildings and other appurtenances when purchased by the present owners
in 1954. Slowly the garden has grown and developed until all the available
land can be said to be in a well organised and managed state, but
obviously the garden is still relatively new.

The stone built cottage faces south west and in front we find a fairly
conventional cottage garden with crazy paving — all very trim and neat.

To the north and west is an area, formerly a field, of irregular contour.
Here informal beds have been made. Planting consists of heathers in
quantity and variety, other ericaceous plants and a good range of modern
shrubs. Conifers are used freely and enough trees to give height and

relieve monotony.

A very pleasing feature is the way natural levels and contours have been retained, thus keeping the top soil where it belongs. So many designers, given such a site, would have had bulldozers in to level things off and grade the banks, and, in so doing would have created problems of compacted sub-soil clay and lost top-soil.

The general layout of informal beds in grass, planted with shrubs and ground cover is in the best of modern taste and it is not surprising to find that John Treasure of Burford House has advised on the work.

A stream runs along the bottom of the garden and this provides moist areas. Some of the beds are set out as low rock gardens.
Growth of trees is very satisfactory. A young specimen of Forrest's variety of *Abies delavayi* is making a foot of growth a year.

Along the side of the entrance drive is a paddock of about three quarters of an acre in which are planted an interesting collection of trees including *Notofagus, Alnus cordata* Leyland cypress, birches, beeches, red and scarlet oaks and others. These ensure continued development for the next century or so.

Morville Hall

Miss A.P. Bythell: The National Trust

Bridgnorth 5km (3 miles) W of Bridgnorth on A458, Bridgnorth — Shrewsbury Road. S of main road at E end of Morville village. Area: 1ha (2½ acres). Altitude: 90m (300ft). Soil: medium loam, lime free. Rainfall: 700mm (27.5in). Open by written appointment with Miss Bythell for NGS and NT.

The approach to Morville Hall is impressive. A large semi-circular drive with cupola topped pavilions at each end and half way round a fine Georgian mansion looking out over the large D shaped lawn to the church beyond.

Although the present building is mid eighteenth century there are incorporated in it remains of earlier ones. A twelfth century Benedictine Priory stood here and materials from this were used by Roger Smith in the sixteenth century to build an E plan house substantial traces of which can still be seen.

The estate was bought by Miss Bythell's father in 1936 and given to the National Trust by her in 1965.

Left: Morville Hall. One of the Martabani jars that add that little extra character to this pleasant garden.

Below: Pitchford Hall. The south front of the fifteenth century house. A few sparse climbers and dwarf shrubs break the hard lines at ground level and provide a little colour.

The house faces slightly south of east and the garden is on what, for convenience sake, we will call the south front. The large walled garden far to the west is now run as part of the farm.

We enter the garden through a wrought iron gate in the wall dividing it from the drive and find ourselves in an unpretentious garden with much charm and almost a 'cottage' atmosphere. A simple straight gravel path runs south from the house to steps leading to the lower garden. On each side of the path are wide mixed borders and beyond these two balanced rectangles of lawn up to the east and west boundaries respectively. The proportions are just right. In the borders are a range of shrubs and plants to provide interest throughout the year. Among those noted were *Hypericum patulum* 'Hidcote', *Potentilla fruticosa, Spiraea x bumalda* 'Anthony Waterer', *Viburnum tomentosum*, ericas, lavenders, and dwarf rhododendrons. Bergenias provided colour and boldness in the spring. The cultivar 'Silberlicht' was particularly fine.

Half way along, the continuity of the borders is broken by two fine old chinese jars, depicted in one of Graham Thomas's delightful pencil sketches in his 'Gardens of the National Trust'. They are believed to be of seventeenth century and were used for the export of various commodities to the Middle East and were known as Martabani jars from the Burmese port of Martaban whence they were shipped.

West of the lawn is a row of ancient yews. They are planted so close together that one suspects they may originally have been a hedge. If so that was centuries ago. Their massed and intermingled branches now provide cool shade for the path leading down to the lower garden.

On the west of the house is a paved garden with a rectangular pool with iris, water lilies, and a particularly healthy stock of goldfish. Just north of this a small lawn with a weeping cherry, probably *Prunus x yedoensis* 'Ivensii', with its masses of small white flowers on slender drooping branchlets in early April.

The lower garden is a semi-formal strip below the retaining wall and planted with roses and lavender. Beyond this is a gravel path and further south a canal-like pool with daffodils in quantity in the surrounding grass. Still further south bordering the meadow is Mor Brook flowing to join the Severn a few miles away.

Oak Cottage Herb Farm

Mr and Mrs J. Thompson

Nesscliffe, 11km (7 miles) NW of Shrewsbury on A5. Area: 0.2ha (½ acre). Altitude: 90m (295ft). Soil: sandy loam, lime free. Rainfall: 760mm (30in). Labour employed: 2 part-time. Open for NGS and at all reasonable times.

This is a delightful place for the plant historian. Here, tumbling over each other, is a collection of plants rarely to be seen in fashionable modern gardens. The main qualifications for admission to this assembly are that the plant must have had an accepted use at some time, and it must not be a hybrid or garden form unless it has antiquity on its side. Thus a Tudor double chamomile would get in, a modern chrysanthemum would not.

The present owners came here in 1970/71 at which time there was no garden, just a piece of ground. The layout is simple and 'cottage'. One has a feeling that it has just grown naturally. As Ruth Thompson says, the theme is one of controlled wildness.

In a collection of this kind listing the various plants is almost meaningless. There are, however, a few that deserve mention. Alliums always interest me and one with large heads and typical onion leaves was of uncertain identity. Skirret grows better here than it does with me. This old vegetable is worth taking in hand by plant breeders. Some plants in a seedling batch are regularly found with little central core. If the roots could be fattened up a bit and their wrinkles removed it would appeal to many discerning amateurs even if it did not find favour with the commercial grower.

Herbs, of course, are a cult with a certain section of modern gardeners and most of the kinds in Britain today will be found here but many people will be interested in the numerous plants no longer in use but with ancient connections. Such things as elecampane, orris root and the apothecaries rose have interesting associations.

The Old Parsonage
Mrs A.F. Porges

Munslow, 11km (7 miles) NE of Craven Arms on B4368. Area: 0.8ha (2 acres). Altitude: 150m (500ft). Soil: lime free. Rainfall: 840mm (33in). Open for NGS.

This garden is a pleasant blend of formal and informal. There is no unified design theme. One gets the impression that developments have taken place piecemeal over a fairly long period but it has the homeliness and intimacy of a garden that is cared for. It is well suited to the late Georgian house. The present owner has been here since 1967.

A fourteen feet high wall on the top or north side of the garden carries a large specimen of *Clematis montana* but there is room for many more. Below this are herbaceous borders with a good range of plants.

Fruit trees, lawn, impressive clipped yew hedges and semi-formal rose beds each contribute their own bit of character. A heather garden has recently been made. Lower down this sloping garden are informal shrub beds with azaleas and other items. There are a couple of good Austrian Pines and other conifers.

The south boundary is largely occupied by a deep quarter acre pool which adds much to the character of the garden.

Peplow Hall
The Hon. R.V. Wynn

4.8km (3 miles) S of Hodnett via A442. Area: including parkland 16ha (40 acres). Altitude: 75m (246ft). Soil: sandy loam, lime free, Rainfall: 760mm (30in). Labour employed: two. Open under NGS.

One approaches Peplow Hall through a fine pair of eighteenth century gates by Jones of Wrexham and passes along an impressive drive flanked by broad expanses of mown grass backed by lime trees to create a wide avenue. Daffodils in great abundance are planted under the trees. As one approaches the house there are large beds of azaleas set well back on each side. The impression one gets on approaching is one of space. The drive is wide and there is nothing cluttering up the front of the house.

This is the west front and the sundial bears the date 1725, the date when the house was built on the site of an earlier house. It was enlarged in 1887 but was restored to its original size by Rollason in 1939. It is a very fine example of Early Georgian building with flat roof and parapet wall. The present owner came in 1978. The garden on the south front is enclosed in a neatly clipped hedge of *Thuja plicata* and contains rose beds with a central fountain feature.

On the east of the house is a large lawn separated from the parkland by a Ha Ha constructed only a few years ago by the immediately preceding owner. There are more rose beds near to the house. North of this is an enclosed sunken garden. Four large rose beds form the corners of a square set in lawn surrounding a central sundial. East of this are topiaries in box and yew.

Two old vineries remain and a modern metal house has replaced some older houses that have been demolished. There are extensive herbaceous borders. iris, pyrethrums and geum 'Princess Juliana' were looking very well at the time of my visit. The kitchen garden is very well cropped and managed.

Below the sunken garden is a rhododendron walk and lawn leading down to the lake. Water for the lake is supplied by the R. Tern through sluice gates. In this area are some fine beech trees, Wellingtonias and sweet chestnuts. There are large areas of daffodils in grass.

Peplow is not a plantsman's garden but there is plenty of interest. It is very tidy and well managed and above all the garden provides a perfect setting for a very fine building.

Pitchford Hall

Mrs Oliver Colthurst

10km (6 miles) SE of Shrewsbury between A49 and A458. Area: 1.6ha (4 acres). Altitude: 80m (260ft). Soil: lime free. Rainfall: 700mm (27.5in). Open for NGS.

One approaches Pitchford Hall through a very fine double avenue of limes. It is an impressive beginning. The drive turns left with St. Michael's Church on the right and enters a gravelled courtyard on the north front of the house. The mid-fifteenth century house must rank among the finest examples of black and white architecture in Britain. The courtyard has borders of roses and clipped domes of golden yew. The present owner came here in 1972 and much of the garden development is from that date.

On the south front the house forms three sides of a quadrangle of lawn with a few climbers on the walls. Further south is a large croquet lawn and beyond that a tree clad bank, beyond which is the walled garden.

To the south west is a unique feature — a house in a lime tree. This house which has recently been restored was known to have been in existence in 1714. The tree, ancient and massive, still has plenty of life in its lower branches.

East of the walled garden is an area with shrub and herbaceous borders and a small range of greenhouses well managed and well stocked. The walled garden itself is used for the usual kitchen garden crops and also for a small tree nursery. On its north side is a fine old orangery now used as a residence.

On the east front below a series of grass terraces is a stream, flowing northwards to Cound Brook and thence to the Severn. To the north-east is another odd feature, a bitumen well.

There are some good cedars, beeches and limes and although Pitchford is not noted for its plant collection there is plenty of interest.

Sansaw Hall

Major and Mrs D.R.B. Thompson

Clive, four miles S of Wem. Midway between villages of Clive and Grinshill. Area: 7.6ha (19 acres). Altitude: 100m (328ft). Soil: sand to medium loam. Acid. Rainfall: 760mm (30in). Labour employed: two plus one part-time. Open for NGS.

The house dates from early eighteenth century (Queen Anne) with substantial additions in 1886 but there is no record of early formal gardens of that period and the house apparently opened out on to parkland at that time. The older trees, especially the oaks, would be of this period or earlier.

In the late 1860's the garden as it is today was laid out. This consists of a vast expanse of well mown lawn dipping down SSW from the house to the lake at the bottom. A sundial is in isolation near the centre of the near part of the lawn. There are numerous very fine Irish yews, a purple beech planted in 1890 and now quite a good specimen, two araucarias, *Metasequoia glyptostroboides, Liriodendron tulipifera*, a particularly fine *Sequoiadendron giganteum*, numerous magnificent oaks, firs, chamaecyparis and many others.

A specimen of *Thuja plicata* is worth a special description. The tree is not old, possibly 40-50 years, and it has not developed layered lower branches as eventually happens with old trees. It was, however, multistemmed from the start and the lower branches, sweeping the ground all round, have a perimeter of about 60 yards. The tree forms a blunt, squat cone of unique character.

It is a characteristic of most of the trees at Sansaw that they have been planted where they have a chance to make specimens and they do not appear to have suffered neglect at any period. They have certainly been well cared for during recent years.

Rhododendrons and maples form large boundary groups and islands. There are some very fine specimens of *Acer palmatum*.

The lake at the bottom has a woodland backdrop. It is supplied by a loop from the main stream. A further lake lies beyond the confines of the garden. There are wild yellow water lilies and various marginal plants. Cornus and other things are planted on the island.

North of the house, opposite the main entrance is a wrought iron gate leading on to a small lawn flanked with trees and shrubs. Maples are conspicuous again here. Near the main drive is another fine Wellingtonia as well as *Metasequoia glyptostroboides, Acer rubrum, Catalpa bignonioides.*

A large stable block has its west wall almost covered by three big fig trees, all carefully pruned and tied in. In front are borders of rhododendrons, azaleas, ericas and such like.

There is no formal bedding. Whether any formerly existed is not certain. There has obviously been some simplification in layout. An area of kitchen garden has been converted into paddocks for ponies. What is most impressive about Sansaw is the impeccable standard of management that is maintained throughout.

This is driven home with real force when we enter the walled garden. Walled gardens today are so often regarded as a liability. In many large gardens they are the first thing to be abandoned when running costs have to be cut.

Fifty years ago the walled garden was the centre of the working garden. Here were applied the growing skills. How delightful to find an old walled garden in which the derelict glass has been completely removed and the balance put into good repair. How wonderful to find an old pit with 8ft pit lights still in use and in sound condition.

Those of us who grew up with this sort of thing must feel more than a little nostalgia on seeing morello cherries as ever on the north wall, peaches on the south and fan trained plums. Not a shoot or leaf out of place, hardly a thing that would not have met the exacting demands of the beginning of the century.

There are two long herbaceous borders, dahlias, a large block of chrysanthemums in addition to a full range of vegetables.

Under glass we find a wide range of decorative plants. Strelitzia, *Begonia maculata*, gerbera, many foliage plants. A supply of material for house decoration is maintained for the whole year round.

Chief credit for the high standards at Sansaw must go to Mr Edwards, the head gardener. The intelligent use of modern methods enables him to achieve with a total staff of two and a half almost as much as was done by 13 men in 1930. But the co-operation of an appreciative employer is perhaps of equal importance.

Stanley Hall

Major and Mrs J.H.N. Thompson

2 miles N of Bridgnorth. Take B4373 and turn R at Stanley Lane. Altitude: 90m (300ft). Rainfall: 700mm (27.5in). Open from time to time under NGS.

The house is 1640 with early nineteenth century additions. Royalist troops were billeted here during the Civil War.

Garden layout has been greatly simplified for easy maintenance and consists mainly of fine specimen trees in mown grass. A paved terrace below lawn level surrounds the house. A large area of lawn provides an open tree flanked vista from the house.

Noteworthy trees are copper beeches, redwoods, Wellingtonias, a notable large *Abies* and Douglas Fir.

The approach drive ¾ mile in length passes through an avenue of horse chestnuts and has masses of rhododendrons on the west side. Behind these is a chain of pools, some almost silted up and not easily accessible.

Swallow Hayes

Mr and Mrs Michael Edwards

7 miles NW of Wolverhampton on S side of A41. Area: 0.6ha (1.5 acres). Altitude: 90m (300ft). Soil: sandy loam, lime free. Rainfall: 840mm (33in). Open usually two Sundays per year under NGS.

Swallow Hayes is an almost perfect example of the modern labour saving garden with shrubs and low growing ground cover plants in informal beds and borders with a central lawn area. This must not be interpreted as saying that this garden is a normal or 'average' modern garden. A plant collection with some 1,600 species and varieties in the space of one and a half acres is obviously exceptional. The first impression is one of overplanting to get quick effects but one then discovers that the garden is used to provide propagating material for a commercial nursery and this keeps plants smaller than would be the case in a normal garden and justifies the high planting density.

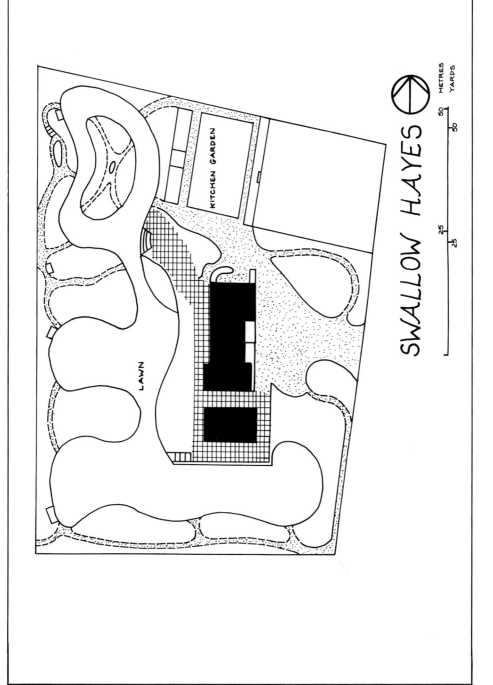

KITCHEN GARDEN

LAWN

SWALLOW HAYES

METRES
YARDS

50

50

25

25

The garden was started in 1968 around a house built a couple of years earlier. There is a gravel entrance drive and a paved terrace area around the house. The siting of the larger trees has been carefully done and although their ultimate growth will undoubtedly change the character of the garden considerably they will not interfere greatly with the smaller plants. There is a tulip tree in the north west corner and *Cedrus deodara aurea*, a scarlet oak and *Liquidambar* along the north boundary. Other potentially large trees include the rare *Fagus sylvatica tricolor, Metasequoia glyptostroboides, Davidia involucrata*, horse chestnut, blue cedar, mulberry and *Pinus strobus*. A weeping cedar is being trained to form an arch. 'Weeping' is hardly the right adjective for this tree — collapsing would seem more appropriate for the branches hang vertically without the slight arching found in most weeping trees.

The south east corner contains a collection of flowering cherries including the cream (almost yellow) flowered 'Ukon', and the wide spreading horizontally branched 'Shirotae' and 'Shimidsu Sakura'. To add variety we have *Arbutus unedo* nearby and on the south wall, hoping for mild winters, is *Fabiana imbricata*, the relative of the tomato that looks like a heather. *Cotinus coggygria* 'Royal Purple' extends the textural range still further and the yellow berried form of our native guelder rose is here also.

Along the south border is a bed of dwarf rhododendrons. *Prunus subhirtella autumnalis* is already a good specimen and the dainty chinese mountain ash, *Sorbus vilmorinii* with pinkish fruits reminds us that it is one of the best trees for the small garden. Other items of interest here are a collection of Exbury hybrid azaleas, *Amelanchier canadensis, Osmarea burkwoodii*, and ornamental crabs.

The south west corner is moister than other parts. Willows have been planted here with hostas, moisture loving primulas, meconopsis and such like plants underneath. Few herbaceous plants are found in this garden and they are mostly concentrated in a bed midway along the west side. Herbaceous plants require more tidying up than do shrubs and they are not so well suited to herbicide treatment.

A little further north is a snake bark maple, *Acer rufinerve*. The white striations are produced by cracks forming in the outer green coloured bark as girth increases. Autumn foliage colour is an added feature. Also in this area is a collection of *Hamamelis x intermedia* cultivars including 'Jelena', 'Magic Fire' and 'Ruby Glow', all winter flowering as are *Garrya elliptica* and *Cornus mas* nearby.

In the north west corner is a group of birches and recently planted dwarf conifers and heathers. More birch and rhododendrons are being planted here.

Near the rose garden by the house is a superb weeping cherry, falling over to ground level and quite one of the outstanding plants when in

Above: Upper Shelderton House. The pool. Conifers, rhododendrons and many other trees and shrubs are carefully sited on the surrounding banks. This 'natural' looking feature has been wholly created since 1971.

Below: Wenlock Abbey. Informal planting in a formal garden with the Priory ruins beyond.

flower.

Climbing plants are now being allowed to use some of the trees for support. A *Rosa banksiae* is doing well as are numerous clematis.

The work in this garden is done entirely by Mrs Edwards and averages about eight hours per week. Labelling has to be correctly and carefully done to avoid errors in collecting propagating material.

This is a garden where every stage of development has been mastered before going on to the next. One gets the impression that weeds have never been allowed to establish themselves — hence no weeds. The timely applications of herbicide to bare areas maintains this condition.

Few amateur gardeners will want, or can afford, to plant such a large and choice collection on such a small space but they can learn a lot about management by just seeing how it is done and they can pick out the items they like best.

Upper Shelderton House
Geoffrey G. Rollason Esq

Clungunford, 5km (3 miles) SW of Craven Arms. Area: 1.6ha (4 acres). Altitude: 150m (500ft). Soil: medium loam, lime free. Rainfall: 840mm (33in). Open for NGS.

This is an old farmhouse, part sixteenth century, but there was virtually no garden when the present owner came here around 1963. The garden is therefore a modern one and has mostly been constructed since 1967.

The situation is particularly pleasing among the South Shropshire hills, a mile or so north of the Hereford border. There are fine views of the surrounding countryside.

A large lawn area on the south side of the house is reduced to wide grass paths as it disappears into woodland. There are shrubs and herbaceous plants in beds, borders and bays. There is a naturalness about the whole design although in borders near the house bedding plants are used to give seasonal colour.

A low rock garden suitably planted forms a middle distance feature and beyond this on the southern boundary is a large shallow pool surrounded by shrub plantings, especially rhododendrons. The shallow water depth is indicated by the almost complete cover of the Fringed Water Lily, *Nymphoides peltatum*, a rare native but well capable of looking after itself when conditions suit it. The pool was constructed in 1971.

South west from the pool is the woodland and rhododendrons area giving the garden as a whole a 'dog leg' shape. Here are planted shelter belts of beech, spruce and Lawson's cypress, and among them beds of rhododendrons. The collection of these is a large one and most groups are represented. The large leaved, early flowering Falconeri group is represented by *R. rex, eximium*, and *fictolacteum. R. sinogrande* is surviving and also flowering early is *R. sutchuenense*.

Flowering later are the many garden hybrids. Among the evergreens may be mentioned the hybrids of *R. cinnabarinum* of which I noted Lady Roseberry 'Dalmeny' form. The range of deciduous azaleas in this garden is considerable and the effect when in bloom spectacular. Spek's Orange, Satan, Berryrose, Golden Sunset and George Reynolds were noted among others.

Numerous specimen trees are making good progress. The purple leaved Norway Maple looked very good as did the several specimens of the white variegated form 'Drummondii'. *Salix matsudana tortuosa* is making good growth. At the end of the rock garden is a small specimen of the short leaved cedar from Cyprus, *Cedrus brevifolia*. This always seems to be a slow grower and one rarely sees a specimen of any size. There are many other items of interest in this well designed garden. Mention may be made of *Metasequoia glyptostroboides* near the pool and an attractive weeping cherry *Prunus x yedoensis* 'Ivensii' near the house. A beautiful small plant that attracted my attention was *Anemone magellanica* 'Primrose'.

Wenlock Abbey
C.S. Motley, Esq.

At Much Wenlock on A458 Bridgnorth — Shrewsbury. Altitude: 150m (490ft). Soil: Medium loam, limey. Rainfall: 760mm (30in).

The earliest record of a religious house at Wenlock was the founding of a nunnery in 680. The present Priory ruins date from the twelfth century with additions up to the late fifteenth century. On the dissolution in 1540 the eastern block, constituting the prior's lodging was preserved. Full restoration of this part took place in the mid. nineteenth century and it is now a private residence of great character and quite separate from the ruined Priory.

The house is built partly in Wenlock limestone and partly sandstone. Stone tiles, very Cotswold in character, and apparently not local have been

Above: Wenlock Abbey. The 'lived in' part that was left intact at the time of the dissolution. The conventional lawn with rose borders seems to suit the fine building.

Below: Milichope Park. The south east front from beyond the lake.

used for the roof. Much of the garden shows its Victorian origin. The main layout was carried out when the property was restored by the present owners ancestors.

On the right of the entrance drive is an enclosed formal garden with an intriguing Italian vase as a centre piece. This is surrounded by a broad gravel path linking the four cross paths which divide the garden into four sectors. Each sector has a central lawn area surrounded by wide borders of shrub roses and herbaceous plants. Doubtless these would have been planted with annual bedding in former years but the gentler effects produced by this less formal planting is much more appropriate in the old Priory setting, the ruins of which are just across the drive. Two fine cut leaved beeches occupy the south and west corner sites and *Vitis coignetiae* covers a good length of wall. There are several attractive magnolias.

A rectangular lawn in front of the L shaped house has a central sundial and borders under the walls planted with roses and some dwarf perennials. Around the corner on the south east side is another semi-formal area — mostly rose beds in lawn and mixed borders.

Layout and planting has obviously been simplified. Many dwarf box edgings have gone but an impressive clipped yew hedge remains. There are two pools just outside the garden proper.

This is hardly a plantsman's garden and it may not contain many rarities but it is a garden of atmosphere in a beautiful setting.

Weston Park
The Earl and Countess of Bradford

Shifnal, on the S side of A5 at Weston under Lizard 10km (6 miles) E of Telford. 13km (8 miles) W of Junction 12 on M6. Area: Formal Garden 1.6ha (4 acres). Temple Wood 9.6ha (24 acres). Walled Garden 1.6ha (4 acres). Amenity Parkland 120ha (300 acres). Altitude: 120m (390ft). Soil: sandy loam, lime free. Rainfall: 840mm (33in). Open most days during summer and at other times.

In the development of Weston Park three dates seem to stand out. The house was built by Sir Thomas and Lady Wilbraham in 1671. 'Capability' Brown and James Paine were engaged in 1762 by Sir Henry Bridgman (later first Earl Bradford) to create the parkland and its features. In 1865 the third Earl laid out the formal terraced gardens and built the orangery.

He also added the present entrance through a portico on the east front. The walled garden is probably of eighteenth century and would coincide with the landscaping of Brown.

Older readers will remember the regular radio programmes in the early post-war years with Roland Smith, Head Gardener at Weston and L.F. Clift. Gone now are those vineries and peach houses and the other frills of that bygone age. The walled garden now produces vegetables by modern mechanised commercial methods with a fraction of the labour formerly required but it may not look quite so pretty.

The terraced garden on the south front is typically Victorian with formal bedding. There are three terraces — the lower one consisting of a D shaped lawn, the curved side with buttressed retaining wall forming the boundary with the parkland to the south. On this lawn is the largest oriental plane, *Platanus orientalis,* in Britain. It is believed to have been planted at about the time the house was built (1671) and one assumes it was at one time in the park. The semi-circular wall seems to have been contrived to bring it into the garden. It is a superb tree.

On the west side of the house is another formal garden and behind it, facing south the very fine orangery, now used for serving teas to visitors. Further west is a large lawn with numerous fine trees. Behind the orangery is the church and Church Pool, bordering the main drive.

Temple wood lies to the east of the house. The original plantings were by Brown. The wood gets its name from the beautiful Temple of Diana designed by James Paine. Visitors with cameras will not easily resist the temptation to photograph the house from the front of the temple with one or both of the Guardian Lions in the foreground.

Behind the Temple is Temple Pool made by Brown by damming the stream.

But it is trees that are today the main attraction at Weston. The Earl himself is a foremost authority on forestry and his Head Forester, Mr Everett, is an accepted expert. The estate is still recovering from the devastating gales of January 2nd 1976 when more than thirty thousand trees were destroyed in total and sixty five giants were lost in Temple Wood alone.

Nevertheless many good trees remain. Oaks, beeches and ashes abound in Temple Wood. I noted *Picea smithiana*, the Morinda Weeping Spruce from the Western Himalayas, *Sequoia sempervirens*, the Coast Redwood from Western North America among others. *Nothofagus spp* from the Southern Hemisphere are now being planted extensively. There are three grand old sweet chestnuts that pre-date 'Capability' Brown by a couple of centuries or so.

South west from the house is Park Pool, the largest of Brown's pools at Weston but still small by comparison with Chillington or Trentham. The setting is, however, excellent and one feels that Weston is one of Brown's greater achievements.

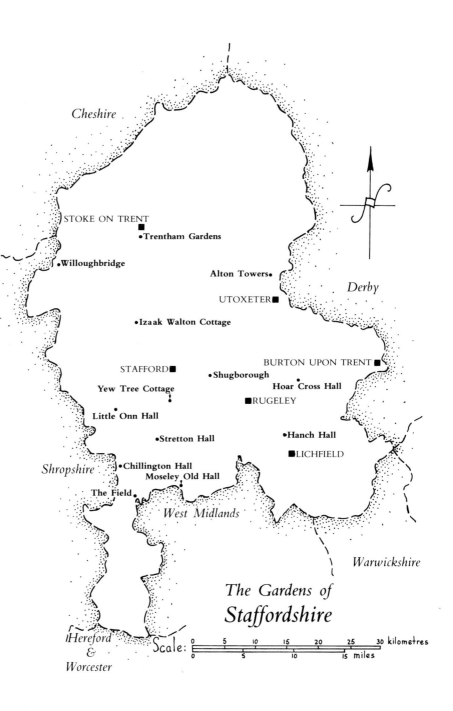

Cheshire

STOKE ON TRENT ■
●Trentham Gardens

●Willoughbridge

Alton Towers●

UTOXETER ■

Derby

●Izaak Walton Cottage

STAFFORD ■
●Shugborough

BURTON UPON TRENT ■

Yew Tree Cottage
●

Hoar Cross Hall
●
■RUGELEY

●Little Onn Hall

●Stretton Hall

●Hanch Hall
■LICHFIELD

Shropshire

●Chillington Hall
Moseley Old Hall

The Field ●

West Midlands

Warwickshire

The Gardens of
Staffordshire

Scale:

0   5   10   15   20   25   30 kilometres
0   5   10   15 miles

*Hereford
&
Worcester*

The Gardens of
Staffordshire

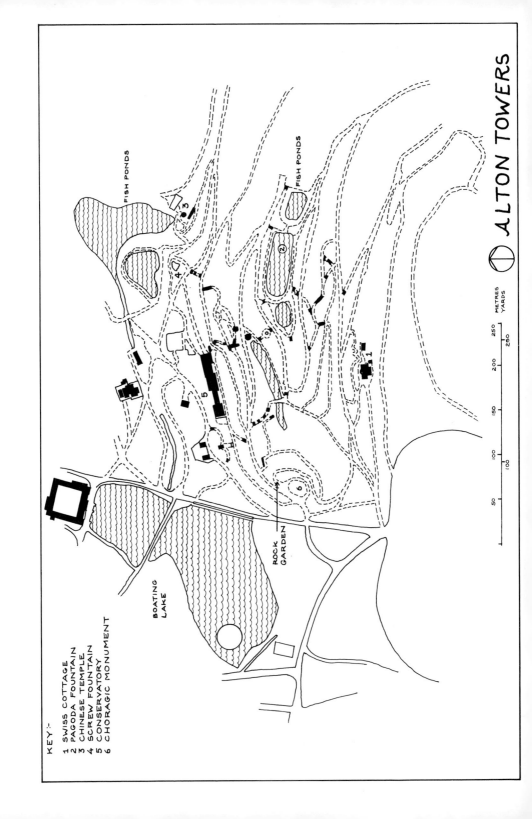

KEY:-
1 SWISS COTTAGE
2 PAGODA FOUNTAIN
3 CHINESE TEMPLE
4 SCREW FOUNTAIN
5 CONSERVATORY
6 CHORAGIC MONUMENT

FISH PONDS

FISH PONDS

BOATING LAKE

ROCK GARDEN

METRES
YARDS

50   100   150   200   250

100   150   200   250

ALTON TOWERS

Mawley Hall. The Herb Garden. Informal plants in a formal setting.

Trentham. The sculpture gallery is a good background for colourful formal bedding.

Alton Towers

Alton Towers Limited

Alton, Staffordshire, 6.5km (4 miles) E of Cheadle on B5032. Area: 200ha (500 acres). Main garden about 20ha (50 acres). Altitude: 180m (590ft). Soil:mostly sandy loam. Lime free. Rainfall: 840mm (33in). Open daily from 9.30 a.m. to dusk from Good Friday to first week end in October.

Alton Towers has been described as having the 'oddest and most spectacular collection of ornamental garden architecture in the world'. It was created by the fifteenth and sixteenth Earls of Shrewsbury between 1812 and about 1835. The story of its origin has been told before and a brief outline will suffice here.

Charles Talbot the fifteenth Earl was among the wealthiest of landowners with his principal seat at Heythrop in Oxfordshire. At Alton (then called Alveton) he had some 10,000 acres of farmland with a bailiff's house, Alveton Lodge, and houses for workpeople. It is said that somebody accidentally called the Earl's attention to this Staffordshire property. How wonderful to be able to forget 10,000 acres and a whole village! Whatever the inspirational source may have been a grand spending spree was triggered off culminating in the building of the neo-gothic mansion, renamed Alton Towers, by John the sixteenth Earl around 1833.

One cannot help feeling that some of the features created by Charles had a slight 'tongue in cheek' suggestion. It seems that they were intended deliberately to shock. J.C. Loudon has frequently been quoted as considering the whole project as 'in excessively bad taste'. But it appears that he was consulted and snubbed. And this would not go down well with Loudon. He writes 'although he (the Earl) consulted almost every artist, ourselves included, he did so only so that he could avoid whatever an artist might recommend'. There may have been a hint of sour grapes here.

Some good architects were certainly employed and some fine buildings erected. Robert Abraham's Conservatory, now undergoing restorations, is a superb building by any standards and his Pagoda Fountain, although rather garish and startling is now brought into scale by the growth of the surrounding trees. Time has, in fact, dealt kindly with Alton Towers. The profusion of foliage has prevented too much being seen at once. Buildings are now incidental to the landscape and not offensive intrusions into open farming country.

The house itself has fared less happily. The architect A.W.N. Pugin was discovered when a young man by the Earl and a close liaison was built up between them. Pugin, it appears, was converted to Roman Catholicism by his employer, the most powerful catholic in the country at that time. The magnificent mansion that resulted has been described as exhibiting a 'complete abnegation of domestic comfort to showmanship'. If that were so it was in good company.

From 1924 the present estate with 500 acres was taken over by a private company and run as a commercial enterprise. In 1939 the house was re-quisitioned by the War Department and used as an Officer Cadet Training Unit until 1945. When de-requisitioned in 1951 the house was derelict and dangerous and was partly demolished. Some restoration is now being carried out and parts of the ruins are accessible to visitors.

It must not be forgotten that Alton Towers is a commercial enterprise. If it did not pay its way it would disappear. There are Amusement Parks, paddling pools, a children's farm, caravan sites and a wealth of other at-tractions. The extraordinary thing is how little one is aware of these activities when in the garden. A garden designer of today would deal less harshly with the creator than did J.C. Loudon. The Earl in his grave is having the last laugh.

From the viewing platform in the West Wing one has extensive views of the parkland and gardens. The ground falls away to the north east and rises again steeply on the other side of the valley. High up on the hill just south of a half hectare pool is the Chinese Temple. A little west of this is the so-called Screw Fountain. This is really a misnomer for although it has helical flutes in its tapering body its main appendages are five tiers of rings over which the water tumbles. A series of zig-zag paths through well wooded country with oaks, sycamore, cedars and rhododendrons leads down to the seven domed conservatory. East of this is a path with a series of yew arches, all very tidily clipped and looking very Victorian. Up above and a little to the west is the 'two storied Stonehenge'. This, in fact is a straight line of stones, not a circle and is just another of the Earl's follies.

In the bottom of the valley is a chain of pools with a large rock garden, reclaimed and planted since de-requisitioning. Here are many small conifers, rhododendrons and other choice items, planted for effect rather

Left: Alton Towers. The top of the Pagoda Fountain. The intricate detail of the structure is best observed when the water is turned off!

Below: Alton Towers. Robert Abraham's Conservatory now fits unobtrusively into the well wooded hillside.

than botanical interest but the collection is quite large. It will become over-crowded in the near future.

On an island further to the east is the famous Pagoda Fountain. This seems to look better when the water is not playing. One can then see better the intricate details of its construction and decoration.

Bedding is less elaborate than would have been the case a century ago but enough remains to provide seasonal colour. A large rose collection is accommodated in neatly edged beds in well mown lawns.

The winding paths on both sides of the valley must total many miles in length. They pass through the changing scenery of lawns, flower beds, and woodland with one or more of the hard surface structures usually in view. There are many fine trees notably cedars, Horse Chestnuts, Wellingtonias, many good specimens of *Chamaecyparis pisifera* and some notable *Picea smithiana*.

Alton Towers is no longer a Stately Home. It is a business. We must be very grateful that so much care is taken to preserve the garden from spoliation, either by neglect or, what could be worse, the introduction of gimmicky features. It has an important place in English garden history and as long as the present management policy is maintained that place will continue.

Chillington Hall

P.R. de L Giffard Esq

6.5km (4 miles) SW of A5 at Gailey, 13km (8 miles) NW of Wolverhampton. Area: see below. Altitude: 120m (400ft). Soil: Keuper Marl. Lime free. Rainfall: 840mm (33in). Labour employed: one full-time. Open May — September. Thursdays and some Sundays. See HHCG.

The Giffards have held Chillington since 1178 but the present house dates from 1724 when Peter Giffard demolished part of a Tudor house and engaged Francis Smith of Warwick to build what is now the south front of the present house. Between 1786 and 1789 Peter's grandson Thomas Giffard, engaged a young architect John Soan, (later Sir John Soan) to complete the house as it is today.

With an estate of this kind it is very difficult to define 'garden'. The mile long oak avenue cannot be overlooked. This was planted by Peter Giffard in 1725. His son, the elder Thomas Giffard engaged Capability Brown who constructed a 30ha (75 acre) lake. There are 140ha (350 acres) of woodland, part of which merges with garden. There is another avenue of mixed trees 1½ miles long. The walled garden is 1.6ha (4 acres). Lawns cover a large area. Flower borders and such like are few.

This is one of the estates where Brown's work has been little interfered with. The house stands in a wide lawn setting, a naked yet noble structure. In 1911 Inigo Triggs was engaged to design a feature to relieve the bareness. He produced a formal rose garden for the south front which is still there. It is of rectilinear design and provides a break in the sweep of lawn. Opinions may differ as to whether it is an improvement.

On the western side of the house is a fine gateway of wrought iron set in a stone facade and giving on to an expanse of lawn. This is the Bowling Green Gate and dates from 1730. The lawn was converted into herbaceous borders by Triggs but has now returned to lawn.

Certain Victorian formal features have long since gone. The woodland encroaches and a garden of new character emerges. Beautiful woodland walks have been created. New plantings of *Nothofagus, Tsuga heterophylla*, the Western Hemlock, Leyland Cypress, numerous oak species and others are being made. The Western Hemlock do very well here. Some specimens must rank with the finest in Britain. There are limes, beeches, yews and rhododendrons.

Brown's lake, always known as 'The Pool' is a feature of special note. It ranks amongst his largest. The bridge near the dam is by James Paine who also designed the Temple in Temple Wood, Weston Park, some five miles away. The drive past the lake is finely wooded with rhododendrons under the trees.

The Field
Mr and Mrs R. Martin

The Wergs, Wolverhampton, 5km (3 miles) NW of Wolverhampton off A41. Turn off by Crown Inn. Area: 1.6ha (4 acres). Altitude: 120m (400ft). Soil: loam to sandy loam. Lime free. Rainfall: 840mm (33in). Labour employed: one full-time. Open occasionally under NGS.

This is a comparatively modern garden. The house was built in 1933/4 on an open field site and the garden was laid out by Mills of Wolverhampton in 1954. For many years this firm constructed gardens for the larger houses in the residential areas of the industrial midlands and became well known for good workmanship and finish. This garden can be taken as fairly typical of his work and is the only one I have discovered for inclusion in this book.

The garden is roughly divided equally between front and rear of the house. The rear is occupied with the approach drive, lawns and shrub planting. The opposite side is where we see Mill's work. There is a large central expanse of lawn looking over a small parkland area. Boundaries are formed by trees and shrubs in informal areas and cultivated beds. There are low rock garden effects with Westmorland limestone.

Few modern shrubs are used and conifers figure prominently. The general effect is pleasing.

Bulbs make a useful contribution in the spring and bedding plants give seasonal colour. The kitchen garden is well cropped and is worth more than casual inspection and the greenhouses are very well managed, as indeed, is the whole garden.

Hanch Hall

Mr and Mrs Douglas Haynes

Lichfield, 6.4km (4 miles) NW of Lichfield on Uttoxeter road, B5014. Area: 12ha (30 acres). Garden proper: 2.4ha (6 acres). Lake: 5ha (12 acres). Soil: sandy loam. Lime free. Rainfall: 840mm (33in). Labour employed: family labour only. Open weekends and Bank Holidays, April — October. See HHCG.

Hanch Hall has its origins in the thirteenth century but is substantially Tudor with a Queen Anne front and additions in Victorian Gothic. The house is interesting to say the least and the view from the Observation Tower is worth seeing.

Like so many other fine old houses it has had its ups and downs. The present owners have within the last four years accepted the challenge of restoration almost entirely on a 'Do it Yourself' basis.

The garden has retained few design features from its earlier history. An eighteenth century Ha Ha has been fully restored and is very effective but lawns and flower borders are typical of the first half of the present century. There is Wistaria on the south front of the house and a very fine sycamore on the lawn in front. A south facing wall on the top side of the west part of the garden has great possibilities.

The outstanding features are the pools: Pool No 1 forms the western boundary of the garden proper. It is about an acre in area and contains yellow water lilies and *Typha latifolia*, the Reed Mace, both native, as well as numerous other marginal plants. There is an attractive walk along the pool margin. Beyond Pool No 1 are two further pools and finally the lake

At the moment no large scale alterations in the garden have been attempted but development is planned. A shrub border has been planted. This site lends itself to a simple modern layout, merging into wild garden around the pool. It could be very fine indeed if treated on labour saving lines with no attempt at following any period other than that of tomorrow.

Hoar Cross Hall
Mr and Mrs W. Bickerton-Jones

Burton-on-Trent, 10 miles N of Lichfield A515 one mile W off main road. Rainfall: 840mm (33in). Open Sundays Easter to October. See HHCG.

Hoar Cross is a garden that was — a garden that isn't. A garden that will be? To be quite fair as it stands at the moment it hardly has a right to be included in this book. Yet it is an intriguing place. One cannot push through the overgrown yew hedges without being haunted by shades of its former grandeur.

The Elizabethan style Victorian mansion was built for Hugo and Emily Meynell during 1862-71. Hugo died at about the time the work was completed but his widow, later Mrs Meynell-Ingram lived there until her death when her younger brother succeeded.

The garden seems to have been superbly maintained in the early years of the century and one supposes that the real decline started in the second World War. By 1950 the house and garden were virtually abandoned and twenty years later the present owners took on the gigantic task of arresting the decline.

So far work has mainly been confined to restoration of the house. It is hoped that the garden will soon receive similar attention.

To return this garden to its former state would clearly be impossible in these days. A well illustrated article in Country Life of 1902 shows a formal garden of almost unbelievable splendour. Elaborate bedding schemes, fountains, yew hedges that seem to go on for ever, a pleached lime walk, all surrounded by shrubbery and woodland with fine trees.

Many fine trees are there still and enough of the garden to indicate something of its former glory. There are six rectangular, yew hedged enclosures each of which once contained a garden of individual character. Now only the water garden reveals much of what it once was.

The Robert Bakewell gates no longer open on to parkland but to arable farmland. They still bear the stamp of the master craftsman nevertheless.

The church, adjoining the Hall was built by Mrs Meynell Ingram in memory of her husband. Most of the work of building was carried out in the period 1872-76 but completion was not until 1901. It is regarded as one of the finest Victorian churches in the country.

Izaak Walton Cottage

Administered by Staffordshire C.C. for
Stafford Borough Council

Shallowford, Stone, between B5026 Eccleshall-Stone and A5013 Eccleshall-Stafford. 6km (4 miles) from Eccleshall. Area: 0.2ha (½ acre). Altitude: 90m (29ft). Soil: lime free. Rainfall: 840mm (33in). Open regularly during summer.

This charming little black and white cottage is Izaak Walton's last surviving bequest to Stafford, the town of his birth. The administration was taken over by the County Council in 1974 but it was not until 1978 that real progress was made to create a garden that would complement the cottage.

The aim is to have a collection of plants that would have been in Britain before 1683, the year of Walton's death. These are mostly planted in rectangular beds set in a lawn behind the cottage. Already a good range of suitable plants has been assembled, including sweet rocket, columbines, gold laced polyanthus, and others. A few of doubtful authenticity are in process of being eliminated.

Another area is intended to house a herb collection and some old roses have been planted in a border on the far side of the lawn.

A small paddock adjoining the garden was purchased in 1978 and some old fruit cultivars have been planted in it. An area has also been reserved for picnics.

Although the whole project is on a small scale it is very interesting and when a really comprehensive plant collection becomes established it will be highly educational. Mr John Rhodes, the Senior Museum Officer has taken a keen personal interest in the garden and he is to be complimented

Izaak Walton Cottage. Carefully restored and with a garden containing plants of Walton's own time a little bit of history has been captured.

on his efforts to create a feature of great interest on a very limited budget.

Little Onn Hall
Mr and Mrs I.H. Kidson

Church Eaton, about 12km (7½ miles) SW of Stafford between A518 Newport — Stafford and A5 Watling Street. Area: Garden 2.4ha (6 acres). Altitude: 110m (360ft). Soil: sandy loam, lime free. Rainfall: 840mm (33in). Open for NGS.

Little Onn has a history both ancient and modern. Mediaeval ruins within a moat, old stew ponds, a late nineteenth century house and gardens laid out at the turn of the century by one of the foremost garden architects provide plenty of material to talk about.

The building of the present house started around 1850 by Col. Charles Ashton who appears to have been a cotton magnate. He died in 1860 and his two unmarried daughters continued for some years to add to the building to produce the fine small mansion we have today. Building throughout was done with the local Penkridge Sandstone in beautiful soft pinky browns and grey greens and workmanship was of the highest order.

When building was completed Thos. H. Mawson of Windermere was called in to design the garden and in his book 'The Art and Craft of Garden Making' (1901) he gives plans and descriptions of the work he was carrying out. Some of his work still survives, relatively unaltered. Some was probably never executed. The story goes that after spending £30,000 the sisters found money running short and called a halt to further developments.

The stable block and the walled kitchen garden now form a separate residence, leaving the original garden and pleasure grounds much as it was at the beginning of the century. The present owners came here in 1971 and from the start the policy was to retain what had been created, tidy up, and plant new trees where needed.

Wrought iron gates halfway along the entrance drive mark the beginning of the garden. A straight fifty yard drive is flanked by grass strips behind which are herbaceous borders backed by clipped yew hedges. The drive leads to the courtyard on the W front. West of this, covering about a third of an acre is Mawson's rose garden. This consists of three square formal gardens with concentrically arranged beds set in crazy paving surrounded by grass strips and separated by wide gravel paths.

Little Onn Hall. The 'Dog Bone' pool on the east front was probably constructed in the 1920's.

There appear to be forty four individual beds in all. A low wall with a belt of rhododendrons on the outside forms the west boundary with the field. A pair of gazebos bearing the date 1898 mark the south west and north west corners of the garden.

A gravel terrace runs along the south and east fronts of the house. On the south front a grass bank leads down to an area of lawn. The Mawson plan shows a formal garden around a sundial. It is doubtful if this was ever done. On the east front is a grass tennis court and further east forming the boundary with the Park is a long belt of lawn on five levels falling from south to north. On the middle level is a water feature, probably constructed in the 1920's. It consists of two small hexagonal pools joined by a narrow channel with a fountain in the middle. It has been nicknamed, not inappropriately the 'Dog bone' pool.

The north side of the house is in many ways the most interesting. A rectangular moat is bridged at its west and east ends to give access to the central island which contains remains of a mediaeval structure thought to be an old penitentiary and now used as a home for peafowl. The southern half of the moat is supplied by a spring and the water flows into the north half which is at a lower level. The centre of the island is occupied by a circular rose garden with lawns around and with yews, rhododendrons and other things along the margins of the moat.

South and east of the moat is a woodland area with rhododendrons, many of them undoubtedly planted by Mawson. He speaks of a fine belt of beech of about forty years growth. The intervening eighty years have taken their toll but some very fine trees remain. Mawson appears to have been very forward thinking in his ideas about wild gardens for he talks of establishing St John's wort, Periwinkles, Ground Ivy, Vacciniums and Gaultherias together with Snowdrops, Daffodils and Wood Anemones. Wm. Robinson could not have done better. The heavy growth of rhododendrons, especially *R. ponticum* has suppressed much of this underplant but where they have recently been cleared primroses and other natives have reappeared.

The north side of the moat is more formal in treatment. A mown strip of grass adjoins the moat and a broad gravel path separates this from a sixty yard long herbaceous border under a south facing wall which is the garden boundary. Beyond this is the walled garden of earlier days.

West of the moat is yet another rose garden, a sunken rectangular feature, and adjoining it on its south side a series of five stone fish rearing tanks, probably mediaeval. Mawson mentions that they were being preserved and it is little touches like this that give a garden that little extra character.

There are few rare plants at Little Onn but with spring bulbs, rhododendrons, roses and herbaceous plants, all in quantity, there is much of interest throughout the year.

Moseley Old Hall
The National Trust

Wolverhampton, four miles N of Wolverhampton off A449. Area: 0.4ha (1 acre). Altitude: 75m (250ft). Soil: sandy loam. Lime free. Rainfall: 760mm (30in). Open regularly see National Trust booklet.

Moseley Old Hall is a Tudor House, encased in brick in 1870 but with much of the interior as it was nearly four centuries ago. Charles II came here two days after the battle of Worcester in 1651. This association is the chief reason for the interest this property arouses.

When the National Trust took over in 1962 there was no garden of consequence and it was decided to create one in the style of mid-seventeenth century, with plants that were in Britain at that time.

The front door is approached by a granite sett path edged with box with cones and spirals of box on each side. There is a knot garden from a design of 1640 with eleven box globes on four feet stems in four: three: four formation in pebble beds. The remaining beds formed by dwarf box hedges are surfaced with gravel contrasting with the gravel of the dividing paths. It is fortunate that no attempt has been made to plant the beds.

On a wooden arbour are trained *Clematis viticella*, and *C. flammula*, the latter one of the few scented clematis although the small greenish white flowers are less showy than some. There is the Purple Leaved Vine and underneath bushes of lavender.

Several old roses, including the Musk Rose and Sweetbriar add period character as do numerous herbaceous plants such as Soapwort (*Saponaria officinalis*) and Bear's Breech (*Acanthus mollis*).

Beyond the arbour is a nut walk and there is the remnant of an old orchard, nineteenth rather than seventeenth century.

Above: Moseley Old Hall. The link with Charles II has prompted this mid seventeenth century layout.

Below: Willoughbridge. The pool with the scree garden above.

Shugborough
The National Trust

(5½ miles) SE of Stafford on A513 Stafford — Rugeley. Area: Garden and Grounds. 6.8ha (17 acres). Park: 80ha (200 acres). Altitude: 80m (262ft). Soil: loamy sand. Lime free. Rainfall: 840mm (33in). Open throughout the year.

The present house was built by William Anson in 1693 and enlarged by his son Thomas in the late 1740s and early 1750s. The younger son George became the distinguished Admiral Lord Anson. Their nephew succeeded to the estate in 1773 and his son was created Viscount Anson in 1806 and his son in turn became Earl of Lichfield in 1831. Viscount Anson employed Samuel Wyatt from 1790 to 1806 to carry out alterations and additions. Other major work has been done from time to time. The fifth Lord Lichfield continues to live in part of the house.

The garden has numerous monuments, mostly erected by the Admiral and his brother. There seems to be little evidence of any noted landscape designers being employed at Shugborough before the mid-nineteenth century. Dorothy Stroud in her book 'Capability Brown' suggests that John Webb may have worked here. W.A. Nesfield, that noted re-creator of the formal garden was probably responsible for the formal terraced lawns west of the house about 1855.

The River Saw flowed along the east boundary of the garden and Thomas Anson cut a new channel. The old channel was used for fish. It tends to silt up and is very slow moving. The two channels rejoin where they empty into the Trent so that the three streams come together at one point shortly before passing under the seventeenth century Essex Bridge.

The Nesfield terraces now have clipped golden Yews on their lawns. Graham Thomas has designed a new rose garden on a site long occupied by roses. It echoes the Victorian period in respect of colour. Violent modern cultivars have been avoided. Some replant problems have been encountered.

An unusual feature is the slab border. This is a long rectangular bed with a zig-zag pattern of paving stones dividing it up into a series of triangles. One kind of plant plus an edging plant is planted in each triangle. This was done in order that flowers may be cut for house decoration without having to tread on the soil.

The grounds consist largely of expanses of lawn with groups of rhododendrons and many fine trees. There are particularly good oaks and limes and some cedars. Pride of place, however, must surely go to the yew. This is a bluntly pointed topped tree some 70 feet high with its lower branches reaching the ground all round. It is solid and dense. In the spring of 1979 I paced the perimeter and found it to be about 175 yards. This gives an area, fully covered, of about 0.2ha or half an acre, surely one of the largest trees in Britain for ground covered.

Daffodils in the turf under the trees are a pleasant feature in the spring.

Stretton Hall

Mrs Monckton

Staffordshire, 0.5km (½ mile) N of A5 at point 3.2km (2 miles) W of junction with A449 Wolverhampton — Stafford road. Area: 2.4ha (6 acres). Soil: sandy loam. Lime free. Rainfall: 840mm (33in). Labour employed: two. Open occasionally under NGS.

The house was built in 1646 and was the home of the Congreve family in its early years. Wm Congreve, the dramatist is believed to have worked here. It is interesting how trees become associated with famous people. Here we have Congreve's Oak, a venerable tree, once in parkland but now the arable farmland has encroached. Why shouldn't we believe that Mirabell and Mrs Millament were conceived under its canopy?

The estate passed into the Monckton family in the eighteenth century and we find yet another connection with the theatre for the owner at the end of that century was a great friend of Richard Brinsley Sheridan.

In 1845 a fine terrace was constructed. It is now an attractive rose garden. There are wide gravel paths and shrub and herbaceous borders and many fine trees.

The walled garden is used partly as a forest tree nursery for the estate and partly as a vineyard. The vines, of the best modern wine varieties, are just coming into bearing. Management is near perfection. One just hopes it is not too far north to produce properly ripened crops.

Trentham Gardens

Trentham Gardens Ltd.

Stoke-on-Trent. Area: including lake 160ha (400 acres) Lake 28ha (70 acres). Whole estate with woodlands 480ha (1,200 acres). Altitude: 98m (325ft). Soil: sandy loam. Not limey. Rainfall: 840mm (33in). Labour employed: about ten, plus glasshouse and nursery staff. Open throughout the year.

The full history of Trentham is too long and involved to be covered here in more than brief outline. The property has long been in the Leveson and Gower families. The original house was built in 1633. The construction of a lake was under consideration from 1695 and by 1703 a 414m (460yd) dam had been constructed and a 4.8ha (12 acre) lake had been formed.

Capability Brown produced plans for Lord Gower for enlarging the lake in 1759 and in due course swept away the formal parterres and straight paths. With his junior partner, Holland, he remodelled the house, the work keeping them busy until 1780 by which time a typical 'Brown' landscape had been created and the old house altered beyond recognition.

In 1833 the then Lord Gower was created Duke of Sutherland but died shortly afterwards. The second Duke immediately began ambitious schemes for alterations and engaged Charles Barry, (later Sir Charles Barry of House of Commons fame) to undertake the work. This involved adding to the existing house and making it into a unified structure.

Fashions in garden design were now changing. Brown's landscape with grass right up to the house seemed dull and uninteresting in an age when so many colourful garden plants were becoming available. The large area between house and lake was therefore laid out with elaborate formal gardens on the Italian style.

Nessfield seems to have joined Barry in this work in 1840 and would have been responsible for detail work but not the broad plan.

When finished the garden consisted of a top terrace with stone balustrades, a garden below with a central circular feature with radiating beds and a flight of curved edged steps leading to the main parterre. The broad central path went southwards down to the lake with a cast of Cellini's Perseus with the head of Medusae as an end stop. This formal garden exists today although minor changes have taken place over the years.

In May 1847, 67 men were employed in the garden and around 1900 a staff of 55 was still maintained but His Lordship's interest was waning and

Trentham Hall was closed as a residence in 1905. The building was offered to Staffordshire County Council and Stoke-on-Trent Borough Council but neither authority were able to accept and demolition started in 1911.

The gardens became a popular place of recreation for the Pottery towns between the wars and features were introduced to attract visitors. It was thus one of the first 'stately homes' to be opened to the public but with the house removed 'stately home' is hardly the correct title.

The formal bedding display in the Italian Garden has been claimed to be the largest in Europe, but the cost of producing 120,000 bedding plants and clearing and replanting twice a year is prohibitive in these days and the quantity has been reduced to 30,000 and permanent herbaceous plants used for the remaining beds. This is an interesting and most commendable development and its effectiveness is enhanced by the manner in which it is carried out.

In the complicated pattern of beds there are 16 very large beds in outer positions. These are the ones in which herbaceous plants are used. The smaller beds are filled with traditional bedding plants. In the summer of 1979 it was very pleasing to see such a wide range of plants succeeding so well. Obviously with a large herbaceous collection it is impossible to mention more than a few. Mr Douglas Brereton, the Garden's Manager, tells me that he has raised seedlings from about 600 packets of seed in 1979, including many quite uncommon items. The Hardy Plant Society have been helpful here.

Plants which I noted as worthy of special mention include *Campanula pyramidalis*, actually monocarpic and at one time much used as a specimen pot plant, a dwarf Oriental Poppy 'Allegro' (seed raised), dwarf Delphinium 'Blue Fountain', Double Field Buttercup, *Ranunculus acris fl. pl.*, some very good forms of *Tradescantia virginiana* and *Anemone japonica*, the two Ligularias, 'Desdemona' and Grenygog Gold, Phlox in variety, *Gentiana asclepiadea*. It was surprising to see *Primula florindae* flourishing but it must be remembered that this lower terrace is very little above the water level of the lake.

This departure from traditional bedding has had a mixed reception. Those who like masses of colour think it a retrograde step. To these people a thousand French Marigolds are a hundred times more attractive than ten. The discerning horticulturist or plantsman holds the opposite view. The question is for whom does Trentham cater? The gate receipts would appear to come mainly from non-garden minded people. Which is a pity for Trentham has much to offer the horticulturist and could offer much more with a little encouragement.

The middle terrace, above the bedding area, is now a Rose Garden and is somewhat spoilt by the recently built but little used Exhibition Hall. The top terrace in front of the Church and Sculpture Gallery has effective displays of bedding plants. East of the Rose Garden is a large shrub area in which related species are grouped together in informal beds, e.g. berberis, buddleia, forsythia, hebe etc.

On the east side of the Italian Garden is a Clematis Walk with a large collection but many of the large flowered hybrids were casualties in the winter of 1978/9 as indeed were many shrubs normally regarded as hardy. Further east still is the Rock Garden and Peat Block Garden, containing many conifers, the smaller rhododendrons, ericas and rock garden plants proper.

The River Trent flows the full length of the garden from north to south and although near to the lake it is no longer joined to it but pursues its own independant course. The gardens mentioned above lie west of the river. On the east is a garden centre, a ballroom and the Spring Garden where bulbs are a feature. At one time Trentham was one of the National Centres for bedding plant trials and a series of long rectangular beds were used for this purpose. This area is now used as a display garden and in 1979 was planted with about 700 dahlias. A row of 25 Magnolias, all different, forms a boundary.

On the far west side, near the entrance to the caravan site are several Demonstration Gardens, showing different types of layout. There are gardens for Flower Arrangers, Women's Institutes, a Herb garden etc.

There are obviously many fine trees at Trentham and there is space here to mention but a few. The inevitable Cedar of Lebanon is here in quantity. Near the north west corner of the lake is a group of fine conifers including *Pinus parviflora, P. ponderosa, P. strobus, Sequoia sempervirens, Sequoiadendron giganteum* and *Sciadopitys verticillata*, all planted around late middle of last century. A fine *Quercus x turneri*, the semi-evergreen hybrid between Holm Oak and Common Oak is near the children's playground. On the east side of the lake near the boathouse is a fine *Pinus nigra* and not far away a Mexican Pine *P. ayacahuite*. A nice specimen of the uncommon Cretan Maple, *Acer sempervirens*, almost evergreen as its name implies is near the west front entrance to the playground and a good tree of *A. cappadocicum* is near the Riverside Café.

Willoughbridge
Willoughbridge Garden Trust

Elds Wood, Market Drayton. On A51 midway between junctions with A525 Whitchurch —
Newcastle under Lyme and A53 Market Drayton — Newcastle-under-Lyme. Area: 4ha (10
acres). Altitude: 140m (459ft). Soil: loamy sand or sandy loam over gravel. Lime free. Rainfall:
812mm (32in). Open daily all the year round 9.30 a.m. till dusk.

The story of Willoughbridge begins in 1937 when Col. Harry Clive
conceived the idea of creating a woodland garden in a 1½ acre gravel pit
abandoned a century earlier. There were some sizeable oak trees, a few
birch and a good deal of scrub and bramble undergrowth. Gradually this
was cleared. Old spoil heaps gave welcome variation in terrain and paths
were made among and around them.

A list of trees and shrubs planted between 1937-1971 has been
published. There is little point in repeating these but on my several visits I
have been impressed with the large specimens of *Magnolia kobus*, flowering
freely and, of course, rhododendrons which are the mainstay of the
garden.

In 1958 a trust was formed to ensure the continued care of the garden
and in 1961 the sloping meadow between the road and the original garden
was taken over and gradually developed as a garden of entirely different
character. Whereas the quarry was well wooded and immediately ready
for planting as a woodland garden the new extension possessed a solitary
ash tree near the main drive and a sycamore on the west boundary.

Miles Hadfield records, in the Guide to Willoughbridge, that John
Codrington was responsible for the plans for development of this new area
from 1967 onwards.

If we start from the Car Park we will notice a bank on the topside
supported by baulks of timber. Here are found many interesting perennials
and dwarf shrubs used as ground cover. *Cotoneaster salicifolia pendula* is
particularly effective. *Rosa californica plena* is also here and we find this
most attractive semi-double pink rose in other parts of the garden also.
Before leaving the Car Park we should note a group of three young
fastigiate beech and a fastigiate elm, still alive in 1979.

A tar macadam roads leads straight up to the old quarry garden. It is
flanked with lawn with large informal beds of trees and shrubs but before
exploring these we will turn left to the area above the Car Park. Here is a
pool with water lilies and good marginal planting. *Rheum palmatum* the

Chinese Rhubarb is particularly effective as is the Willow Leaved Pear, *Pyrus Salicifolius*.

Above the pool is the Scree Garden. This is most effectively planted with thymes, dianthus, thrift, campanulas, helianthemums and *Parahebe catarractae* against a background of Pines and birches. Sedums and sempervivums are particularly well used.

Whereas the original quarry garden provided mainly a spring display the garden now has abundant colour and interest from early spring to autumn. Many trees which one day will dominate the garden are getting well established. We find cedars, tulip tree, liquidambar, catalpa, ginkgo, many cherries, malus, sorbus as well as conifers in variety.

A collection of camellias has been planted and are protected by screening.

The variety of herbaceous plants is considerable. There are many geraniums and I was particularly pleased to find that uncommon plant *Veratrum viride*, surely one of our finest green flowers. What a plant for the flower arrangers if it could be produced in quantity.

Willoughbridge is a young garden. Its character will change markedly as trees and shrubs mature but its foundations are so well laid that it will be of interest for centuries to come.

Yew Tree Cottage
Mr and Mrs H.W. Rogers

Dunston Heath, about 3km (2 miles) W of Junction 13 on M6. Area: 0.6ha (1½ acres). Altitude: 100m (328ft). Soil: neutral. Rainfall: 840mm (33in). Open for NGS.

This garden, attached to a late eighteenth century cottage, has been developed by the present owners over the last twenty five years but a substantial portion is a product of the last few years.

The aim has been to create a number of small intimate gardens separated by hedges and fences so that one never sees everything at once. Paths, some in grass, some in paving, wander about and disappear around corners.

On the south side is a small lawn with rose beds and seasonal bedding plants. An attractive pool and rock garden with a backing of shrubs is south of the lawn.

The largest lawn area is north of the house and here a raised bed, built up rather like a huge trough is colourful in the spring with aubrieta, alyssum etc. All around are plants in immense variety. Conifers range from the accepted dwarfs to small specimens of other kinds that will one day get too big for their site. Planting has been for immediate effect and thinning will soon be necessary. Most of the ericas in commerce appear to be here and there are many plants one does not often see outdoors so far north, as for example *Convolvulus cneorum* and *Callistemon* spp. There are several specimens of *Acer pseudoplatanus* 'Brilliantissima' with their characteristic umbrella heads of pinky gold. A small tree that shows promise is the purple form of cut leaved beech *Fagus sylvaticus* 'Rohanii'.

Bedding plants are produced by the thousand and add colour in their season. Herbaceous plants are little used.

The Gardens of
Warwickshire and West Midlands

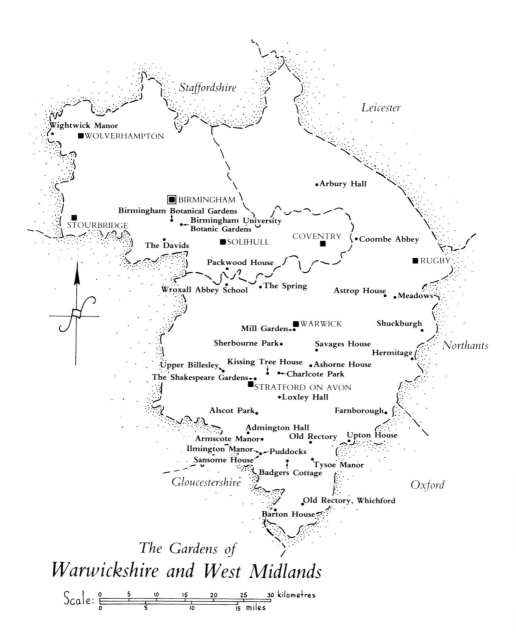

Staffordshire

Leicester

Wightwick Manor
■WOLVERHAMPTON

■BIRMINGHAM
Birmingham Botanical Gardens
Birmingham University
Botanic Gardens

•Arbury Hall

■STOURBRIDGE

The Davids

■SOLIHULL
Packwood House

COVENTRY

•Coombe Abbey

■RUGBY

Wroxall Abbey School •The Spring

Astrop House
•Meadows

Mill Garden ■WARWICK
Sherbourne Park•
Savages House

Shuckburgh

Hermitage
Northants

Upper Billesley• Kissing Tree House
The Shakespeare Gardens•• Ashorne House
←Charlcote Park

■STRATFORD ON AVON
•Loxley Hall

Alscot Park•

Farnborough•

Admington Hall
Armscote Manor•
Ilmington Manor•• Puddocks
Sansome House

Old Rectory Upton House

•Tysoe Manor
•Badgers Cottage

Gloucestershire

Oxford

•Old Rectory, Whichford
Barton House•

The Gardens of
Warwickshire and West Midlands

Scale: 0 5 10 15 20 25 30 kilometres
0 5 10 15 miles

Admington Hall
Mr and Mrs J.P. Wilkerson

Shipston-on-Stour, 10km (6½ miles) S of Stratford-upon-Avon, between A34 and A46. Area: 2.4ha (6 acres). Altitude: 75m (246ft). Soil: clay loam calcareous. Rainfall: 660mm (26in). Labour employed: one full-time, one part-time OAP plus casual and Mrs Wilkerson. Open each year for NGS and GS.

The approach drive with cherries and other trees along it takes one to the east of the house between two rows of clipped, flagon shaped yews. This prepares one for a formal Victorian garden but formality soon ceases and we find an attractive, informal garden of quite exceptional merit.

Although the house is essentially Georgian there are traces of Jacobean origin at the rear. It is said that a Sir Thomas Overbury once lived here, but not the distinguished essayist who was poisoned in the Tower, and who was born at Compton Scorpion a few miles away. One assumes it was a descendent of *the* Sir Thomas.

Standing at the south front of the house there is a wide area of drive and a large open lawn beyond which is a recently constructed Ha Ha.

On the distant field boundary is an old gateway with a pair of very fine horse chestnuts. These mark the entrance to the old drive which came straight up to the south front. The change over probably occurred at the beginning of the present century.

Widely spaced in front of the house are a fine pair of Cedars of Lebanon. They are set sufficiently east and west respectively to avoid interference with the view or to obscure the south facade. On the east side of the front lawn is a modern style mixed border with a good herbaceous collection backed by shrubs. Two wide spreading *Amelanchier canadensis* were particularly attractive at the time of my visit.

It is, however, on the west side that the most important feature of this garden is found. There was probably a pond of sorts in a small patch of woodland centuries ago. In 1936 Col. and Mrs Horton purchased the

Admington Hall. The Stream Garden. The stream margin is planted with primulas, caltha and lysichytum. Mown grass paths pass through naturalised daffodils under the trees.

property and after the war diverted a nearby stream to create channels and supply an enlarged pool. The present owners have, since 1970, developed the area with great care and very good taste.

Considerable planting has been done along the water channels. Among plants noted were some particularly fine *Caltha polypetala*, with flowers double the size of our native Marsh Marigold, various Primulas including *P. japonica, P. denticulata, P. viallii* and others.

Both white and yellow skunk cabbage *Lysichytum camschaticum* and *L. americanum* respectively, flourish. *Gunnera manicata* and *Rheum palmatum* create bold features.

Elms, once a feature here and the site of a good sized rookery, have gone of course, but there are still plenty of mature trees, including limes, beeches and horse chestnuts and the rooks still seem to manage. Extensive new tree plantings have been taking place in this natural woodland area west of the pool.

Primroses, daffodils, *Anemone blanda* and such items are naturalised in grass around the water garden and a weeping willow is becoming a note-worthy feature.

North of the house is a small enclosed garden, once a formal rose garden, now mostly lawn. The walled kitchen garden lies east of the house and here visitors will find growing to a standard rarely seen nowadays. In two heated greenhouses pot plants are grown to perfection with meticulous attention to detail.

This is a garden where everything seems to fit. So often, even in fine gardens one finds little jarring features that seem out of place. Not so at Admington.

Alscott Park

Capt. and Mrs James West

Stratford-upon-Avon, three miles S of Stratford, on A34 (West side). Area: 2ha (5 acres). Altitude: 45m (150ft). Soil: clay loam. Alkaline. Rainfall: 660mm (26in). Labour employed: two full-time. Open occasionally for NGS.

The house, a good example of Roccoco Gothic, was built between 1750 and 1765 by an earlier James West and has remained in the family ever since. The deer park has much of the character of the period. A fine orangery also survives from the eighteenth century but with a new glass roof. Some Victorian features have disappeared and some new twentieth century ones have been added.

A large sweeping expanse of lawn right up to the south front of the house has some good cedars on it and three fine sweet chestnuts. One of these, on the east side, is quite magnificent. The trees are well away from the house.

Also well away on the south lawn is a new feature consisting of a wide central grass drift flanked by mixed borders of shrub roses, shrubs and herbaceous plants. This covers quite a large area. The choice of plants and their siting shows excellent taste. It is a good example of modern planting.

The walled kitchen garden is well maintained. The old glass of last century has been demolished and in part replaced by modern structures. An attractive feature here is an arch of young apple trees, forming a cul-de-sac with an end stop of roses.

West of the kitchen garden and using its wall as its east boundary is another new development. An enclosure has been created by planting yew hedges on the west side and south end. These were planted in 1964 and have now matured well. At the north end of this garden is the old orangery. Wistarias cover its front. Tacsonias, passifloras and *Plumbago capensis* were flourishing inside, and standing outside in tubs were oranges and other citrus fruits to be moved inside on the approach of autumn in the traditional manner of the seventeenth century. In many gardens so called 'orange trees' are grown in tubs. Close inspection reveals that they are portugal laurel.

Some portugal laurel, however, have been planted to create an exaggerated perspective. They will be clipped into hemispheres but three a side (six in all) are probably not enough to create the desired illusion.

On the west facing wall are rose 'Albertine', honeysuckles, and Wistarias. The latter are of great age. One has a trunk girth of 1.2m (4ft).

Two large pools, believed to be old fish ponds, surviving from monastic times are on the east side and a nineteenth century bridge crosses at this junction. Just beyond here is a planting of new trees, including London planes, Norway maples, *Acer griseum, Sorbus mitchellii, Parottia persica*, red horse chestnut, *Sequoia sempervirens*, and others.

A fine old lime avenue is now passing its prime and a mixed lime/beech avenue has been planted as an ultimate replacement.

The west side of the house has a small enclosed garden with lawn and rose borders. On the house itself are *Vitis voignetiae, V. vinifera apiifolia* and *Hydrangea petiolaris*.

On the north side is one of the many rivers Stour flowing into the Avon two miles away.

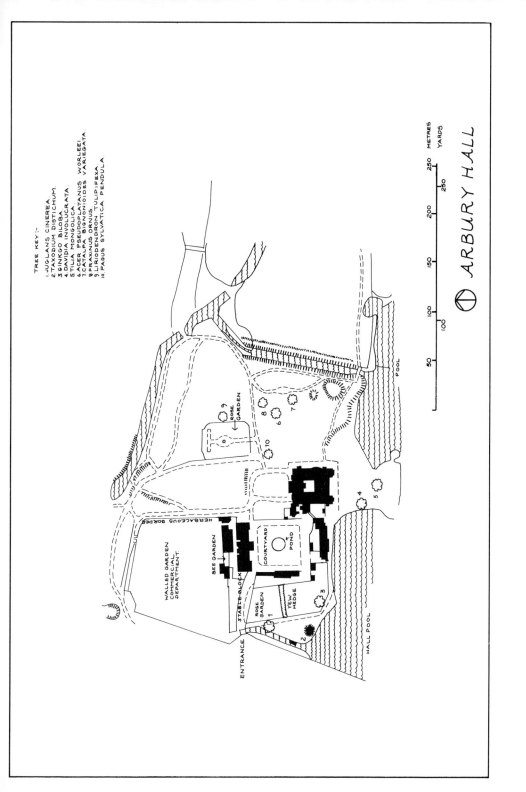

TREE KEY:—

1. JUGLANS CINEREA.
2. TAXODIUM DISTICHUM.
3. GINKGO BILOBA.
4. DAVIDIA INVOLUCRATA.
5. TILIA MONGOLICA.
6. ACER PSEUDOPLATANUS WORLEEI.
7. CATALPA BIGNONIODES VARIEGATA.
8. FRAXINUS ORNUS.
9. LIRIODENDRON TULIPIFERA.
10. FAGUS SYLVATICA PENDULA.

250 METRES
250 YARDS

200

150

100
100

50

⊕ *ARBURY HALL*

POOL

ROSE GARDEN

9

8

6

7

10

4

5

WALLED GARDEN
COMMERCIAL
DEPARTMENT

HERBACEOUS BORDER

BEE GARDEN

STABLE BLOCK

COURTYARD

POND

ROSE GARDEN

1

YEW HEDGE

3

5

2

ENTRANCE

HALL POOL

Arbury Hall

F.H. FitzRoy Newdegate Esq.

Nuneaton, 3.2km (2 miles) SW of Nuneaton off B4102. Follow AA direction signs. Area: 5.6ha (14 acres). Altitude: 120m (400ft). Soil: sandy loam. Lime free. Rainfall: 700mm (27.5in). Labour employed: three. Easter Sunday to October. Sundays, Bank Holidays. See HHCG.

The Arbury Estate has numerous historical connections of importance. The original house was built by Sir Edmund Anderson, Lord Chief Justice to Elizabeth I. Finding the house too far from London he arranged an exchange of property with John Newdegate of Haresfield, Middlesex in 1586. Thus began the Newdegate connection with Arbury.

The house remained unaltered until the latter half of the eighteenth century when Sir Roger Newdegate had the house 'Gothicised' by Sanderson Miller and others. This is the superb mansion we have today. The same Sir Roger founded the Newdegate Prize for poetry at Oxford.

Another historical event which must be mentioned is the birth of a daughter to Robert Evans, the estate bailiff, at South Farm in 1819. She was christened Mary Ann and was later to become the distinguished novelist George Eliot. Arbury is 'Cheverel Manor' in 'Scenes of Clerical Life' and Sir Roger is Sir Christopher Cleverel.

The gardens we see today are also largely the work of Sir Roger. He created a canal system seven miles in length, linking a chain of lakes, without the help of 'Capability' Brown. Much of this water still exists but some sections of the canals are dry and mining subsidence has affected levels in some places.

The entrance drive leads into the stable block courtyard, a large rectangular area the north side of which consists of the stable block, in the designs for which Christopher Wren was involved. A row of Hidcote lavender runs along the front. Two sides of the courtyard have rows of pleached limes. The central area is lawn and in the middle is a round pond with shelving sides containing the South African Water Hawthorn, *Aponogeton distachyus*. The flowers of this plant are scented but as they are borne only a few inches above the surface and usually well away from the edge the claim can rarely be put to the test.

North of the stable block is the old walled garden now run commercially and with separate staff to that of the private garden. Some of the old glass has been retained and some new erected.

Outside the east facing wall of the walled garden is a large herbaceous

Above: Arbury Hall. The south facing wall with Hall Pool just visible on the right. The Wall is well clothed with a large fig, wistaria, climbing roses and *Chimonanthus praecox*.

Below: Arbury Hall. The Old Rose Garden, with formal beds around a central pond. The whole area is enclosed by walls and hedges.

border and further east wide sweeping lawns with many fine trees. There are fine purple beeches. East of this is a woodland area with remains of old canals. Rhododendrons are prominent here. Enclosed in this area is an old formal rose garden covering about half an acre. There is a small central pond.

Moving a little to the south we are on the east side of the house itself and here are wide lawns. A weeping elm still lives (1979) but it is the last of several and it can hardly be expected to survive much longer. There is a nice specimen of *Fraxinus ornus*, the Manna Ash, with leaves of typical ash form and sprays of whitish flowers in late spring and the uncommon *Catalpa bignonioides* 'variegata' is worth special mention as probably the largest leaved variegated tree we have. Another variation on a common theme is a Golden Sycamore, *Acer pseuodoplatanus* Worleei, a pleasant tree indeed. There are some good cedars.

The loss of substantial numbers of elms has opened up new vistas and advantage has been taken of this in new plantings.

The whole of the south boundary is taken up with water. The large Hall Pool to the south west is separated from the newly resurrected pool to the south east by an elaborate piece of rockwork dating back to the Sir Roger period. On this is a davidia and the rare Mongolian Lime, *Tilia mongolica*.

The south side of the south wall of the stable courtyard, lying west of the hall is well covered with wistaria, a large fig, climbing roses and *Chimonanthus praecox*. This wall overlooks Hall Pool and it is a particularly attractive part of the garden.

West of the courtyard is a three cornered, partly-walled garden. There are climbing roses on the walls with H.T. and Floribundas in front. A yew hedge runs crosswise and divides the garden into two. Steps lead up to the north end to a formal rose garden with a central sundial and clipped yews. There are some good magnolias on east and west boundaries.

On the outside of the west wall are numerous clematis, camellias, hydrangeas. A canal forms the west boundary of the garden and Hall Pool the south. An area of lawn along this boundary has a few notable trees. *Ginkgo biloba*, always interesting, *Taxodium distichum*, the Swamp Cypress and, I am informed, *Juglans cinerea*, the Butternut.

North of the entrance drive and south of the old walled garden is a narrow strip called the 'Bee Garden' which contains some interesting shrubs. The entrance to the commercial department passes through this little garden.

Arbury is not a plantsman's garden although there are numerous interesting items. Its location on the fringe of an unexciting industrial area does not encourage visitors. Few people go to Nuneaton for a holiday. Yet Arbury is very beautiful: the architecture is superb; the garden management excellent for these difficult days.

It would have been easy to have attracted crowds by introducing popular features such as has been done in so many places. One is grateful that such temptations have been resisted. Visitors to Arbury go to see a stately home in as unspoilt a state as possible. They are not disappointed. Some go out of homage to one of Britain's greatest novelists.

Armscote Manor
Mr and Mrs J.F. Docker

Stratford-upon-Avon, 1km (¾ mile) W of A34 Stratford — Shipston Road. 6.4km (4 miles) N of Shipston. Area: 2.4ha (6 acres). Altitude: 70m (234ft). Soil: clay loam, calcareous. Rainfall: 660mm (26in). Labour employed: one full-time. Open each year for NGS.

There appear to be two incidents in the past history of this house that have come down to us, both with a religious flavour. The house was built around 1590, probably by a John Holford who appears to have had sympathies with the Gunpowder Plot plotters although we have little precise information on this point. The second, and much better documented, is that of George Fox's arrest in this house in 1673. It would appear to be one of the later of his numerous arrests which started in 1649. The swing from Catholic to Quaker shows an extreme change of allegiance during seventy years.

This is a garden where beautiful high stone walls play an important part. It is also a garden with more than an average area of herbaceous borders which in these days of shrubs and ground cover makes an interesting change.

The house faces south and opposite the front door is a straight paved path leading to the street through a door in the boundary wall. The path is flanked by lawn and on the east side is a double red hawthorn of exceptional size. Further east is a wide border of roses and herbaceous plants forming the boundary of the south garden. On the west of the path is the walled kitchen garden entered through a circular gateway.

The main lawn extends westwards from the house and north of the kitchen garden and is again bounded by walls with wide herbaceous borders in front.

A wrought iron gate through the west wall leads into an enclosed garden with a broad straight sided central lawn. At the far (west) end is a semicircle of tall clipped yew with domes on top and a central vase feature;

an excellent eye-stopper. Wide herbaceous borders are on each side of the lawn. The north border is backed by a hedge of Lawson's Cypress, the south one by assorted shrubs. When at its summer height this is a most delightful garden.

North from the west lawn a gap in the wall leads into a formal garden with rectangular rose beds in grass around the edge and a sunken central area, in the middle of which is a rectangular pool. The garden is surrounded partly by walls, including house walls and partly by tall yew hedges.

North from the formal rose garden is a wilder area which forms the outer boundary on the north and north west sides and joins up with the entrance drive on the east. It consists of undulationg rough mown grass, with daffodils in the spring and trees ranging from very old apple trees, which give a touch of maturity, to many trees quite recently planted. At the west end of this area, north of the Lawson cypress hedge are three good young whitebeams, several flowering cherries, and a *Catalpa bignonioides*. On the north side are three erect, almost fastigiate maples which appear to be *Acer pseudoplatanus* 'Erectus'. At the east end many limes, birches, weeping willows, alders and *Liquidamber styraciflua* have been planted since a large number of elms were lost. A sizeable walnut and a promising *Pyrus salicifolia* are at the house end of the drive.

South of the drive are more old fruit trees and a large block of newly planted trees in variety. The present owners have been here only since the end of 1977 and tree planting seems to have been their main contribution so far. The value of this will be appreciated in years to come.

Ashorne House
Mr and Mrs A. John Sidwell

Ashorne, 5 miles S of Warwick. W of A41 Warwick — Banbury road. Area: 3.2ha (8 acres). Altitude: 65m (213ft). Soil: medium loam over marl, neutral to alkaline, variable. Rainfall: 660mm (26in). Labour employed: three and a boy. Open under NGS.

Ashorne House was built as one of the grander farmhouses in 1740. The present owners have been here since 1971.

The general layout is that of a vast expanse of lawn, some superb mature trees and well sited new plantings. There are considerable herbaceous borders of traditional type and many bulbs in grass in the spring. Seasonal bedding is absent.

Muscaris and other small bulbs cover the high bank on the west side of the drive as one enters. Here also are some stately Austrian pines. The drive comes in on the north front of the house and north from this steps lead down to a sunken lawn with a high bank beyond planted with shrubs. Here is a very attractive low branched beech and moving to the east one of several very fine horsechestnuts. These have been fortunate to have had room to grow and to have escaped the activities of those people who delight in removing lower branches from every tree in sight. The branches now sweep gracefully to the ground with those upturned tips so characteristic of this fine tree when it is allowed to have its head.

Another feature here that is particularly pleasing is the underplant. Mrs Sidwell, who has a love of plants in her blood being descended from the Smith's of Tresco, is fond of native wildings. Under the trees cow parsley, *Anthriscus sylvestris*, the keck of Warwickshire, grows unmolested and unmown until it gets too untidy. One sees another example of this with masses of native lesser celandine growing among heathers. Not, as Mrs Sidwell says, quite the best combination but she likes celandines.

Moving around to the east side we find some good *Robinia pseudoacacia*, just about in their prime, and beyond this an enclosed garden with high hedges of *Chamaecyparis lawsoniana* and golden privet. A broad strip of lawn runs up the middle with a little temple at the north end. Herbaceous borders flank the lawn on each side and the proportions of every feature are just right. In the summer these are a feast of colour and give that variety in form and texture that only herbaceous plants can. Near the temple are several young liquidambers which are doing well.

On the south side is the main lawn which is great by any standards. Near the house it is in the form of a series of terraces with mown banks. In the south east corner is another horse chestnut and matching it in the far south west is an enormous ash. Nearer to the house is an Austrian pine to the south east and a fine lime to the south west with a weeping ash and an Irish yew nearby.

The south boundary is formed by a stream which may one day supply water for a pool but plans for this are still nebulous. Many new tree plantings have been made along this boundary and I noted birch, willows and alder among others. Near the western boundary a group of young Serbian spruce, *Picea omorika* look very promising.

West of the house are some old fruit trees, remains of a one time farm orchard and beyond more herbaceous borders under the boundary wall. Paeonies are a feature here as also are roses.

Beyond the west boundary is the village cricket field which Mr Sidwell owns. More tree planting has been done here, beyond the boundary line.

In the north east corner is the kitchen garden with a large greenhouse containing a good range of house plants and other items. A plant of the commercial passion fruit, *Passiflora edulis*, threatens to take over and that vine relative, a *Tetrastigma sp.*, will soon want more room than can be spared. There is a good cymbidium collection. An interesting feature here is a small greenhouse within the larger one. In this are housed plants with a higher temperature requirement and include *Calanthe, Dieffenbachia, Maranta, Codiaeum* and others.

The standards of management here are obviously high with adequate staff under Mr Batty, who is a third generation head gardener.

Astrop House
Mr and Mrs A.J. Harvey

Frankton, 1.6km (1 mile) S of B4453 Leamington to Rugby about 1.3km (8 miles) from Leamington 10km (6 miles) from Rugby. Area: 0.6ha (1½ acres). Altitude: 100m (330ft). Soil: deep line free sandy loam overlying calcareous lower lias clay. Rainfall: 660mm (26in). Open under NGS and local charities.

This is a sixteenth century cottage enlarged in 1956. The original garden was minute but has gradually been extended.

Today the garden is L shaped and consists of informal beds and marginal borders of varying width set in lawn.

Armillaria killed the largest tree in the garden, a weeping willow, a couple of years ago and numerous large elms on the boundaries went down with Dutch elm disease leaving the garden more open than had been expected.

There are a few mature silver birch and several young ones. A blue cedar, *Cedrus atlantica glauca*, thirty three years old, is now the most imposing tree and a much younger deodar is making efforts to catch it up. A good specimen of *Eucalyptus gunnii* was feared killed in the 1979 winter but has broken well from the main trunk to about eight or ten feet from the ground. An eight year old Weymouth pine, *Pinus strobus* is looking particularly happy as is a Colorado spruce, *Picea pungens glauca.*

Chamaecyparis lawsoniana is used as a boundary screen and among cultivars of this species I noted *C.l. erecta* and *C.l. columnaris* looking particularly well.

Some of the beds are planted with heathers of which there is a very good selection. Shrub roses in about fifty species and varieties are an important feature and the whole range of shrubs and ground cover is very wide.

Shrubs of special note include *Magnolia stellata, Cornus mas, Amelanchier canadensis, Pieris forrestii, Cotoneaster watereri,* and *Hydrangea villosa.* Among the smaller subjects may be mentioned cyclamen, Hellebores, Iris spp.

This garden is a good example of the modern owner/designed/managed garden.

Badgers Cottage
Dr and Mrs G.P. Williams

Idlicote, 2 miles E of Fosse Way at Halford (about 10 miles N of Moreton in Marsh). Area: 0.13ha (⅓ acre). Altitude: 96m (320ft). Soil: clay loam. Alkaline. Rainfall: 660mm (26in). Open occasionally under NGS. See Yellow Book.

This is mainly a plantsman's garden and is an excellent example of this type of small garden managed without paid labour. Cottage and garden were derelict eight years ago (1973) when the present owners purchased the property.

The seventeenth century thatched stone cottage is close to the village street so that the garden lies behind on the south west side. Layout is in the current style with a basic lawn and informal planted areas encroaching. There are no narrow grass strips or paths and the relationship of lawn to planted areas shows an appreciation of scale and proportion

An artificial bog garden with a strip of free water has been created on buried polythene and primulas, ligularias and astilbes are quite happy there. Numerous stone troughs contain encrusted saxifrages and other choice alpines.

A substantial part of the cultivated area is taken up with herbaceous plants. These include the usual 'run of the mill' plants and a few less common items to give something of interest over a long season.

Some old fruit trees serve as supports for *Vitis coignetiae*, Clematis and climbing roses. A *Betula utilis* planted four years ago is now 4.5m (15ft) high. Other young trees getting established are a fastigiate hornbeam and a few conifers. *Buddleia alternifolia* is being grown as a standard and *Acer pseudoplatanus* 'Brilliantissimum' as a bush.

There is a small kitchen garden screened by a row of dwarf pyramid apples.

This garden has not been overplanted as have so many modern gardens in order to gain immediate effect. One has a feeling that most of the 'permanent' features really are permanent and that the temporary fillers will slowly disappear as required.

Badgers Cottage. This recently created small garden has a large plant collection and is a pleasure to visit.

Right: Barton House. The west lawn with Japanese Larch and daffodils.

Below: Coombe Abbey. Nessfield's formal terrace and parterre of the 1860's forms a buffer between the house and Capability Brown's parkland of the previous century.

Barton House

Dr and Mrs I.A. Bewley Cathie

Barton-on-the-Heath, 4.8km (3 miles) E of Moreton-in-Marsh. 3.2km (2 miles) W of A34 at Long Compton. Area: 2ha (5 acres). Altitude: 123m (410ft). Soil: clay loam, lime free. Rainfall: 660mm (26in). Labour employed: one full-time, if obtainable. Open for NGS.

This is our most southerly garden in Warwickshire being only 1½ miles from the Gloucester Border and in typical North Cotswold country. It is, however, decidedly atypical in its soil for instead of the usual calcareous soils of the Oolite it is lime-free and rhododendrons are a feature.

Like so many fine old houses it has grown with the passing years. The central block, without its present facade dates from 1558. The north wing was added by Inigo Jones in the early seventeenth century. The ill-fated Sir Thomas Overbury, a friend of Jones, lived here at one time. Further additions were made in 1840 and 1898. The chimneys are the contribution of the present owner who came here in 1946.

A couple of Scots Pines by the entrance gate survive from three said to have been planted in 1745. It was, apparently, a local custom to plant this tree to indicate loyalty to ones' Sovereign. The drive entering from the east forms an ellipse around a central area of lawn with a round pond in the middle and borders of rhododendrons on each side. South of the drive is a very good Wellingtonia with low sweeping branches. A little nearer the house is a weeping ash.

North of the drive behind a hedge is a little secret garden with many rhododendron species, and early hybrids among which were noted *R. wardii, R. augustinii, R. argyrophyllum* and the three forms of R. x *nobleanum*. Above on the wall of an Inigo Jones barn is a large sundial.

The south front of the house, with a beggars niche by the door, looks out over a large raised lawn with twelve domed yews, about two feet high, in orderly arrangement. The beggars niche perhaps demands explanation. It was where food left-overs were placed for the less fortunate passers-by.

Further south a tall yew hedge screens the tennis court beyond. In the south-east corner is a large rhododendron collection including *R. williamsianum*, with rounded, heart shaped leaves and dainty pink flowers early in the season, *R. fulvum* with rusty backed leaves and *R. makinoi*, even rustier. *Magnolia x solangeana* 'Picture' with a broad petalled flower, almost globose in form looked very good. There is a sorbus collection including the attractive white fruited *S. prattii*.

West of the house is the main lawn, a wide stretch of grass uncumbered except for a particularly good specimen of Japanese Larch. On the west boundary is a Ha Ha with a broad border in which bulbs are naturalised. In addition to a large collection of the smaller daffodils, especially the old Leedsii and Barrii types, *Fritillaria meleagris* is present in quantity. Five golden Irish Yews are spaced along the boundary.

South of this is a bowling green said to have been constructed in the 1840's to relieve unemployment in the village. It is screened by a yew hedge with golden yew end and corner blocks.

On the north side of the west lawn is a mixed border with a path beyond and a further border under the wall which is, in fact, the wall of the one acre walled kitchen garden, still kept going although obviously not up to the standard formerly maintained.

This is a very pleasing garden to wander around. There is a large area of lawn giving a feeling of space and yet one keeps finding little corners where interesting plants are tucked away.

Birmingham Botanical Gardens

Birmingham Botanical and Horticultural Society Ltd

In Westbourne Road, Edgbaston. Area: 4ha (10 acres). Altitude: 135m (450ft). Soil: lime free. Rainfall: 700mm (27.5in). Open daily.

We have to thank the altruism of the early midland industrialists for many of the cultural and recreational facilities of Birmingham. The story is not entirely one of grime and squalor, as is sometimes supposed. It was in 1829 after some years of hesitancy that the Birmingham Botanical and Horticultural Society was formed and a lease taken from the Calthorpe Estate for the site which is still occupied by the gardens. Throughout the years the gardens have been maintained by private funds, often with a struggle to survive.

Many people distinguished in the horticultural world have been associated with the gardens over the years. The original design was by J.C. Loudon and had all of Loudon's plans been possible to execute a conical plant house two hundred feet in diameter and one hundred feet high would have been built before the Kew Palm House or Paxton's Conservatory at Chatsworth.

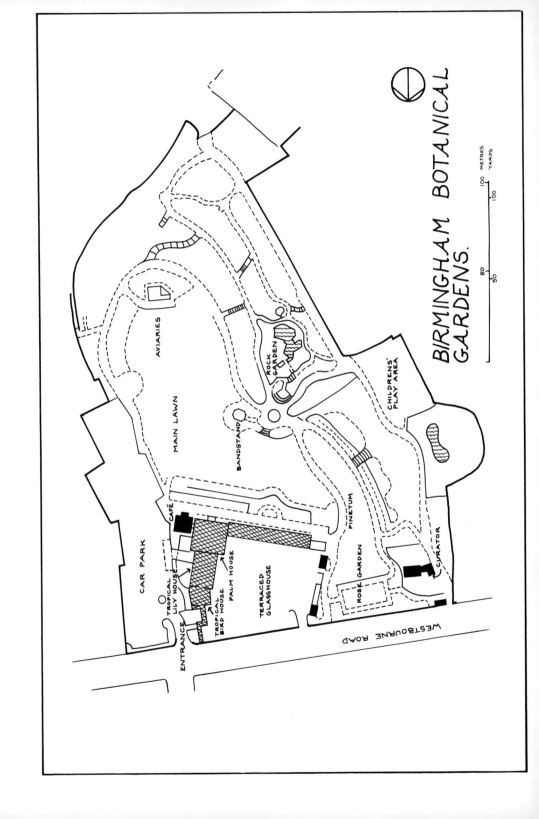

BIRMINGHAM BOTANICAL GARDENS.

100 METRES
100 YARDS
50
50

CHILDRENS' PLAY AREA

AVIARIES

ROCK GARDEN

MAIN LAWN

BANDSTAND

CAR PARK

CAFÉ

TROPICAL LILY HOUSE

TROPICAL BIRD HOUSE

PALM HOUSE

TERRACED GLASSHOUSE

ENTRANCE

PINETUM

ROSE GARDEN

CURATOR

WESTBOURNE ROAD

The gardens have been and still are a training ground for students. E.H. Wilson was a student here towards the end of last century before going on to Kew and later to become our greatest of all plant collectors.

Today the struggle to survive continues but it is a noble effort and Birmingham is fortunate to have such an attraction so close to the city centre. The Society is registered as an educational charity and special facilities are offered for school parties.

One passes through the tropical bird house, for birds are an additional interest here into the lily house where tropical Nymphaeas flourish in the heated pool. The educational aspect of the gardens is emphasised by the presence of rice, banana, cotton, sugar cane, cocoa and many other warm climate economic plants.

The palm house contains a good selection of warm temperate plants and, once again, economic plants are given space. The terrace glasshouses run east to west along the top of the gardens and include sections with succulents, pelargoniums and, at the west end, a collection of half-hardy shrubs not quite able to withstand winters outside in Birmingham. I noted *Prostranthera, Pomaderris, Leptospermum, Crinodendron patagua, Datura sanguinea,* and *Rhododendron fragrantissima.*

In front of the terrace glasshouses is a south facing border and many slightly tender items flourish here including *Itea ilicifolia, Cytisus battandierii,* and *Callistemon linearis.*

Looking south from the terrace one sees the broad expanse of the main lawn slightly east of centre. The walk down the east boundary is screened from the car park by a beech hedge on the left. On the right is the main lawn. A copper beech, low-branched, gnarled and twisted adds character. The lower part of the main lawn is planted with daffodils.

Continuing along the east boundary we pass through shrub borders in which rhododendrons add colour in their season. There are some fine large camellias. Near the southern end of the gardens is a wild, water garden area where, against a background of rhododendrons such marginals as *Gunnera manicata, Lysichytum,* and *Rheum* create bold foliage effects.

Near the west boundary is the rock garden constructed in 1895 in memory of Sir Hugh Nettlefold. Water for the rock pool is supplied by a natural spring, the overflow of which is piped to create an area for moisture loving perennials. This is a well designed feature and is well maintained.

The rose garden is in the north west corner and in the nearby boundary wall two old scots pines seem to have existed on almost nothing for long before living memory — natural Bonzai specimens.

An excellent guide is published with a large plant list.

Birmingham University Botanic Gardens

Director: Prof. J.G. Hawkes
Curator: Mr. A.D. Radley

In Edgbaston Park Road close to the University Campus. Area: 3.5ha (8.75 acres). Altitude: 137m 9450ft). Soil: naturally lime free. Rainfall: 735mm (29.4in). Open occasionally to public or by appointment.

The gardens were formed by combining those of two private houses, Winterbourne and part of Westmere. The Westmere portion is mainly devoted to research and is not normally open to the public.

Although the obvious main function of any university botanic garden is research and education they are not without popular appeal and this is particularly the case with Birmingham. The steep bank of ericas near the car park is a sort of thing we might find on varying scales in many good gardens and the central fountain surrounded by a circular bed of dwarf roses in the Walled Garden is a typical private garden feature.

The main feature within the Walled Garden is the area devoted to the origin of garden rose varieties. Here are to be found original species and early hybrid forms from which the modern rose has been developed.

It is interesting to note that the habitat range, already naturally quite wide, has been extended by special features. A raised scree garden of tufa and limestone chippings in which many choice alpines are grown illustrates this point.

A larger scree area lies east of the Walled Garden. Here attempts have been made to imitate natural terrains and create sites for plants with special needs.

An educational feature of interest to many is an area of geographical beds showing trees and shrubs from the different continents.

A new rose garden has been planted (1975) with modern cultivars which complements the area in the Walled Garden.

The tree and shrub collection is quite large and rock and water gardens extend further the range of plants. To many the wild garden at the eastern end will have the greatest appeal. With abundant moisture many interesting plants can be grown. Beyond this boundary is the Nature Reserve managed by the Birmingham Natural History Society. Permits are required to enter this area. It is hard to believe that all this is less than two miles from the Birmingham city centre.

An excellent guide is produced and for that reason long lists of plant names have been omitted from this description.

Charlecote Park
The National Trust

Four miles E of Stratford-upon-Avon on B4088 between its junctions with B4086 and A429.
Area: 1.2ha (3 acres) Park about 220 acres. Altitude: 39m (130ft). Soil: sandy over gravel.
Neutral to slightly acid. Rainfall: 660mm (26in). Labour employed: one full-time. Open
regularly for NT.

The garden at Charlecote has a less notable history than the park. The oft
repeated story of the young Shakespeare's poaching episode and the
dramatist's later lampooning of Sir Thomas Lucy in the character of
Justice Shallow in 'Henry IV' and 'Merry Wives of Windsor' is well
known.

The Lucy family were at Charlecote from 1247 but they appear to have
been descended from Thurstane de Cherlecote who was there a century
and three generations before.

It seems that the garden was never large. The dutch style water garden
and parterre of the late seventeenth century on the cover of the guide book
occupies an area little different from that of today. This is reproduced
from a painting of Ian Stevens and shows the Gatehouse much as it now
is. This magnificent structure dates from the mid sixteenth century. The
house itself has been altered from time to time over the centuries.

'Capability' Brown was engaged to carry out certain work but was not
allowed to remove two avenues, one of lime and another of elm. The lime
avenue remains today running westwards from the house. The elms, alas,
have gone the way of all elms. He did, however, change the course of the
little river Hele at the point where it joins the Avon south of the House.

Dorothy Stroud in her book 'Capability Brown' records that on 29th
September 1757, 'Mr Brown began making alterations upon Wellsborn
Brook'. This was the name by which the stream was then known. Even
today one is more likely to hear locals speak of Wellesbourne Brook than
River Hele. Brown also filled in the pools of Ian Steven's painting and
constructed a 'fosse' which is presumably the Ha Ha existing today.
Dorothy Stroud also records the planting of cedars on the lawns around
the house. One or two of those still standing on the lawn north of the
forecourt could be of this age but the others are more likely to be
nineteenth century plantings.

The garden passed through the usual phase of Victorian formal bedding
and became somewhat neglected over the years of the Second World War.

The National Trust took over in 1946 and slowly have created a garden of interest and character.

One enters the Park from the Barford Road along the drive where the elms once were and passes through the Gatehouse with its two cupolas and clock tower into the large rectangular forecourt on the east front of the house. There is a central drive flanked by broad lawns. A border under the south facing wall contains a range of modern shrubs and herbaceous plants. A large Wistaria is on the house. A row of ancient clipped yews is along the north facing wall.

Northwards from the forecourt is a raised lawn on which are six cedars of Lebanon, previously mentioned, and still further north is an area of old shrubbery now being planted as an interesting wild garden.

Further north is a lawn covered promontory on which are two very old mulberries. The western edge of this north garden is occupied by a border of plants mentioned in the works of Shakespeare. The whole northern area is surrounded by a Ha Ha — possibly the one constructed by Brown.

On the west side of the house the garden runs down to the river Avon and is enclosed in a stout stone balustrade. This encloses a small semi-formal rose garden, with rosemary, rue and *Euphorbia myrsinites* adding a little extra character.

Before leaving this delightful bit of Warwickshire mention might be made of another item of horticultural interest. Charles Maries, that great collector of plants from Japan and China, was born in Hampton Lucy, just over the river from Charlecote Park. Why not a small memorial garden planted with subjects that he introduced? And what better place for it than Charlecote?

Coombe Abbey Country Park
Coventry City Council

Coventry, just outside the Coventry city boundary on A427 Coventry — Lutterworth Road. Altitude: 70m (230ft). Soil: sandy loam, lime free. Rainfall: 660mm (26in). Open daily throughout the year.

Coombe Abbey has suffered many ups and downs in its long history. Its foundation by the Cistertian Order was in 1149-50 and it remained a religious house until the dissolution of 1539. Some time before 1618 William Craven purchased the property and it is recorded that his son, the first Earl Craven was given permission by Charles I to enclose over 600 acres of land around the house to form a park. The Craven occupation was to continue for over three hundred years until the death of the young Earl in 1921.

In 1684 Captain Wm. Wynne was engaged to modify the house and he gave it the present west front. At the same time many trees, mainly oak and beech were planted in the Park.

In 1770 Capability Brown began two schemes for the sixth Lord Craven, one at Benham in Berkshire and the other at Coombe. The Coombe work involved damming the little Smite Brook to form a lake of eighty six acres. This involved building an earthen dam thirty feet high and was probably one of his greater works. Brown's weirs penstocks and bridges remain today as evidence of his industry. Many trees were also planted to create a typical Brown landscape. The formal parterres were swept away. Between 1771 and 1776 Brown received £7,650:9s from Lord Craven for work at Coombe.

By 1860 the urge to create more formal and intricate patterns with plants came to Coombe as elsewhere and William Eden Nesfield was engaged to carry this out as well as making additions to the house. He laid out the present terrace and parterre on the west front, created a formal canal, linking Brown's lake with the parterre, and also made the moat on the south side. In addition to his work in the grounds Nesfield also added an east wing which was demolished in the early 1930's.

It is probable that Nesfield's work included the making of a ridge of high ground known as the 'hillock'. Some mystery surrounds the creation of this feature. It is thought that the soil removed during the moat and canal extension might have been used but experts agree that there would not have been sufficient soil for that purpose.

The suggestion that Brown might have made the hillock is ruled out by the fact that no trees that could have been planted before Nesfield are found on it. So far as we know it was uncharacteristic of Nesfield to move soil just for the fun of it. The mystery remains.

There was obviously a great flurry of tree planting during the second half of the nineteenth century and it is assumed that Nesfield played an important part in this. Most important of all are the Wellingtonias, *Sequoiadendron giganteum*. The numbers of these must run into a hundred or more, some very fine specimens and all in good health. The above mentioned hillock is covered in them. There must be few places in Britain that can boast so many.

Nothing of note is recorded about Coombe until the sad death of the young Earl in 1921. This marked the end of the Craven connection with Coombe and the beginning of the decline.

After various occupants the estate was acquired by the City of Coventry and has now been developed as a countryside park with apparent great success. There are, of course, the usual children's play areas, picnic areas and such like but all visitors must be impressed by the way the old features have been preserved. In spite of the need to cater for the masses one still has a 'stately home' feeling when walking around.

The Coombe Abbey of today is approached by a long drive flanked by very broad areas of mown grass behind which are double rows of trees. The outermost row on each side is of horse chestnuts, the inner row of limes. The trees are so far back from the drive that the 'avenue' effect is lost. Recently young red twigged limes have been planted in front of the older trees to form a new avenue when the useful life of the older trees is past. These, being nearer to the drive will produce a better proportioned vista.

The drive leads straight over the bridge crossing Nesfield's moat into the south courtyard. On our right is the 12th century cloister more or less intact; on our left the Tudor restored cloister. Little else remains of the earlier buildings. The courtyard has a small central pool surrounded by lawn and box edging.

The west front is probably much as Nesfield left it. The wide upper terrace leads down to the parterre through which a broad paved path flanked by seasonal bedding leads down to the canal. On each side are elaborate patterns in clipped box almost a yard high. A photograph in Country Life of 1909 shows a more complicated arrangement with the box much lower but the general character remains. The area is surrounded by neatly clipped yew hedges with mushroom headed specimens at intervals.

Along the canal edge are a few incense cedars, *Calocedrus decurrens*. Northwards from here is an old mulberry, a fine beech and many other trees, and, just beyond is the hillock, mentioned above, with its superb Wellingtonias. A black walnut, *Juglans nigra*, is nearby. This is a tree that should be more commonly planted.

Much new planting is being done, especially along the path near the lakeside leading to the picnic site. This is an open field surrounded by woodland. Near the woodland margin are the remains of several aged sweet chestnuts, still living and growing but very old and gnarled. They might date from the enclosure by the first Lord Craven.

Ones' pleasure at seeing attempts made to preserve a fine old garden is mixed with sadness at what cannot now be saved. The old walled garden to which the public do not have access and which is now being turned over to farm use is stark and almost bare. Two ranges of peach houses, glassless and derelict, the remains of once extensive vineries and nothing more.

The Davids

Mr and Mrs L.J. Cadbury

Hole Lane, Northfield. Hole Lane runs S off A38 Bristol Road midway between Selly Oak and Northfield. The Davids forms the corner site with entrance gate a short distance up Hole Lane on right. Area: 7.2ha (18 acres). Altitude: 144m (480ft). Soil: Keuper Marl, about neutral. Rainfall: 735mm (29in). Labour employed: one full-time. Frequency of opening: normally once per year for NGS and once for local fete.

Lying two miles north of the huge BL Austin works at Longbridge, five miles south of Birmingham city centre and actually bordering the busy Bristol Road, one hardly expects to find such an oasis as this. By the use of heavy screen planting it has been possible to create an atmosphere of seclusion and isolation and the visitor can easily forget the close proximity of the industrial world.

The house is partly nineteenth century but was added to substantially by the present owners when they purchased the property around 1928. The garden has been created wholly since that time. Only some very good oaks and other native trees provide a link with an earlier period.

From Hole Lane the entrance drive starts in a westerly direction but curves to the south and finishes at the north front of the house. The whole of the north west boundary with the Bristol Road consists of a grassed tree area with an especially dense boundary belt. Some of the oaks, horsechestnuts and beech are of a fair age. Many trees are much younger as, for example black and lombardy poplars. The same pattern is continued in an L shape around the south west boundary, thus providing a wide buffer against intrusive sounds.

On the south west of the house is a paved terrace looking over a sunken garden of great charm. The main axis of this is open lawn which leads directly to a long paved path bordered by an avenue of silver birch now about fifty years old. Viewed in the opposite direction the house forms an end stop to the vista.

The sunken garden itself has low retaining walls, two and a half feet high, on three sides at the house end and clipped yew hedges at the other. Within the walled area are four L shaped rose beds and rose borders under the walls. In front of the yew hedges are two long, parallel herbaceous borders and here, also, is to be found the finest tree in the garden, a grand specimen of English oak.

Rising to the east of the birch/sunken garden feature is a large expanse of lawn on which are two cedars, *Cedrus deodara* and *C. atlantica glauca*, now some twenty years old.

The boundary with Hole Lane south of the house has another dense evergreen belt, mainly conifers in which *Chamaecyparis lawsoniana* predominates.

Most of the lawn area is free of trees which emphasises the spaciousness of this most attractive garden. A small pool near the south east boundary has steep banks on three sides. Here are some good oaks and beech and masses of our native daffodil in the sring.

On the south west boundary of the lawn is a mixed border with some interesting shrubs and small trees. I noted magnolias, amelanchier, dentzia, elaeagnus, and an attractive low flat topped cherry, rather like 'Shirotae'.

There are masses of small bulbs in the spring. Crocus, chionodoxa, ipheon, small narcissus and others make this a colourful garden in the spring although the peak season is midsummer.

Farnborough Hall
The National Trust

8 miles S of Southam on A423 Coventry — Banbury. Area: 6.5ha (16 acres). Altitude: 150m (500ft). Soil: medium loam. Neutral. Rainfall: 660mm (26in).

Farnborough lies in the pleasant part of south Warwickshire close to the Oxford and Northampton Borders in that upland belt which includes the Middle Lias scarp of Edge Hill four miles to the south west.

In the early fourteenth century the manor of Farnborough came into the possession of a John Raleigh, an ancestor of the illustrious Sir Walter and it remained in the family until 1683 when it was purchased by Ambrose Holbech. The west front of the house is late seventeenth century but the south front was altered by William Holbech in 1745-55 and this is the front we see today. It is built in the warm brown local ironstone which is such a feature of the villages on the Middle Lias.

The Holbech family have been in continuous occupation ever since. In 1960 the property was transferred to the National Trust and Mr Geoffrey Holbech who endowed it still resides in the Hall.

The Farnborough garden could be described as 'not so much a garden, more a country walk' but it is a fine walk none the less and has much of interest. Above all it has the ability to give one a feeling of quiet repose which fussily tidy beds of gaudy flowers can never do.

Water abounds at Farnborough. As one approaches along the entrance drive two pools, Lady Pond and Island Pool lie to the left. Near the edge of the Lady Pond is a fine tulip tree.

The drive continues into a small forecourt on the NNE front of the hall. A circular lawn occupies the middle of the forecourt. There are mixed borders around the edge and climbers on the walls.

Westwards from the house lies the main lawn with a magnificent cedar *Cedrus libani*, aged but very sound with a large branch arising at ground level and pointing southwards. Near here is the site of an old conservatory. The back wall has been retained and it adjoins a formal garden with box edged rose beds. A large tree paeony is on the adjoining path. Just beyond here is an ice house.

North west from the main lawn one has a view over a Ha Ha to a large distant lake, Sourland Pool. This is connected to yet another lake, Rookery Pool which forks and spreads in narrow channels south west of the house.

But the great feature of Farnborough is the long terrace running in gentle curves south of the house for half a mile. The western edge of this consists of a series of alcoves and bulges flanked by cherry laurel. The laurels are flush with ground level on the terrace top but four or five feet high from the field below. The falling ground runs down to Rookery Pool which is more or less parallel with the terrace and a quarter of a mile away.

Half way along the terrace is an Ionic temple on the right and further along on the left an oval temple with an upper storey approached by a flight of stone steps. At the end is an obelisk with the date 1751.

All the time we have been walking along the terrace we have had a woodland strip on our left. Returning along this strip under horse chestnut, lime, yew, beech, oak, holly, sycamore, sweet chestnut, we find ground cover of great variety. I noted *Daphne laureola*, *Campanula latifolia*, *Ruscus aculeatus*, scruffy as usual, *Lilium martagon*, *Doronicum pardalianches* with sanicle and many other natives. Daffodils, bluebells and winter aconites have colonised large areas.

Hermitage
Mrs M. Watson

Priors Marston, 8km (5 miles) SE of Southam — on Welsh Road. In triangle formed by Southam — Banbury — Daventry. Area: 1.6ha (4 acres). Altitude: 1216m (540ft). Soil: clay to loam. Lime content variable. (See below). Rainfall: 660mm (26in). Labour employed: one full-time. Open occasionally under NGS.

Thirty years ago this was a broken down smallholding. Mrs Watson and her late husband started changing the order of things around 1948-50, but things proceeded slowly at first. The site is an attractive one on the upland belt which forms the Warwickshire boundary with Northamptonshire. There are, however, problems.

The geology is Lower Lias clay overlaid by Middle Lias. The Lower Lias is fairly high in lime. The Middle Lias in this area is lime deficient. This means that where the overlay is deep enough lime hating plants may be grown. But there is more to it than that. The underlying clay is impervious to water whereas the Middle Lias produces a free draining loam of good structure. Water therefore moves freely down until the clay is reached, when it emerges as a spring. Badly drained areas are therefore present in this garden and planting has to take account of this.

The late Mr Watson was an engineer and a farmer and it is a tribute to his great practical knowledge that he retained all the natural contours however steep and awkward some may have seemed. Less knowledgeable designers would have had bulldozers in to level things off and created a site impossible to manage. As it is we have a garden of great interest with a variety of habitats, wisely planted and skillfully managed. It is among the best gardens in our area created since the Second World War.

There is a small orchard on the left of the drive as one enters the garden and approaches the east front of the house. Opposite the front door a flight of steps gives on to a rising lawn area with yew hedges behind. A large herbaceous border is on the left. A wide grass path wanders uphill to the right (south), following the undulations of the original field. We are here moving into the lime free part of the garden and with applications of peat rhododendrons are grown successfully.

On our left is a semi-formal paved area backed by a curved yew hedge with a seat in front.

Following our grass path up further we pass a fine White Beam and a huge Kanzan cherry with the wide spreading habit of an old tree. It is difficult to believe it is only 30 years old.

Above: Hermitage. The Lower Pool with effective marginal planting.

Below: Ilmington Manor. Informal steps and paving with lavender and roses are one of many attractive features in this garden.

Near the top of the garden is a pool, naturally maintained by springs. This is a woodland area and the pool is shaded, but the Water Hawthorn, *Aponogeton distachyus* covers much of its area. Gunneras and Lysichytum provide their characteristic foliage textures. Oaks, silver birch and other trees with daffodils in grass underneath occupy the top north east corner.

Down below, near the entrance drive is the lower pool. An old willow leans across. Margins are heavily planted with candelabra primulas, rodgersias, hostas, variegated *Iris pseudacorus*, ligularias and many other plants that enjoy this environment.

Nearby a specimen of *Metasequoia glyptostroboides* is doing well. A *Catalpa bignonioides* suffered from the 1976 drought and again from the 1979 winter but it was just beginning to break in mid-June 1979 and there seemed some chance that it would make up some of its leeway.

The south side of the house opens on to a lavender edged terrace and beyond is the main lawn. The extreme boundary is a mini arboretum with larch, birch, beech, Norway Maple, and others, mostly native. There is a row of young walnuts on the east boundary of the lawn. On the west side is a sunken area with moisture loving plants including gunneras.

Ilmington Manor

Dennis L. Flower Esq.

Near Stratford-upon-Avon, 13km (8 miles) S of Stratford-upon-Avon between A46 and A34. 6.4km (4 miles) NW of Shipston on Stour. Area: 1ha (2½ acres). Altitude: 120m (400ft). Soil: clay loam over clay. Limey. Rainfall: 660mm (26in). Labour employed: one full-time. Open occasionally under NGS.

The house dates from 1600 but when purchased by the present owner's father, Mr Spenser Flower, in 1919 it had become somewhat run down. The garden consisted of a small area around the house and some rough orchard. Complete restoration and extensions to the house and the laying out of the garden date from this period.

We now have a garden in which the formal, semi-formal and informal blend into one. Stonework echoes the fine Cotswold stone of the house itself.

The drive has a row of hornbeams on the left as one enters. A semi-formal garden on the right consists of a rectangular pool with low stone wall surround and corner piers containing plants. A neatly trimmed and edged lawn surrounds this and a low outer wall with appropriate planting encloses the whole feature.

We pass this and enter the forecourt. This is a large expanse of gravel with a central lawn feature edged with stone and with a low stone vase in the middle. Leading off to the south is a broad grass walk with herbaceous borders on each side and a pair of clipped yews at the far end.

West of the house, up some stone steps a narrow paved path flanked with thyme and lavender leads to the Rose Garden. Clipped yew hedges and topiaries mark the boundaries. The central feature of the rose garden is a sundial in a circular area of Rose 'Max Graf' with stepping stone cross paths. The whole is surrounded by beds of roses set in grass. Scillas and chionodoxas provide colour in the spring.

A semi-formal garden, long known as the Dutch Garden because it was largely planted with tulips is now being remodelled and planted with dwarf shrubs. A large lawn area beyond contains masses of daffodils, various shrubs and an interesting rock garden.

Between here and the herbaceous borders described above are the upper rose borders, fairly formal straight line areas with wide grass paths. The rose collection in this garden is quite large and includes H.T. Floribunda, and shrub types.

A few trees are worth noting. There are three Scots Pines near the entrance drive and a fine old pear suriviving from the days when fruit trees were the main occupants. It is not sufficiently appreciated how good a tree the pear is. A vigorous variety on wild pear stock will hold its own with any ornamental tree. Elegant of form, lovely when in flower and among the best for autumn colour, it is sadly disappearing. The wild pear might well be considered as a replacement for some of the dead elms. There are three walnut trees on the south lawn. A notable shrub is *Cornus mas* with its yellow winter flowers on its bare branches. The Ilmington specimen is one of the largest I have ever seen.

This garden has something of interest throughout the year. Spring bulbs, roses and herbaceous plants ensure this.

A recent development is the construction of some pools totalling one acre in area.

Kissing Tree House

Mrs J.B. Priestley

Alveston, Stratford-upon-Avon, 4km (2½ miles) E of Stratford-upon-Avon on A4086. Area: 1.2ha (3 acres). Altitude: 36m (120ft). Soil: sandy loam, lime free. Rainfall: 660mm (26in). Open occasionally under NGS.

The house dates from about 1790 and has been in the present owner's possession since 1959. An earlier owner 'turned the house round'. In other words made a front entrance on what had been the rear of the house. This involved destroying an elaborate Italian style parterre which dated from the turn of the century and replacing it with a circular entrance drive having a central grass area with a bed in the middle. On the far side from the house is a stone columned pergola covered in wistaria and beyond this the walled garden with two three quarter span greenhouses of fine traditional construction. How good to see glass cut with curved bottom edge — perhaps not economic today but functional. A Muscat of Alexandria grape vine is well tended.

Wide herbaceous borders lie to the east and on the south side is a wide expanse of lawn with rose beds, shrub areas and a few good trees including sweet chestnuts which probably date back to when the house was built. Bulbs are a prominent feature in the spring.

Loxley Hall

Mr and Mrs Gregory-Hood

In village of Loxley, 4 miles SE of Stratford-upon-Avon. N off A422. W off A429. In triangle formed by Stratford — Wellesbourne — Ettington. Area: 1.6ha (4 acres). Altitude: 228ft. Soil: clay. Calcareous. Rainfall: 660mm (26in). Garden staff: 3 part-time.

The house is of William and Mary period with additions made in 1860. The present owner's father purchased the property in 1928.

Apart from a few trees the garden is substantially a creation of the present owner during the last fifteen years.

On entering the drive one finds the church on the right above a bank

Above: Loxley Hall. Modern sculpture, a massive metal and slate effort by Philip King, reminds us that gardens have uses beyond that of just growing plants.

Below: Wroxall Abbey. Christopher Wren's alcoved wall is probably unique. The old fruit trees are being replaced by roses.

covered with snowdrops in the spring. Along this bank are the stumps of elms killed by Dutch Elm Disease. Much as one regrets the loss of elms there are occasions when their disappearance seems an improvement and this is the case here. Whether one looks up to the church from the drive or down from the churchyard the more open situation is pleasing.

The church dates from 761 with Norman additions and 18th century alterations. It is well worth a visit.

There is a lawn at two levels in front of the house and this is separated from the field by a Ha–Ha which has become somewhat filled in with the passage of time and its stock protection is now supplemented by a wooden fence.

Most of the Victorian features have been removed by the present owner and there is a modern shrub border on the west side of the lawn, backed by the east wall of the kitchen garden. In front of the south wall is a broad herbaceous border which is threatened with removal if labour shortage makes this necessary. At the present time it is very well managed.

A fine specimen *Ginkgo biloba*, upwards of a century old stands near the south corner of the lawn and beyond that is a sizeable *Sequoiadendron giganteum*.

Yew hedges are used to create enclosures in which are displayed modern sculpture. At the time of my visits some massive exhibits of large blocks of slate bolted together, by Philip King, were quite impressive. It is good for we botanists to be reminded that gardens are also amenity areas, and not only places where plants grow. An enquiry reveals that the owner is also the proprietor of the Rowan Galleries in London.

One interesting feature is the laburnum lawn in which numerous laburnums are associated with beds of blue iris with great effect.

A further touch of originality is a garden, mainly of shrub roses which are allowed to roam at will around a central sunken paved area in which are displayed appropriate sculptures. A few evergreen shrubs are included to widen the interest and I noted some cotoneasters, *Senecio* 'Sunshine' and *Elaeagnus ebbingei*. This is a most successful feature.

Along the north boundary is a row of Scots Pines and between these and the enclosed laburnum garden is a tree and shrub area, mostly recently planted. Here I noted *Cupressus macrocarpa*, *Cotinus coggygria*, *Parottia persica*, *Hamamelis mollis*, *Cryptomeria japonica elegans* and many others.

To the east of these, beyond a beech hedge, is a row of old pear trees, now supporting *Clematis montana* and roses, and nearby is an aged mulberry on crutches but still looking quite healthy.

Meadows
Mr and Mrs R. Law

Draycote, Rugby, 5 miles SW of Rugby. 1 mile S of B4453 Leamington — Rugby Road. Area: 0.6ha (1½ acres). Altitude: 80m (260ft). Soil: heavy loam, alkaline. Rainfall: 660mm (26in). Open occasionally for NGS.

This is a modern style garden around a bungalow built in 1962 on open farmland. Design and construction was carried out by Bernhards of Rugby.

The most important feature is the stream which not only provides sites for a good range of waterside plants but also supplies a pool with a collection of waterfowl.

There is a heather garden and a little patch of dwarf conifers. Shrubs are planted around the entrance drive and climbers and wall shrubs break up the hard lines of the bungalow.

The Mill Garden
Mr and Mrs A.B. Measures

At 55 Mill Street, Warwick. Area: 0.3ha (0.75 acre). Altitude: 45m (150ft). Soil: slightly alkaline. Rainfall: 660mm (26in). Open frequently throughout the summer. Proceeds for charity.

Historic old towns have many little corners that have resisted the effects of time. The most significant change is that old cottages, built for workpeople, have, with careful modernisation, become residences for the more affluent. Such a place is Mill Street. Leave your car in a car park and walk down to the far end. You will find yourself under the Castle wall with the River Avon just ahead.

Few gardens can have such a superb setting. Whichever way one looks there are no unsightly objects beyond the boundary that one feels one must try to hide. There is the magnificent Castle itself a few yards away, a picturesque ruined bridge, and the river with its backdrop of trees on the other side. It is a garden designer's dream.

The house is part fourteenth century and the present owners have been here since 1938. The garden therefore is entirely their creation.

Before entering the garden take a look at the wall on the right. It faces slightly east of south and is covered with climbers and wall shrubs. One finds *Solanum jasminioides album, Phygelius capensis* eight feet high, roses and clematis as well as bold herbaceous plants such as *Onopordon* and Globe artichoke. This is not really part of the garden. It is one of Mr Measure's extra-mural activities.

The garden itself is a series of informal, partially enclosed areas. One passes through a shrub flanked gap or a bamboo curtain to find something different. Near the house are raised beds with the more easily grown alpines such as *Sedum spp, Geranium dalmaticum*, campanulas and gypsophila. Interesting annuals are also used *Phacelia campanularia* of a blue that sets the standard for gentians to aim at and *Leptosiphon* with its extraordinary colour range. These are what I call 'plantsman's annuals' as distinct from the bedding annuals of our parks.

Not that the latter are absent from this garden for we find Perilla, petunias, begonias and castor oil plants all adding colour and interest in odd corners. Fuchsias, very well grown, occupy baskets and other containers. But none of this is overdone. It is all in good taste.

There is a fine border of hostas with other moisture lovers including *Veratrum album* and nearby a large plant of the dyers weld, *Reseda luteola* just to show that this is not a garden limited to gaudy colour.

The riverside is well used. I cannot recall seeing *Gunnera manicata* quite so fine anywhere. Shrubs and small trees, well sited and tended, all make their own contribution to the general scheme. There are good collections of lacecap hydrangeas and ferns in the slightly shaded areas. This is a garden of great variety and great beauty.

The Old Rectory

Mr and Mrs D. Whaley

Oxhill, 17.5km (11 miles) SE of Stratford-upon-Avon. 1.6km (1 mile) S of A422 Stratford — Banbury Road. Area: 0.6ha (1½ acres). Altitude: 80m (270ft). Soil: heavy lias clay. Rainfall: 660mm (26in). Family labour only. Open for NGS.

The garden is a simple rectangle on the east side of an early eighteenth century house. A wall forms the north boundary, a *Thuja plicata* hedge the south. A stream runs along the bottom forming the east boundary. The upper part is mown lawn, the lower rough mown grass.

A good specimen walnut is on the lawn and a nearby Cedar of Lebanon, not too happy, has been cut back from time to time to give the walnut more room. An old Irish Yew, boldly upright, adds character. A large horsechestnut by the streamside forms a focal point when viewed from the house.

Bordering the lawn under the south facing wall is an herbaceous border. A small round pond, near the lower side of the lawn, has a paving and lavender hedge surround. Nearby is a good specimen of *Viburnum burkwoodii*, scenting the garden in the spring.

Nearer the south boundary are informal beds of shrubs and shrub roses. A shrub rose bed is graded in colour from white at one end to red at the other.

A few old fruit trees remain from earlier days. Such is the bare outline of a very pleasant and unpretentious country garden which the present owners have substantially created since 1967.

The Old Rectory

Mrs Scott-Cockburn

Whichford, 10km (6 miles) SE Shipston On Stour. 3.2km (2 miles) E of A34 at Long Compton. Area: 0.3ha (¾ acre). Altitude: 120m (400ft). Soil: medium loam over clay. Some lime. Rainfall: 660mm (26in). Labour employed: one part-time for lawn mowing and kitchen garden only. Open occasionally under NGS.

Set on the North Cotswold fringe in pleasant rolling country the village of Whichford is an attraction from the start. The house has had a somewhat chequered career. It is part Tudor and part 1720. After a period as a Rectory it became a farmhouse and later it was two derelict cottages. The present owner took possession in 1968 and house and garden have been reborn from that date.

The garden slopes fairly steeply down to a stream which has been enlarged to create a pool through which the water flows. This is an attractive feature and allows the cultivation of the usual waterside plants.

There is a large shrub border with ground cover plants. Grey foliage is used extensively. *Viburnum tomentosum* 'Lanarth' has made a good specimen, its compact tabular form makes this one of our best shrubs for the smaller garden. It is pleasing to find that in the 1979 winter some rather tender shrubs which I had seen two years earlier were only slightly damaged and are now recovering well. That larged leaved broom, *Cytisus battandieri* with its deliciously scented yellow bosses in midsummer and *Ceanothus burkwoodii*, one of the best of our blue flowered summer shrubs are two notable examples. *Carpentaria californica* also came through with only slight injury. On the other hand many hebes were killed outright. Shrub roses are an important feature and do well on this well bodied soil.

Many small items, bulbs and other herbaceous plants are grown in the border on the south side of the house. Lilies have been tried in various situations but in the end only L. regale, that most useful of all lilies and L. candidum really thrive. The latter species is never seen better than in the gardens of Cotswold cottages.

There are no very large trees but that rather odd poplar, *Populus candicans* 'Aurora' is growing fast and some cherries are becoming large enough to give that extra dimension so necessary to make the complete garden.

Vitis 'Brant', one of the best vines for autumn colour and the new clematis 'Yellow Queen' are notable climbers.

Behind the house, on the north side, the steep bank is kept up with retaining walls, creating terrace beds planted with shrubs. There is also a formal paved rose garden with radiating beds in this area.

This garden is typical of the better kind of owner — managed amateur's garden. The range of habitats offered makes it specially interesting.

Packwood House
The National Trust

Hockley Heath, 2km (1¼ miles) E of Hockley Heath on A34 Birmingham to Stratford-upon-Avon road. Area: 2ha (5 acres). Altitude: 120m (400ft). Soil: clay with free lime. Rainfall: 700mm (27.5in). Open from April to September. Wednesday to Sunday and Bank Holiday Mondays. See National Trust Guide.

Packwood House is a timber framed Tudor building which has been rendered over and variously altered. The property was in the hands of the Featherston family for some 300 years and it is probable that the original building was erected by a William Featherston in the mid sixteenth century.

The yew garden is the feature for which Packwood is noted and the story that it was planted by John Featherston between 1650 and 1670 and that it represents the Sermon on the Mount has been copied from book to book and rehashed in popular magazines repeatedly over the last half century or so. Now Graham Thomas has exploded all these myths in his 'Gardens of the National Trust'. Apparently by merely looking through readily available documents he has established that although the mount was there before 1756 the main planting of yews was not until 1850 when they were put in as small topiary specimens surrounding a newly planted central orchard and this was after the removal of an old worn out orchard. We must be grateful to Graham Thomas for his work on this problem.

Visitors enter from the east side through a pair of brick pillars into a forecourt with a central paved path leading to the east front of the house. On the right is a stable and office block built by John Featherston in the 1670's. It carries a rather fine sundial. The forecourt is mostly a clear expanse of lawn with colourful mixed borders of flowers.

The south garden is reached through a doorway from the forecourt. This is the main part of the present garden and consists of two distinct parts. The northern half near the house is mainly open lawn. The southern half is the famous Yew Garden.

Taking the northern half first we have a rectangle with a gazebo in each corner. The oldest of these is c1680, the others are of more recent date but they make a well matched set. They are one of the special features of Packwood.

In the height of summer the most colourful feature is the sunken garden. This consists of a rectangular pool below the level of the surrounding lawn. The sloping banks around it are planted with the brightest of bedding plants and the whole is surrounded by a low, perfectly square clipped, yew hedge.

Herbaceous plants occupy borders in front of the south facing wall. Under the west facing wall are five rectangular rose beds separated by buttress hedges of yew with a box hedge along the front. Not perhaps the most desirable kind of construction either from the point of view of microclimate or labour requirement. It is possible, of course, that micro-climate does not matter. There may be enough sulphur dioxide in the air to keep block spot and mildew at bay. It is, after all, close to the industrial midlands.

The division between the north and south parts is effected by a raised terrace linking the two southern gazebos. This has a paved middle path and herbaceous borders on each side. An odd clematis or two hang over the wall. The south side of the wall has ten pairs of niches for bee skeps. They are clearly shown in a drawing of 1756 and probably go back to an earlier date.

South of this wall is the Yew Garden. So much has been written about this and so much nonsense talked that it is not my wish to add to it. Readers wishing to learn more are referred to the work mentioned above.

A word about the mount will not be inappropriate. Mounts were a common feature of mediaeval and early post-mediaeval gardens. They were of varying designs and usually had some sort of structure on top. In this case it is a large mushroom headed yew. A spiral brick path flanked with clipped box winds its way up to the top.

On the west side of the house is the part of the garden first developed. It contains a dipping bath which seems to have long been known as the 'Roman Bath'. There is also a sundial on a central lawn area and over the fence to the west is a substantial lake.

Packwood is a unique garden in many respects and even if some features are not so old as was once claimed it is still a garden of great interest.

Puddocks
Miss Helen Syme

Frog Lane, Ilmington, S of Stratford-upon-Avon between A46 and A34. 6.4km (4 miles) NW of Shipston-on-Stour. Area: 0.2ha (½ acre). Altitude: 120m (400ft). Soil: clay with free lime. Rainfall: 660mm (26in). Labour employed: some casual. Open occasionally under NGS.

This is one of those delightful little gardens that is within the compass of anyone with a little energy and a fair amount of good taste.

The house is a converted barn; the garden a former orchard and a few old fruit trees remain.

A circular entrance drive surrounds a central paved area with a few dot plants and stone troughs. Shrubs and herbaceous plants occupy the border around the drive. *Rosa rubrifolia*, rugosa type shrub roses and other roses, *Mahonia japonica*, philadelphus, clematis and other things are all in accord with the Cotswold stone.

The garden proper is behind the cottage. A little stream runs down the boundary and crosses the middle of the garden. This provides planting sites for astilbes, hostas, numerous ferns, mimulus and candelabra primulas. The double white buttercup *Ranunculus aconitifolius plenus* is a noteworthy plant of wide appeal, yet still not common.

At the top end of the garden is a raised paved area approached by stone steps flanked by *Juniperus sabina tamariscifolia*. There are numerous other small conifers and a pear tree supporting a 'Kiftsgate' rose.

The plants here are all easy going subjects requiring no special attention when planted in the right place. There is no need to rush out in the middle of the night with a sheet of glass to protect some obscure rarity. There are none. It is not often that I mention weeds but in the stream the little water fern, *Azolla*, forms a floating raft of bronzy green. Miss Syme regards it as a weed. I thought it looked quite attractive but I understood her point of view. What surprised me was to find it so abundant after the hard winter of 1979.

Sansome House

Brian E. Suckling Esq

Ilmington, 13km (8 miles) S of Stratford-upon-Avon between A46 and A34. 6.4km (4 miles)
NW of Shipston-on-Stour. Area: 1.4ha (3½ acres). Altitude: 120m (400ft). Soil: clay loam.
Limey. Rainfall: 660mm (26in). Labour employed: one full-time. Open occasionally under NGS.

The house is part 1727 but has been substantially reconstructed by the
present owner who has been here since 1964. The garden has been wholly
reconstructed.

A principal feature is a very large curved shrub border planned by
Hilliers who also supplied the shrubs. There is a rose garden and space is
found for herbaceous plants. A rock garden was constructed by Joe Elliott.

The whole plant range is obviously wide and it is widened by the
creation of specially prepared beds for rhododendrons.

This is a well managed garden with much of interest through all the
year.

Savage's House

Mrs S. Hickson

Bishops Tachbrook, 4km (2½ miles) S of Leamington Spa on A452. Area: 1.6ha (4 acres).
Altitude: 60m (200ft). Soil: pebbly sandy gravel. Lime free. Rainfall: 660mm (26in). Labour
employed: one part-time. Open occasionally under NGS.

The house, which dates from 1558, was in the Savage family for many
years, hence its name. Walter Savage Landor took the name 'Savage' on
marrying into the family and lived here for some time. Mrs Hickson has
been here since 1935.

On acquiring the property the present owner immediately engaged
Brenda Colvin to redesign the garden. The present garden is much as Miss
Colvin left it.

The entrance drive runs east to west and at the garden end are some
very fine double white cherries planted at the time of the re-making of the

garden. The house looks over a lawn to the south with box hedges on each side. There is a cedar on a raised area at the far end. A wide grass path with fruit trees alongside runs eastwards from the main lawn.

On the east front of the house is a raised lawn area. Herbaceous and shrub borders are separated by mown grass paths. Two old mulberries remain from an earlier garden. The outer boundary of this area has a tall holly hedge with a brick path alongside. Brick paths are also used around the house and show some signs of crumbling after almost 45 years. Clipped box domes on square bases add dignity to the area around the house, especially on the east side.

There is a *Magnolia grandiflora* on the house, a tulip tree, shrub roses and a useful range of shrubs. Two young blue cedars, three metres high will make their presence felt in years to come.

A woodland wild garden on the south west side has had its character changed by the loss and removal of 26 elms, mostly large trees. The area is now being redeveloped in keeping with the changed circumstances. Numerous trees of other species are still there and more planting is being done.

The Shakespeare Gardens

The Shakespeare Birthplace Trust
Five properties in or near Stratford-upon-Avon

One of the main functions of a garden of an historic building is that it should provide a pleasant place for visitors to walk around. It should be an acceptable setting for the building but not necessarily part of it historically. This philosophy, in part, lies behind the planning and maintenance of the gardens of the five properties administered by the Shakespeare Birthplace Trust. There is, however, another policy superimposed on the above basic philosophy and that is to provide a link with the works of Shakespeare and to provide examples of gardens typical of Shakespeare's time. The two policies become confused.

The show piece of these gardens is the Knot Garden at New Place, Shakespeare's last home. This is a copy of a genuine Tudor design and the boundaries of pleached apples, vines and figs with the sweetbriar hedge provide a perfect framework. The knots are in dwarf box, hyssop and other plants just as they would have been in later Tudor times. It is when the filling of the beds has to be tackled that problems arise. Genuine plants of the period would look rather an unkempt lot by present day standards with very few plants other than carnations in flower after midsummer. The problem is overcome by using modern bedding plants and their use under the circumstances is fully justified. Sticklers for historical accuracy however, may wince a little and wish that the standard roses, at least, might be old varieties rather than modern hybrid teas. The use of genuine Tudor roses would, however, be impracticable.

East of the Knot Garden at New Place is the Great Garden. The southern boundary consists of a series of rectangular beds backed by hedges of yew and divided by buttress hedges of box. The layout is elaborate and the management near perfect. In the height of summer the display of bedding and herbaceous plants is very fine and is much admired.

An old mulberry, split and concreted up is said to have been propagated from the original tree planted in this garden by Shakespeare himself in 1609. A young tree has been planted to provide continuity in future centuries.

Hall's Croft was the home of Shakespeare's daughter Susanna and her husband Dr John Hall. A paved area where teas are served has odd bushes of lavender and rosemary. Beyond it are twin herbaceous borders with a central paved path. Once again management is of the highest standard and the effect impressive. A large central lawn provides adequate space for visitors to walk about. A bed around two old mulberry trees was filled in the summer of 1981 with bedding Zonal pelargoniums. Rather garish, I thought and wished for something a little softer. But this is a fine garden and serves its purpose well.

The Birthplace Garden is smaller and here are to be found many of the plants mentioned in the plays and poems. Being mentioned by Shakespeare does not necessarily mean that he knew it as a growing plant. He certainly would not have seen a cedar growing in Britain. F.G. Savage, 'The Flora and Folk Lore of Shakespeare' (1923) discusses this at length under many of his entries.

Whilst one can justify attempting a collection of plants mentioned by Shakespeare it might be more realistic to set aside one of the properties for a collection of Tudor plants, whether they are mentioned in his works or not. When one sees how attractive these plants can be when properly handled it seems that something is being missed. The Herb Garden at Sissinghurst is planted almost entirely with plants in Britain by the early seventeenth century. They would look horrible crammed into a knot garden but in the Sissinghurst setting they are beautiful.

Ann Hathaway's Cottage at Shottery and Mary Arden's house at Wilmcote have pleasant cottage gardens, mainly Victorian in character with plants of no clearly defined period but mostly post Tudor. One of these might well be used for a wholly Tudor plant collection.

Sherbourne Park

The Hon. Mrs C. Smith-Ryland

5km (3 miles) S of Warwick off A49. Area: 3ha (7.5 acres). Altitude: 42m (140ft). Soil: slightly alkaline. Rainfall: 660mm (26in). Open for NGS and at other times.

This is a good example of a modern garden with informal plantings of shrubs in borders around areas of lawn. There are, however, a few other features which give this garden a distinct character.

The house is Early Georgian (1740) and when the present owner took the garden in hand in 1959 there was little of interest apart from some very good trees. The garden has been extended considerably and many new trees planted.

On the east front is a wide gravel drive and beyond that a large open lawn with a Ha-Ha on the field boundary. The illusion of continuity with the level pasture beyond is particularly good. Some so-called Ha-Ha's are little more than retaining walls between different levels of ground. The illusion is then lost.

A border on the east front of the house has a useful range of climbers and other plants. *Euphorbia wulfenii, Helleborus argutifolius, Philadelphus microphyllus*, climbing roses and clematis were noted

An iron gateway leads through to the main garden on the south front. Standing at the house and looking south we see another wide, open lawn flanked with borders to begin with and then opening out to further lawn along the southern boundary of the garden. The section of the boundary opposite the house is another Ha-Ha and in the field beyond two belts of trees have been planted to create a vista which will improve as the trees mature. It is very effective. Once again one has the feeling that parkland is within the garden.

The borders of the top lawn are stocked with a wide range of modern shrubs well sited and well managed. The west border is backed by a wall and an iron gate leads through to the swimming pool garden. This is attractively planted and *Romneya coulteri, Cytisus battandieri*, and *Solanum crispum* were particularly effective. South of the pool shrub borders form a 'neck' in the lawn and lead to the southern boundary. *Viburnum juddii* and hydrangeas are prominent.

West of the swimming pool garden is a sunken garden consisting of lawn with a collection of *Sorbus* spp on a rectangular plant. South of this are steps leading up to the south lawn with two rows of *Pyrus salicifolia* planted to create exaggerated perspective. As there are only four a side plus two very widely spaced at the beginning one wonders whether there are enough to create the effect desired. Furthermore is it necessary when plenty of space is available anyway?

Further west we reach the churchyard wall and in front of it a neat formal parterre edged with box in patterns of diamonds and half diamonds. The four main beds are filled with roses, the corner beds with grey foliage plants.

South of this still against the churchyard wall, is a yew enclosed semi-formal garden with four upright junipers around a central sundial. The outer borders are filled with silver and white plants. *Carpentaria californica*, *Olearia scillonensis*, white *Potentilla fruticosa* and white hebes are typical plants. These two gardens add a little formality to a mainly informal garden.

We pass through another iron gate to the area south of the church. This consists of a large area of rough mown grass around an L shaped pool extending around to the west of the church. Trees in great variety have been planted here and climbers are becoming established on the south wall of the churchyard. This is the area of most recent development and the water will be a feature of great interest when marginal planting is mature. The church provides a pleasant background but having gone around the outside we may dwell on this building itself for a time. It is the fifth church on the site and was built by Gilbert Scott in 1863.

Shuckburgh Hall
Sir Charles Shuckburgh

Daventry, on A425 mid-way between Southam and Daventry. Area: about 2ha (5 acres) but merging with woodland. Altitude: 150m (500ft). Soil: clay loam. Lime free. Rainfall: 660mm (26in). Labour employed: owners plus part-time gardener. Mowing done by contract. Open about four times a year on the first Sundays in May, June, July and September.

This is the most easterly garden in our area and is one of that group of interesting gardens of the Middle Lias upland belt near the Northamptonshire border. Here the Middle Lias is sufficiently deep to give free drainage and complete freedom from lime.

The site is an ancient one with written records as far back as 1100, and the present house dates from that period. Alterations and additions have been made from time to time. The front is 1825-30. The Shuckburgh family have been in continuous occupation from the beginning. The church within the grounds has foundations c. 1200. It was wrecked by Cromwell and restored in 1830. Although this is the Parish Church it is a 'peculiar', that is to say, it does not come under the jurisdiction of the Bishop.

The garden is in part a Victorian survival. Large areas of lawns, but with less flower beds than a century ago, occupy much of the space. A belt of oak woodland with many fine trees gives protection from south and west.

Within the garden proper are some superb larches, some of the finest I have seen and more recent plantings include *Davidia involucrata*, *Ginkgo biloba*, *Catalpa bignonioides* and *Paulownia imperialis*. A *Metasequoia glyptostroboides* dates from 1949. All of the above seem to be essential occupants of mid-twentieth century gardens, and why not? They are all trees of character. The dictates of fashion are very sound sometimes.

These recent plantings are the work of Sir Charles as is also the 1½ acres of rhododendrons and wild garden on the wood margin with a wide range of modern shrubs and underplants. This is in the best modern style of natural gardening and is in a perfect setting.

A small rock garden near the entrance drive adds welcome colour as one approaches. Another 'rockery', essentially Victorian, is the 'Redan' which was built by Sir Charles' grandfather Sir George Shuckburgh on his return from the Crimean War. The central 'Citadel' is protected by the surrounding fortifications. Today the only battle that goes on is the struggle between the plants for possession of territory. This can be war to the death from the plant's point of view. To the human observer it seems very peaceful.

The Spring
Miss H. Martin

Upper Spring Lane, Kenilworth. Lies E of A452 Kenilworth — Birmingham and W of A429 Kenilworth — Coventry. Area: 3.2ha (8 acres). Altitude: 90m (295ft). Soil: Sandy loam, lime free. Rainfall: 660mm (26in). Labour employed: Three men including handyman. Open under NGS.

The house was built in 1870 and the present owner's father bought it in 1910.

The garden underwent some replanning around 1925 but there have been no very substantial alterations since that time. It certainly belongs very much to that period.

Austrian pines flank one side of the drive as one enters. Nearer the house they give way to beech with daffodils in grass underneath. The drive terminates at the west side of the house where there is a good specimen Wellingtonia, probably as old as the house.

The south front looks over a large wide lawn with a Ha Ha on the field boundary. Rhododendrons form a boundary on the right beyond which is the entrance drive. To the south east is a large block of Ghent azaleas and still further beyond two of the finest oaks one could wish to see. It is not usual to find oaks with the lower branches sweeping the ground. Here in an open site they have been left untouched and massive branches spread out in an arc with masses of twigs at lawn level.

East of the house is a traditional herbaceous border and further east a rock garden, now planted mainly with heathers. There is a small central pool and an outer screen of rhododendrons, junipers and other shrubs.

On the eastern boundary is a well constructed formal rose garden of considerable size. The straight sided beds, square, oblong or L shaped are set in extremely well laid paving to a standard far above that usually found. A sundial occupies the central position. Unfortunately roses are not very successful in this garden. The soil is better suited to rhododendrons. The rose garden is surrounded by a low wall on which are aubrieta, yellow alyssum and similar things.

There are fruit trees in grass with daffodils underneath and on the north side a walled kitchen garden well cropped and managed.

This garden contains few rarities but it is a very pleasant place with plenty of colour in its season.

Tysoe Manor

Major and Mrs Geoffrey Sewell

19km (12 miles) SE of Stratford-upon-Avon on S side of A422 Stratford — Banbury road. Area: 0.8ha (2 acres). Altitude: 120m (390ft). Soil: heavy lower lias clay. Rainfall: 660mm (26in). Labour employed: one part-time man. Open for NGS.

The warm brown ironstone of the Middle Lias provides one of the most beautiful building materials in Britain. Tysoe Manor is an excellent example of how it has been used over the centuries for we have a house that has grown from west to east and finally to the north and taken around six hundred years to do it. The west end dates from between 1250 and 1350 and still has one original window and internal timbers of that date. In the seventeenth and eighteenth centuries more was added and finally in 1930 the west end was extended northwards to form the back wing.

Although the stone is from the Middle Lias the soil is derived from the strata below. This is a calcareous clay, impossible to cultivate when wet but flocculating beautifully when properly handled, and capable of yielding very heavy crops and growing fine trees.

The present owners family came here in 1928 and found almost no garden of consequence. Now after half a century we have a mature low labour garden enhancing and enhanced by the beauty of the house.

The large top lawn is on the south front of the house. South and west of it is the lower lawn which we can reach either by a sloping grass path or stone steps each flanked by a pair of Irish yews. A few old fruit trees on the lower lawn remain from the days when it was an orchard and misteltoe has been successfully established in the apple trees.

There are large informal beds with a good range of shrubs and shrub roses with a few herbaceous plants as fillers. *Viburnum burkwoodii, Cotinus coggygria, Potentilla fruticosa* cvs, *Osmarea burkwoodii*, beautifully scented, and *Cornus* spp. in particular were noted. *Viburnum rhytidophyllum* with its big bullate leaves has attained a large size. A blue cedar is now getting going after a slow start.

To reach the north side of the house we pass a thicket of a very vigorous mock orange. This is probably a variety of *Philadelphus coronarius* and is often found in Cotswold country but I have never been sure of its identity. In my own garden it has been known to make ten feet of growth in a year. It is highly scented.

A large cherry, 'Kanzan', planted in 1938 has now got over its funnel shape and is spreading widely. Otherwise the north side consists of a small upper lawn with a retaining wall and steps leading down to a small rose garden below. Once again a pair of Irish Yews are at the sides of the steps.

Go eastwards along the lower lawn and we observe two fine walnuts. One of these is truly magnificent and probably two hundred and fifty years old. It is perhaps true to say that it is the finest piece of vegetation in the garden. Other trees of note are some Scots Pines and beeches at the drive entrance and a weeping willow of 1935 planting on the east of the drive.

The south wall of the house has several well trained climbers, notably *Piptanthus laburnifolius, Pyracantha* sp., roses, wistaria and a magnolia which appeared to be *M.x soulangeana*.

Upper Billesley
Mrs Robert Ansell

Stratford-upon-Avon, 5.5km (3½ miles) W of Stratford-upon-Avon, just N of A422 Stratford
— Alcester road. Area: 0.6ha (1½ acres). Altitude: 80m (260ft). Soil: calcareous clay loam.
Rainfall: 660mm (26in). Labour employed: casual only. Open under NGS.

Both house and garden have, over the years, grown and developed. The house dates from the mid seventeenth century and was built in the local Lower Lias limestone. Originally rather a fine farmhouse it had the single gable of the east front increased to three, the brick chimneys were rebuilt (or faced) with stone, the cold grey of the lias was relieved by the introduction of a little Cotswold Oolite and we now have a very lovely small stately home.

From the outbreak of war until 1968 the garden was neglected and although the basic framework has not altered the garden can be regarded as a creation of Mrs Ansell over the last dozen or so years.

The main part of the garden is behind the house facing slightly south of west. A wide paved terrace runs the length of the house and as the garden beyond slopes from north to south we find steps leading up from the terrace at the north end and down to a sunken rose garden at the south end. The terrace is partly of lower lias which is having its usual flaking problems when used for this purpose. There is also a good deal of random rectangular York stone in this garden. Mrs Ansell is planning to relieve the bareness of the terrace by some form of planting.

Going up the steps at the north end we follow a straight paved path edged with lavender which leads to the hard tennis court. About two thirds of the way along is a small sundail. North of the path are some oldish fruit trees in grass with daffodils in the spring.

South from the sundial we pass through an opening in a tall clipped yew hedge to the top lawn. This is a large, unencumbered expanse of grass with a large ash tree in the corner. A rock garden has recently been constructed in front of the tennis court. A screen of norway spruce has been planted on the far west boundary. Still further west is the former kitchen garden which may one day be developed as a wild garden.

Looking down from the top lawn to the house the garden is seen to be on three levels. The top path we have already traversed. Two flights of steps lead down to the sunken rose garden, crossing a terrace with a large herbaceous border and lawn in front. Percy Cane designed this area in 1969–70 but it has since been somewhat modified.

Upper Billesley. A real country house garden, unpretentious and homely.

The rose garden is on the site of a former stockyard and was constructed about 1920. Old photographs show that it has not been altered in design since the original layout. There was once a small rectangular pool in the centre. It is now filled in but will one day have in its place some other feature, perhaps a bird bath. Paved paths run diagonally across the rose garden and four grass strips come in from the sides but do not reach the centre.

South of the rose garden is an attractive old barn, reminding us of the farmyard origin of the garden and further south a well designed and well concealed swimming pool garden. Hedges of leyland cypress, privet and pyracantha are on three sides. A collection of *Geranium spp* fill surrounding borders and several willow leaved pears, *Pyrus salicifolia*, fill in a gap.

From here, east of the barn is a newly developed paved garden, really a continuation of the main terrace. Here we find some interesting shrubs including the pineapple broom *Cytisus battandieri*, that very attractive yellow flowered summer jasmine, too seldom seen, *Jasminum revolutum* and, on the barn wall and already learning to climb, *Hydrangea petiolaris*.

On the east front of the house is a croquet lawn and below a semicircular drive with a belt of trees and shrubs between. The main drive up from the road is bordered by an avenue of horse chestnuts planted in 1930.

This garden is still developing and will become very attractive indeed, especially if, as one hopes, the wild garden is properly developed.

Upton House
The National Trust

Edgehill, Warwickshire, on A422 Stratford-upon-Avon — Banbury. 21km (13 miles) Stratford.
11km (7 miles) Banbury. Altitude: 210m (700ft). Soil: medium loam. About neutral. Rainfall:
660mm (26in). Open April — September. See National Trust Guide.

Upton House was built by Sir Rushout Cullen in 1695 and it is thought that the architect/builder may have been Francis Smith of Warwick. Cullen also seems to have constructed a series of rectangular pools, which in modified form, still survive. Cullen's family was of Low Country origin and one cannot help comparing these pools with the Dutch style water gardens such as Westbury which were exactly contemporary. Cullen died in 1730 and after a lapse of some years the estate passed into the hands of the Child family. Robert Child (1739-82) added to the house and enlarged the lower pool. He also built the porticoed temple at the far end of it, probably to designs of Sanderson Miller of nearby Radway.

Little seems to have happened to Upton in the nineteenth century but about 1898 it was bought by Mr A.R. Motion. In 1927 the second Viscount Bearstead purchased the property and engaged Percy Morley Horder to remodel the house and carry out certain work in the garden. In 1948 he gave the property to the National Trust with a large endowment.

The wide south front of the house looks over double terraces, which were designed by Horder, on to a large expanse of lawn. Beyond the lawn edge is gently rising meadow land. As one continues to walk southwards one becomes aware that the meadows are farther away than appeared at first sight and between them and our lawn edge is a deep coomb. The first thing to come into view is the large rectangular canal-like pool at the bottom, then by degrees the south facing bank almost under our feet becomes visible. Before investigating this in detail we may note that on the west side of the lawn is a group of Cedar of Lebanon that date from the Child period of mid-eighteenth century. On the east side is a colourful sloping border of small shrubs and rock plants in considerable variety.

From the south west corner of the lawn a stone balustraded stairway descends to the terraces below. This is another of Horder's designs and is a fine piece of work. The first terrace is a broad grass path with a brick retaining wall, of late seventeenth century date, and six feet high, supporting the lawn above. Climbing roses are trained on the wall. On the lower side are lavender and various grey foliaged plants. Below this is a sloping bank containing many bearded iris and choice shrubs which include *Berberis spp, Phlomis fruticosus, Acers, Mahonia* and others.

Another high brick wall, this one standing free, is below the bank. On its south side are many clematis and in front surely one of the largest delphinium borders in Britain. Below this, and still sloping away steeply is the kitchen garden. This latter feature is one of the things that makes Upton almost unique.

In most large gardens kitchen gardens are put away from the pleasure grounds, often a long way away, and frequently behind walls. How the kitchen garden at Upton came into being is not known. Why it has been allowed to remain is a mystery but we must be thankful that it has. The management of it is near perfect and in these days of shrubs and ground cover how good it is to see well cultivated soil.

On the east side, behind a clipped yew hedge running straight down the slope is a double herbaceous border with a central grass path leading to the edge of the pool. At the top end is a little secret garden planted with bedding plants.

West of the kitchen garden is a small area enclosed by yew hedges which once contained too greenhouses, frames and other appurtenances. At some period early in this century they were removed but the hedges have been left and little formal gardens created in the space. This again is surprising. Any noted garden designer would have swept the whole lot away and incorporated the area into the whole garden as a unified scheme. Not so Upton.

The large rectangular pool has been mentioned. Beyond this is a grass walk and yet another brick wall of Sir Rushout Cullen's period forms the south boundary.

West of the area so far considered is another coomb running at right angles to the main one and below the cedars. This, at one time, contained three of Cullen's rectangular pools. The lower one has been drained and is planted with a collection of flowering cherries. The middle one remains but is less severely formal than it once was. From a grotto in the north west corner emerges a stream, known as the Monks' Well, which provides the water for the pools.

This whole area has been developed as a natural woodland garden with the added attraction of the water. Magnolias, cercidiphyllums, bamboos and other choice shrubs have been planted. A 'Kiftsgate' rose and clematis of the 'montana' group cover large trees on the western boundary. The usual waterside herbaceous plants flourish.

There remains one further pool, almost a lake, which is best reached from the road and not the garden. This is the pool which was enlarged in the mid eighteenth century by Robert Child following the Capability Brown style of the period. The formal lines of the Cullen's original have disappeared.

Wightwick Manor
The National Trust

Wolverhampton, 4.8km (3 miles) W of Wolverhampton off A454 (Turn off at Mermaid Inn). Area: 4ha (10 acres). Altitude: 75m (250ft). Soil: sandy loam. Lime free. Rainfall: 760mm (30in). Open regularly for NT.

When Samuel Theodore Mander, a Wolverhampton industrialist built the half timbered house in 1887 and engaged Wm Morris and his Pre-Raphaelite friends to do the interior decorations he was following in a tradition going back at least as far as Josiah Wedgewood and Matthew Boulton. Many of these pioneer manufacturers were appreciative of culture. It is the Pre-Raphaelite associations that make the house interesting today.

The garden is fairly solidly formal Victorian around the house. Alfred Parsons R.A. who was for many years a close associate of Ellen Willmot and illustrated her book 'The Genus Rosa' as well as painting many water colours of her Warley garden was responsible for the original garden layout particularly the rose garden. This consists of a central octagonal arbour with rose beds around it. There are clipped yews with topiaries on top, some erect Irish Yews and dome topped golden yews. Several old yews have recently been cut back to restart growth. The whole Rose Garden is enclosed in clipped yew hedges.

A grass walk leads down to the pools below. It has yew and 'Golden Queen' Holly planted alternately on one side and berberis on the other. A parallel grass walk bordered by clipped yew hedges leads from the entrance drive.

The south terraces are the work of Thomas Mawson and were constructed around 1910. The top terrace has an oak balustrade in front of which are five little rectangular bays separated by yew buttresses. These little gardens contain plants from the gardens of famous men i.e. Tennyson, Morris (Kelmscott), Kempe, Shelley and Dickens. Beyond these are two rows of clipped barrel shaped yews with some low domed ones beyond. A large Norway Maple and a fine beech add height.

Below the formal gardens on the west side is an area of rough mown grass with two pools at the bottom backed by well wooded slopes. Rhododendrons in quantity border the pools.

Many commemorative trees have been planted, each with its appropriate plaque. King George V (when Duke of York), seems to have started the fashion in 1900.

Wroxall Abbey School
Principal: Mrs I.D.M. Wiles

10km (6 miles) NW of Warwick on A41. Area: 11ha (27 acres). Altitude: 120m (400ft). Soil: lime free. Rainfall: 700mm (27.5in). Open for NGS.

Of the old Priory fragmentary ruins only remain today. A Tudor house was built here by Richard Burgoyne and this was later purchased by Sir Christopher Wren for his daughter. There is a garden reputedly designed by Wren. Wroxall is proud of its Wren connection. Around 1861-6 the house was demolished by a northern industrialist, James Dugdale, and the present house erected nearby. The school moved here from Rugby in 1934.

The entrance drive approaches from the east, through an avenue of limes, to the courtyard car park on the east front. On the south and west fronts there is a wide gravel terrace with grass banks leading to the areas below. This, on the west front, is a large lawn with groups of trees near the boundary and a large group of rhododendrons. The south front has a D shaped formal garden with a balustrade on the curved south boundary. There are two large rose beds, a pattern of lawn strips and gravel paths, eight clipped domes of box and two mushroom headed yews. This is a typical formal Victorian garden and no doubt is of about the period of the house.

Below the balustrade is a large grass area with a natural looking pool on the southern boundary. There are many rhododendrons near the south-west boundary.

Moving eastwards we pass behind the priory ruins into the area south of the drive. There are many good trees here but pride of place must go to two Lebanon Cedars. One of these is quite outstanding and presumably would date from the eighteenth century.

North of the drive is the little church with an old mulberry at its east end. A clipped yew hedge conceals a partly walled garden, once a kitchen garden and still retaining some old espalier apples which form a partial screen to the tennis court. The Wren garden is at the north end and consists of a wall with a series of deep alcoves in which are planted fruit trees and, more recently, roses. I cannot recall having seen a similar wall elsewhere and it is not surprising to learn that it was conceived by an imaginative artist trying to do something different.

Index

INDEX